Praise For *How To Ru(i)n A Record Label*

"It's so rare to get to have an independ[...] [...] a
scene, a place like Gilman Street, wher[...] [...]ng
out my favorite records at the time, w[...] [...]r]
Isocracy..."
– **Billie Joe Armstrong, Green Day**

"Larry writes incisively and tellingly about an era he didn't just witness, but helped define."
– **Danny Penman, author of *You Are Not Your Pain* and *Mindfulness For Creativity***

"A brilliant book by one of the greatest tastemakers in the history of punk rock."
– **Grant Lawrence, award-winning broadcaster and author, former lead singer of the Smugglers**

Praise for *Spy Rock Memories*

"Livermore writes with deference for his time spent on Spy Rock, finding a way to keep nostalgia from clouding his experiences, and the book's breezy nature finds its middle ground between music memoir and personal essay. Spy Rock Memories paints its characters in lush details, allowing for readers to be welcomed into the culture of Iron Peak, just as Livermore was all those decades ago."
– ***The AV Club***

"Spy Rock Memories is an unflinching look at life in Northern California's Emerald Triangle, a world usually hidden from view. Part social history and part personal history, it is as critically insightful as it is hopelessly romantic."
– **Aaron Cometbus, *Cometbus***

"Larry was always deemed the troublemaker up on Spy Rock for telling and writing the truth."
– **Tre Cool, Green Day**

"Livermore's book Spy Rock Memories provides a glimpse at Livermore's trials and tribulations as a brutally outspoken, city-punk, post-hippy, trying to survive in an unforgiving environment that proved to be just as deadly and threatening as it was beautiful and nurturing."
– ***The Willits News***

HOW TO RUIN A RECORD LABEL

THE STORY OF LOOKOUT RECORDS

LARRY LIVERMORE

Don Giovanni Records

ISBN (paperback): 978-0-9891963-4-5
ISBN (hardcover): 978-0-9891963-5-2
e-ISBN: 978-0-9891963-6-9

Cover art: Patrick Hynes
Cover design: Nolen Strals
Layout: Doan Buu
Author photo: Kenneth Bachor

Third printing

I would like to offer my heartfelt thanks to my long-suffering editor Zach Gajewski, to Murray Bowles for his invaluable work in documenting the East Bay scene and allowing us to use his photos here, to David Hayes for being my partner in getting Lookout started, to Aaron Cometbus for all his help and support, and to Tim Yohannan, who despite our well-publicized differences, helped create the environment in which our music and culture could thrive.

Special thanks, of course, go out to Christopher Appelgren and Patrick Hynes. Even if Lookout could have survived without them—which is doubtful—it wouldn't have been nearly as much fun. I also want to thank all the musicians and artists who worked with us, the fans who attended the shows and bought the records, and you, of course, for being here to read about it.

Contents

A Note To The Reader   ix

Intro: Escape from Zug Island   xi

1 If You Build It They Will Come   1
2 All These Friends, All These People   11
3 A Broken-Toed Kickoff   23
4 Life At The Maxipad   33
5 1988, Stand Up And Take A Look Around   45
6 Enter The Weasel   57
7 The Rodeo   69
8 Too Much Golden Light   79
9 The Berkeley Way   91
10 My Brain Hurts   10
11 Buffy And The Hanks   115
12 East Bay To The World   127
13 The Queers Are Here   137
14 Not Just Boys Fun   149
15 Get Ready For Action   161
16 Welcome To Paradise   173
17 The Year That Broke Punk   185
18 Moving On Up   197
19 The Office   209
20 Iceland   221
21 As The Weasel Turns   233
22 Journey To The End   245
23 After The Gold Rush   255
24 There Is A Light That Never Goes Out   267

Outro: The Neon Boneyard   279

A Note To The Reader

If you picked up this book to find out who played bass on your favorite band's obscure second demo, or how many copies of so-and-so's 7" were pressed on red vinyl as opposed to purple, you've come to the wrong place.

How To Ru(i)n A Record Label is a highly personal account of my time at Lookout Records. It leaves out many people and events that could and maybe should have been included, some because they slipped my mind, others because there just wasn't enough room.

To those who might feel I represented their words, actions, or motives in a less than flattering light, I can only say that I did my best to recall things as they actually happened. In doing so, I drew on a combination of personal correspondence, fanzines, flyers, and recollections—mine and those of others—all of which can be fallible. I didn't set out to hurt or "get" anyone, only to illuminate and arrive at the heart of the story.

Whether I failed or succeeded, what I've written here is but one facet of a many-sided memory. If you feel hard done by, if you remember things differently, if you feel I overlooked the best or most important parts, by all means pick up a pen or keyboard or camera or microphone and tell the world how you saw it.

Intro:
Escape From Zug Island

Detroit felt like a strange and wondrous place when I was growing up, if not an especially pretty or pleasant one. You could literally hear the gears of industry grinding. The air was foul with thick, stinking clouds of red and black smoke, and the river streaked with fluorescent streams of toxic waste. The ground shook with the dull, booming roar of dynamite from the salt mines beneath our feet.

I found the noise, the smells, the raucous upheaval more than a little intimidating, but this, adults reminded me, was the price of prosperity. "When you're old enough to start looking for a job," they'd say, "you'll thank your lucky stars you were born here."

I wasn't so sure. Asked when she decided to leave Detroit, actress Lily Tomlin reputedly said, "As soon as I realized where I was." I'd reached a similar conclusion by the time I was four or five.

I nagged my parents, demanding to know why we couldn't move somewhere nicer, but they just laughed at me. Retreating inward, I taught myself to read and spent long hours with my head pressed up against the family radio, idly twirling the dial in search of something—anything—worth listening to.

That's how I discovered doo-wop, and the first stirrings of rock and roll. On muggy summer nights I'd chase fireflies around my front yard and watch the teenagers on the corner work out harmonies and dance moves to the latest hits.

It was on one such night that I spotted a mysterious orange glow spilling up from the horizon, covering nearly half the sky, before slowly fading away. The light was soft, ethereal, mesmerizing. I could hardly take my eyes off it.

"What's that?" I asked my dad, hoping he'd spin some yarn about angels or wizards setting the world on fire, but he shrugged and said, "Oh, they're just emptying the blast furnace out on Zug Island." I had no idea what he meant, but the day would come when I'd find out.

When I was 13 I joined a gang, but not, unfortunately, the singing and dancing kind I'd been hoping for ever since seeing *West Side Story*. These guys were more into breaking stuff, running smash-and-grabs on local stores, and fighting turf wars against kids with the wrong kind of haircuts.

At my parents' house in mid-6os Detroit.
(Photo most likely by Mom or Dad)

It wasn't the brightest way to spend my adolescence, but at least I had something to believe in, to feel a part of. At 15 I started carrying a gun, thinking it would make me a badass rather than the skinny scaredy-cat I secretly knew myself to be. It was an ancient gun, with no safety catch; how I managed never to shoot myself remains somewhere between a mystery and a miracle. The one time I tried to use it on someone else, my tight jeans saved the day: I wasn't able to get it out of my pocket fast enough.

Graduation night was spent tooling up and down the Dix-Toledo Highway in a '58 Chevy convertible, the radio blasting the Rolling Stones' "Satisfaction" as I took potshots at the McDonald's golden arches. By then guys were drifting away from the gang in favor of girlfriends, cars, and jobs. Soon afterward, they started getting drafted and shipped off to Vietnam.

I was one of the few who didn't have to go to war, having already been in enough trouble that the army didn't want me. With my old buddies gone, I sometimes hung out with the kids who'd been forming British Invasion-style bands in basements and garages around town. I watched a couple of them, the Satellites and the MC5, face off in a battle of the bands on a local tennis court.

The Satellites won, but the MC5 impressed me more. Though my own age and from the same working class background, they carried themselves with the swagger of stars. A few weeks later I saw the Supremes, three girls from the projects who had just racked up an unprecedented five Number One hits in a row.

Detroit was an extremely segregated place in those days, so the sight of thousands of black and white people dancing, cheering, and singing along together was as astounding as it was inspiring. I was equally impressed by the Supremes' label, Motown Records, a homegrown affair that was finally putting Detroit on the map for something besides ugly cars and pollution.

In a perfect world I would have immediately gone out and joined a band or started a record label myself, but I hadn't yet gained that kind of confidence. Besides, I'd fallen in with a new, more violent gang. To let them see me sporting the clothes or hairstyle favored by my musician friends would have been near-suicidal.

After my glue-sniffing-induced spiritual makeover.
(Photo by Jann Merecki)

I drifted further down a rathole of alcohol and crime until 1967, when, while sniffing glue and listening to the Beatles' *Revolver* album, I had a spiritual experience that turned me overnight into a raving hippie lunatic. I spent the rest of the year living on LSD and cheese sandwiches, shoving flowers in people's faces, and haranguing passersby about world peace. It was all a lovely dream until the night two gun-wielding plainclothes cops jumped out of the bushes and hauled me off to jail.

Facing heavy-duty drug charges, I jumped bail and ran for it, hiding out first in New York, then in California. When I finally landed in front of a judge, I was offered a choice between a lengthy prison term and a suspended sentence conditioned on doing something I'd never managed before: holding down a steady job.

That was how I wound up in the slag pit on Zug Island, breaking rocks with a jackhammer that weighed nearly as much as I did. Later I was promoted to the coke oven, where we produced fuel for the blast furnace that lit up the Detroit skies.

My job was to monitor the temperature and pressure gauges—basically to make sure the oven didn't blow up—but I spent most of my time high on mescaline or LSD, staring out at the city lights that twinkled like fairy dust through the fiery haze. When I could find a secluded corner, I read and re-read the opening pages of Dostoyevsky's *Crime and Punishment*, never managing to make much sense of them.

It was 1969 now, and the title song of the new Stooges album summed up my predicament exactly. I felt trapped, as if my life might as well be over.

One chilly day as winter was setting in, I called in sick, dropped ten hits of acid, and flopped down on my bedroom floor to contemplate my fate. The radio was tuned to the FM station that let DJs play whatever they felt like; every song, it seemed, contained a hidden message aimed directly at me.

"The West is the best," sang the Doors, "Get here and we'll do the rest." "Your time has come to shine," Simon and Garfunkel told me, "All your dreams are on their way." I knew what they were talking about. Ever since the halcyon summer I'd spent there while dodging the law, I'd been desperate to get back to California.

If only I hadn't screwed everything up. It might be years, if ever, before I could do that now.

"But you have no choice," Bob Dylan retorted.

Afternoon rolled into evening, the battle still raging inside my head. "What will I do when I run out of money?" I protested. "Where would I live? How would I eat?" A long, lugubrious King Crimson song echoed my concerns with a chorus of "I fear tomorrow I'll be crying."

It had been years since I'd set foot in a church, but I suddenly seized on the

Bible verse about the lilies of the field. "They neither toil nor spin," Jesus had said, "but never was Solomon himself arrayed in such glory."

That did the trick. I'd had my fill of toiling and spinning, I decided; it was time to take my chances in the lily fields of California. Giving or throwing away almost everything I owned, I traded my shiny new motorcycle for a decrepit VW bus and hit the highway.

It wasn't all smooth going. I'd barely arrived in the Golden State when I found myself handcuffed in the back of a patrol car and on my way to jail, thanks to the two Benzedrine capsules I'd stashed away in the van in case I needed them for late night drives.

The cops cut me loose a couple days later, but only after they'd stolen most of my money, leaving me with $35 and a bag of brown rice to start my new life in Berkeley. My fears about how or if I would survive never completely left me—I suspect that's the case with most people who've ever been poor—but from then on things would be . . . all right.

Some people might be embarrassed to admit they were swayed into uprooting their whole existence by some song lyrics and an imaginatively interpreted Bible verse, but I'm not. I'd tapped into a power that led me out the gates of Zug Island into a life I'd never imagined possible. I've followed it ever since.

1.
If You Build It They Will Come

In 1985 I was living up on Spy Rock, an off-the-grid hippie wilderness about as close to the middle of nowhere as you could get and still be anywhere. I was publishing a magazine called *Lookout*, and singing and playing guitar for a band called the Lookouts. We'd just recorded our first demo tape, and this guy named David Hayes wrote to order a copy.

A month or two after I sent it to him, he wrote back to say he was putting together a cassette compilation of Northern California bands, and invited the Lookouts to be part of it. I don't remember him actually saying he *liked* our band, but we were part of the scene he was documenting, so a couple of our songs wound up on his *Bay Mud* tape. We continued exchanging letters, and a tentative friendship sprang up.

I'm not positive when David and I met in person, but I think it might have been when the Lookouts played at Own's Pizza in South Berkeley, on May 29, 1986. It was the first time our band had made it down to the big city, or, for that matter, anywhere out of Mendocino County.

Where we lived, punk rock shows were all but nonexistent. The only way there was likely to be one was if we put it on ourselves. But it wasn't easy finding places to play in San Francisco or the East Bay, either. Venue after venue would get trashed by unruly crowds or shut down by the police.

New Method, an anarchist and peace punk warehouse in Emeryville, where I'd been hoping the Lookouts might land their first Bay Area gig, had recently suffered both fates. So now shows happened in random places—pizzerias on the brink of going out of business, for example—whose owners knew nothing about the mayhem they might be letting themselves in for.

But for some reason that night in 1986 was different. Not a hint of trouble, and big smiles all around.

The lineup—No Means No, Victim's Family, the Mr. T Experience, Complete Disorder, and the Lookouts—was a mixed bag, bands you might not expect to see on the same bill. But somehow it all flowed together beautifully.

Victor Hayden, a vaguely mysterious, almost Devo-esque character who I'd met at New Method, had helped organize the Own's Pizza show. As a bunch of us milled around at the front door afterward, not quite ready to go home, I heard him say, "We need to find someplace we can do this all the time."

I wasn't the only one, but I'd like to think I was one of the first to say, "Yeah, let's do it!" None of us realized it just then, but that was the beginning of the Gilman Street Project.

Victor's idea might have never progressed beyond wishful thinking if it weren't for Kamala Parks, barely a year or two out of Berkeley High, but already adept at making things happen on the East Bay punk scene. A few days later, Victor told me Kamala had found a vacant warehouse in West Berkeley.

"It's perfect," he said. "Now we just need to convince Tim."

"Tim" was Tim Yohannan, *Maximum Rocknroll's* irascible but mostly benign dictator-for-life. *MRR* had started as a radio show in the 1970s and began publishing a monthly magazine in 1982. Through sheer persistence and punctuality—until then nobody had heard of a zine that came out unfailingly on schedule—it had grown into one of the most powerful punk rock institutions on the planet.

Despite its low cover price and dirt-cheap advertising rates, *MRR* raked in an astonishing amount of cash. But surplus income didn't end up in Tim's pockets or the magazine's own coffers; instead, he recycled it into musical and political causes he thought were worthwhile. Victor and Kamala set out to persuade him that converting the West Berkeley warehouse into a punk rock club fit that bill.

"We'll need about $10,000 to get it up and running," Victor thought. It wound up being more like $40,000. Tim was dubious at first—for starters, he thought the club should be in San Francisco, not the East Bay—but once he decided to get involved, *MRR* began footing the bills and money was no longer an issue.

Next came the physical work of actually building the club. I wielded a jackhammer for the first time since my Zug Island days, and nearly electrocuted myself trying to install some wiring. Meanwhile, a revolving cast of punks, misfits, and weirdos tried to come up with rules and principles for how Gilman Street should be run.

It could—and probably would—have devolved into nothing but collective chaos if Tim had not been at the helm. Everyone was allowed his or her say, no matter how bizarre or off-the-wall, as long as they wound up agreeing to do things Tim's way. Sometimes we had to vote and re-vote half a dozen times to come up with that result, but we always did.

His semi-authoritarian tactics earned him the nickname of "Chairman Tim," and some of his more vocal critics even accused him of being a Stalinist. Tim's cheerful reply: "It's true! I have a poster of The Stalin hanging on my bedroom wall."

He was referring to the Japanese hardcore band, not the Soviet strongman, but Tim was a collectivist at heart. He believed in democracy when it produced the desired result, but naked totalitarianism was fine too, if that was what got the job done.

Not all of Tim's ideas proved realistic. Scornful of "rock star egos," he hoped to break down the traditional hierarchy separating performers from audiences by making bands who played Gilman help out with unglamorous jobs like cleanup and security. That lasted about as long as you'd imagine.

Another experiment that survived only a month or two was a ban on advertising. The theory was that people wouldn't know who was playing on any given date, but that they'd show up to be part of the club rather than to be passively entertained. A few too many chilly midwinter nights in a mostly empty warehouse put an end to that plan. David Hayes became Gilman's de facto calendar maker, and also produced many of its most memorable flyers.

David developed a unique, disarming style, employing comic techniques without ever becoming cartoonish. This might have been a talent he'd had all along, but it came to life and blossomed at Gilman.

That was how it worked for many bands, too. When Gilman opened on Dec. 31, 1986, the Bay Area punk scene was far from dead, but it wasn't exactly thriving. Bands came through town on tour, of course, playing commercial venues like Ruthie's Inn or the On Broadway, and there were a few local bands "big" enough to open for them. Beyond that, you were mostly looking at disaffected teenagers who'd count it a success if they packed in enough friends and classmates to fill somebody's garage or basement.

Gilman got off to a slow start; on its first night, the room was never much more than half full. But in the weeks and months that followed, it began to feel like that catch phrase from *Field Of Dreams*: if you build it, they will come.

The East Bay scene had been small and insular; go to enough shows and you'd soon know everyone, at least by sight. But once Gilman opened, kids nobody had ever seen began showing up. And by kids I mean *kids*, mostly high school-aged, but some as young as 12 or 14. Word had obviously gotten out: here was a place where you wouldn't be laughed at or turned away for being uncool, where being strange or unusual was considered a character asset, where you could wear your weirdness as a badge of honor.

It also didn't take long to figure out that almost anyone could get a gig at Gilman. You didn't need special connections, you didn't even need to be good. As long as you looked like you were having fun and didn't take yourself too seriously, people would give you a chance. Not surprisingly, newly formed bands were soon coming out of the woodwork.

Some old school bands didn't fare so well. The Naked Lady Wrestlers, who'd been around since the beginning of the 80s, were greeted with catcalls and boos despite being among the most gifted musicians—from a technical standpoint, anyway—to play Gilman in those early days.

Granted, they invited most of that abuse by bragging about how great they were, taunting the audience, and insulting the newer, younger bands. Supposedly it was all a joke, but they seemed genuinely distressed at being shown up by kids who were still learning to play their instruments.

The band that really worked the Naked Lady Wrestlers' nerves was Isocracy, four high schoolers from the far-flung East Bay suburb of El Sobrante (Spanish for "the leftover"). I'd met Isocracy a few months before Gilman opened, when their drummer and chief mouthpiece, John Kiffmeyer (aka Al Sobrante), plaintively asked me, "How do bands get to play shows?"

I wonder about that myself, I told him, but since the Lookouts had a gig at San Francisco's Club Foot that week, I offered Isocracy the first ten minutes of our slot. I wasn't even sure they'd show up, but just before we were due to go on, I spotted them carrying their equipment up Third Street. They'd made the hour and a half trip from El Sobrante via bus, BART, and, for the last few blocks, on foot.

Isocracy made a mess.
(Photo by Murray Bowles)

Jason Beebout, their lead singer, had such a bad case of stage fright that he more or less hid out behind our bass amp. All four members of the band looked like they'd rather be at the dentist getting their teeth drilled, but it took only a matter of months for the once-timid teenagers to transform themselves into masters of the Gilman universe.

It might sound like I'm exaggerating, but no one who was there during the first months of 1987 could deny that Isocracy were the club's first superstars. Their music might still have been in a developmental stage, but they made up for it with a show that was nothing short of spectacular. Or, as some preferred to call it, trash-tacular.

Trash was the essence of the Isocracy experience. There was the verbal kind, delivered in the braying foghorn tones of Al Sobrante and the free-association ramblings of Jason, who'd come so far out of his shell it was hard to believe he'd ever had one.

But the band became even better known for the massive amounts of physical junk—basically anything cheap or free, from silly string and police tape to reams of office paper and bags of flour—that they dumped on the audience, who promptly threw it right back at them.

It was a tough act to follow. The Naked Lady Wrestlers were one of the few bands foolish enough to try, but they failed abjectly. If they hadn't been so loud and arrogant about putting down "those no-talent kids," you almost could have felt sorry for them.

The Naked Lady Wrestlers show their disdain.
(Photo by Murray Bowles)

Isocracy milked the abuse for all it was worth, until the Naked Lady Wrestlers unwisely challenged them to a battle of the bands. It was set up like a wrestling match, and refereed by rubberfaced loudmouth and *MRR* record reviewer Walter Glaser.

The bands took turns playing songs, after which the audience would vote on who had won that "round." Isocracy scored a unanimous victory. It was all in good fun, of course, but it also represented a changing of the guard. This was not your dad's punk rock anymore, not even your big brother's. Gilman belonged to a new generation.

I was still spending the majority of my time up on Spy Rock, which had been my home for most of the 8os, but I hated missing any of the Gilman action. Getting there, though, meant a three and a half hour trip each way, and, if I was too tired to drive back after the show, sleeping in the camper shell on the back of my pickup.

I was complaining about this to Dave MDC ("Millions of Dead Cops," "Multi-Death Corporations," etc.), who told me he was about to get evicted from his apartment in San Francisco unless he could find three new roommates right away.

David Hayes wanted to move out of his parents' house in the suburbs, and our mutual friend Joe Britz, a disgruntled fanzine editor from Brooklyn, was eager to relocate to the Bay Area. A week later the three of us took up residence at what would become known as the Rathouse.

Why the "Rathouse"? There was David's pet rat, not to mention the appearance of the place, which ranged from "comfortably lived in" to "Whoa, did Isocracy just play here?" Lastly, it was a play on the German word *Rathaus*, which means "city hall."

I still spent several days a week at Spy Rock, but my Rathouse base made it possible to get more wholeheartedly involved at Gilman. David, Joe, and I launched a house zine, *Tales* (sometimes *Tails*) *From The Rathouse*, and whiled away many a night with rambling discussions about where this whole punk rock thing might be going.

That could have been when the idea of starting a record label first came up. It was mostly just idle speculation; there weren't enough bands—or fans—for it to make sense. Once you got beyond Isocracy, and maybe Nasal Sex and Rabid Lassie, who was there, really?

Well, there was my band, the Lookouts, but I was already, much too hastily in David's opinion, putting out our own LP. "You should have done a 7" first," he kept saying. Too late, I realized he was right.

One Planet One People came out in April of 1987, bearing the imprint of something called "Lookout Records." No such company existed; I'd just slapped the name on there to make it look more "official." The album didn't sell anywhere near enough copies to break even, and that, I assumed, was the beginning and end of my life in the music industry.

In June of that year, I sublet my room at the Rathouse and took off to Europe for a couple of months. While I was away, *Maximum Rocknroll* asked David to put together a double 7" compilation to showcase some of the Gilman bands and raise money for the club.

He wrote me a letter telling me about it, and mentioned a band called Operation Ivy, who he said were becoming "the new stars of Gilman Street."

"Bigger than Isocracy?" I wrote back.

"Way bigger," came the answer.

That was as much as I'd heard about Operation Ivy until I got back to Gilman in mid-August. I'd barely walked in the door when a kid I knew only as Tim—"that floppy boy," I always called him—ran across the room and jumped up into my arms. He weighed about as much as a bag of feathers.

"Yo Larry, I'm in a band!"

Tim's previous band, Basic Radio, had broken up just before Gilman opened. Judging from the way he was always tearing around the dance floor and hugging everyone in sight, you'd think he was the happiest kid alive, but I knew he'd been desperate to start playing music again.

"That's awesome, Tim!" I said.

"Yeah, I don't go by Tim anymore. People call me Lint now."

"Lint?"

"Yeah, you know, like the stuff in the bottom of your pocket. Larry, you gotta check us out. We're playing today. Are you gonna stick around and watch?"

"Sure, of course. What's your band called?"

"Operation Ivy."

I stood at the back of the room, not expecting much. After all, they'd barely been together three months.

By the time they went into the first chorus, I was up front singing along to words I'd never heard before. It was one of those moments I'd experienced only a handful of times in my life, when music moved beyond the level of entertainment or inspiration, and opened a door to dimensions previously undreamed of.

Afterward, as I leaned against a wall catching my breath, Lint walked up and asked if I'd liked his band. I still marvel at how I opened my mouth to say, "That was really good," only to have a completely different set of words come tumbling out:

"Do you guys want to make a record?"

David Hayes at the Rathouse.
(Photo by Larry Livermore)

I have no idea why I said it. All I knew was that there needed to be an Operation Ivy record, and somehow I was going to make it happen.

A day or two later David Hayes sidled up to me and said, "Now that you've promised Operation Ivy you're going to put out their record, maybe you should try listening to their demo tape."

I hadn't even known they had a demo. When I put on the cassette David gave me, my heart sunk. It was good, all right, but not *that* good. It sounded like what it was: a decent first effort from an almost brand new band. It bore little resemblance to the transcendent spectacle I'd witnessed at Gilman.

Me and my big mouth, I thought. But I'd given Op Ivy my word, and I wasn't going to take it back. Besides, not wanting Isocracy to feel left out, I'd asked them to do a record, too.

The whole thing would have turned into a giant fiasco if David hadn't come to the rescue. I was good at big talk and crazy ideas, but he knew how to make things actually happen.

He'd been wanting to put out a 7" for Corrupted Morals, so I suggested we join forces and do all three bands together. He agreed. Hearing that Crimpshrine had recorded enough songs for an EP, I decided what the heck, let's make it four, and just like that, we were in the record business.

2.
All These Friends,
All These People

I've been to shows in bars and nightclubs, garages and basements, arenas and stadiums, not to mention barns, parking lots, and backyards. Each had its moments, its highs and lows, its bad points and good.

Gilman Street stood apart from them all.

Walking through that front door was unlike entering any music venue, club, or hangout I'd ever known. It felt like coming home. And it wouldn't have been home without a family, even if this family was, as the MDC song put it, a little weird.

The first person you'd encounter, collecting money or checking membership cards, might be 14-year-old Robert Eggplant, who made the 20-mile round trip from Pinole on his skateboard. Another lobby regular was Claude, a preternaturally intelligent 15-year-old who people assumed—mistakenly, as it turned out—to be either insane or permanently drug-fried.

Claude and Eggplant in the front hall at Gilman. In the doorway: Pat "Skin" Mello, credited with "Irritating Comments" on the first Op Ivy EP. (Photo by Murray Bowles)

Reading aloud from Nietzsche or speed-rapping about space aliens and conspiracy theories, Claude made such an endearing nuisance of himself that his name became synonymous with unstructured nonsense (hence the Crimpshrine record *Quit Talkin' Claude*). He was the one who observed, while tripping on acid, "Dude, your face is bright purple, like you're turning into a giant eggplant," which was how Robert had gotten his name.

So much joking, gossiping, and story-swapping took place just inside the door that you could easily spend the whole night there without ever seeing a band play. To the right of the lobby was a room that would later become the club's "office," but for the first couple of years functioned as a less noisy hangout space, with kids bouncing, flopping, crawling, and sprawling across the filthy cushions, couches, and carpets.

Across the hall was the Gilman store, aka "The Stoar," typically presided over by jazz pianist, and (it was claimed) onetime beatnik, Vivian Sayles, helped out by her teenaged kids, Nina and Jake. You never knew what might be on sale there: anything from homemade baked goods to 7"s and demo tapes to the club's unofficial soft drink, Jolt Cola ("all the sugar and twice the caffeine").

Eggplant and Claude, like many younger punks, seldom had the four or five bucks it cost to get in, so they'd volunteer to work in exchange for free admission. I could afford to pay, but wound up working most nights anyway, all too often on the security detail.

Security was one of the most vital and least pleasant jobs, especially during that first year. We hadn't realized how much of a challenge it would be, having naively assumed that because we'd banned alcohol, racism, sexism, and violence, punks who were into those things wouldn't want to come to our shows.

We were mistaken. Many old school chaos and gutter punks took our policy as a personal insult. They'd turn up and demand to be let in, but when they were, it was a near-certainty they'd be fighting or breaking things before the first band was through.

The most persistent of them—and definitely the biggest pain in the ass—was a Sid Vicious clone known as Screamer. Despite repeatedly being thrown out, and eventually being given a semi-permanent ban, he kept coming back. It was as if he thought everyone at Gilman had amnesia and wouldn't remember what he'd done the last ten times he'd been there.

"You can't keep me out," he'd argue. "This is a punk club and I'm a punk."

This was a potent argument. It even worked sometimes, especially if someone inexperienced was working the door. The question of who was or wasn't a punk, and whether we had the right to exclude anyone from shows, occupied many an angst-ridden hour at our Saturday afternoon meetings.

The debate wasn't only about people like Screamer. It became obvious that trouble was more likely to erupt when certain bands played. Confrontation and disruption were central principles of punk rock, so it was inevitable that someone would always be trying to take things one step further, for instance when Frank Discussion of the Feederz tossed a dead dog into the audience.

Some people thought that was hilarious; others were angry or hurt. It also earned us unflattering publicity in the mainstream press. But the truly thorny issue was what to do about bands who, for reasons that weren't always clear, attracted fans who seemed to think it wasn't a punk show unless you were beating the shit out of somebody.

What made it especially difficult was that you couldn't always predict which shows would bring in a problematic crowd. Speedmetal and oi bands were an obvious trouble magnet, but what about MDC? Despite his cop and capitalism-hating lyrics, Dave MDC was a pot-smoking, Grateful Dead-loving hippie who preached the virtues of peace, love, and anarchy.

Yet it was a rare MDC show when some sort of violence didn't break out, forcing Dave to stop the music and plead with his fans not to kill each other. Archetypal peace punkers Christ On Parade inexplicably developed a huge following among South Bay gangbangers, who, on what might have been Gilman's worst night ever, took over the pit and began assaulting and robbing people.

The cops arrived en masse and shut down the show. It was obvious the police were needed; the young suburban teenagers in attendance were helpless against the gangbangers, many of whom were carrying weapons. But it brought up much agonizing and hand-wringing about "punks calling the cops on punks."

"We're not calling the cops on punks," went the counter-argument. "We're calling them on assholes."

This was how I felt about it, especially after being sucker-punched by one of Screamer's minions as I tried to pleasantly and respectfully explain why he couldn't come in.

Then there were the skinheads.

In the 1980s, skinhead culture was still a big thing. While some skins were out-and-out Nazis, others simply suffered from an overdose of testosterone, and still others might be all right as individuals, but turn vicious when traveling in packs. And of course, there were those who meant no harm, to whom boots, braces, and shaved heads were simply a way of expressing themselves.

Unfortunately, when skinheads showed up at the door, it was hard to tell which kind you were getting. "Diamond Dave" Whitaker, a counterculture presence since the 1950s—and renowned for introducing a young Bob Dylan to marijuana—ran a one-man campaign urging "Beats, Hippies, Punks, and Skins" to "unite." But the only kind of uniting that appealed to certain skinheads involved their fists and punk rockers' faces.

We tried taking skins at their word when they promised to behave, but it was usually only a matter of time before they had taken over the pit and started beating people up. If we tried turning them away, they'd attack the volunteers at the front door.

Between Screamer's crowd and the skinheads, it began to seem like the cops were at Gilman every weekend, whether or not anybody had called them. This wasn't the impression we'd wanted to make on the City of Berkeley, who could yank our operating permit if the club became too much of a nuisance.

It's kind of amazing how patient the police were with us, and city officials as well, especially considering how we'd sold them on the club as an alcohol and drug-free "center for the arts." The word "punk," as far as I can recall, was never mentioned.

They might have guessed, though, when a couple dozen of us strode into the City Council chambers in a trail of flashing spikes, safety pins, and multi-colored hairdos. Many members of our delegation spoke more reasonably and articulately than you might expect from looking at them, but I always thought the speech that turned the tide in our favor was by Kamala's decidedly non-punk dad.

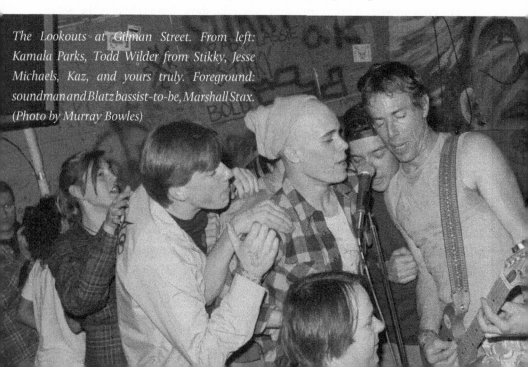

The Lookouts at Gilman Street. From left: Kamala Parks, Todd Wilder from Stikky, Jesse Michaels, Kaz, and yours truly. Foreground: soundman and Blatz bassist-to-be, Marshall Stax. (Photo by Murray Bowles)

"Don't turn your backs on these kids," he urged. "They represent what Berkeley has always been about, the opportunity to grow and express yourself in ways that might not be understood or tolerated anywhere else."

He looked and sounded like a classic Berkeley liberal, but the quiet nobility and passion of his words rekindled my affection for a town I thought I'd fallen out of love with long ago. Until then I'd assumed we were just saying what needed to be said to get our club past the bureaucracy. Now I started seeing Gilman not as an aberration or departure from Berkeley tradition, but as its logical next chapter.

As we neared our first anniversary, even the most jaded cynic had to admit something special was unfolding in that West Berkeley warehouse. Any remaining doubts should have been erased by the October release of *Turn It Around*, the *MRR* compilation David had put together.

The two 7"s might have sounded a little thin and tinny, thanks to cramming so much music onto such tiny slabs of vinyl, but the energy and spirit came blasting through. *Turn It Around* had little in common with the dark, negative aesthetic that had dominated 80s punk rock. Bands wanting to be taken seriously had once needed macabre names and artwork filled with festering corpses; now we had Sewer Trout singing "Wally and the Beaver Go To Nicaragua."

Even Rabid Lassie's anti-Reagan polemic was remarkably good-natured; it asked only that we follow the legal, constitutional procedure and "impeach the president." Punks from an earlier era would have been calling for his head on a stake.

Some took this as a sign punk was getting soft or being co-opted. I preferred to think of it as growing up. Not in the negative sense of giving up or giving in, but recognizing that everything didn't need to be turned into a moral dialectic, that it was possible to change and improve society without completely dismantling it.

This was the approach I saw our record label taking. I wasn't planning to go head-to head with Warner Brothers or Atlantic, let alone try to replace them. But neither did I see the need to stay so far underground that only the most determined and knowledgeable scenesters could find us.

When asked, as I would be many times over the years, why I wanted to start a record label, I'd glibly but truthfully answer that I was sick of the music I found in stores and heard on the radio. If I wanted any decent records, I concluded, I'd have to make them myself.

It wasn't that I didn't have dreams. Who doesn't? In a just world, I thought, Operation Ivy would be vastly outselling the schlock artists then dominating the airwaves. But like punk rockers from time immemorial, I was conditioned to think small and expect the worst.

So I would have been thrilled to sell a thousand copies each of our first four 7"s. If we managed that, we'd break even, and maybe make enough of a profit to put out a couple more records one day.

If we didn't? Then I'd be even broker than I already was. I'd sunk the last of my savings into pressing those records. David, who made his living as a bike mechanic, didn't earn enough to have savings.

I knew it was idiotic to gamble what little I had on such an uncertain venture, but what was the point of money, I kept asking myself, if I didn't put it to use doing something I loved? Despite there being a pretty good chance I'd lose everything, I went ahead and did it anyway.

Luckily, both David and I had a knack for doing things on the cheap. There weren't many bargains to be found when it came to pressing records, but we could produce passable covers for a fraction of the normal cost by xeroxing the cover art onto sheets of legal-sized paper, folding them, and stuffing them into 7" plastic bags.

It didn't hurt that I'd made friends with the manager of the all-night copy shop, who gave us huge discounts and a place to hang out while we worked. Without this and a few other "deals" and hookups (many of our early layouts were produced on *MRR*'s state-of-the-art computers, with or without Tim's permission), we might never have got off the ground.

David and I did a lot of strategizing about how to get our label going, but maybe not enough about where we expected it to go. David was not big on philosophical discussions, so I may have mistakenly assumed that because we shared similar views about bands and DIY ethics, we were on the same page about everything else.

One thing we didn't agree on was what to call the label. David, inspired by his bicycle roots, thought it should be Sprocket Records. I argued in favor of Lookout.

Lookout would give us more name recognition, I pointed out. Not so much because of my band, who enjoyed a spotty reputation at best, but *Lookout* magazine was widely read, and earlier that year I'd begun writing a *Maximum Rocknroll* column called "Lookout! It's Lawrence Livermore."

Was there some egotism involved? No doubt. I'd been operating under the Lookout banner long enough that it had become an integral part of my identity. But at the same time, I honestly felt the name would have a broader appeal. Some punk rock labels made themselves as obscure or obnoxious as possible to guarantee they'd never get "too big" or too popular, but that was never my intention.

I wasn't trying to hide the fact that we were a punk label, not that anyone would be fooled if I had. But I saw no reason why we needed to cater only to punks. Good music was good music. You shouldn't have to wear a certain costume or subscribe to a certain ideology to enjoy it.

David finally agreed to go with the name Lookout Records. Maybe he saw the wisdom of my reasoning, or, more likely, he just got tired of arguing about it. Once the decision was made, he threw himself into creating some of the instantly recognizable images that would define the label.

One was the Lookout logo, with its smiley face and "o's" turned into eyes. I'd come up with the eye thing in an early issue of *Lookout* magazine, but it was David who turned it into a usable design. It figured prominently in our first *MRR* ad, coupled with his cheeky tagline: "No one buys 7" records anymore, so we're putting out four of them."

Tre Cool and Kain Kong of the Lookouts. Lower left corner: Lint.
(Photo by Murray Bowles)

When the bands went into the studio, David was there to ride herd. There'd be no time or money wasted on knob-twiddling and guitar-tone experiments while he was around. David didn't enjoy talking on the phone, so I made most of the arrangements with the pressing plant, the mastering lab, the printers, that sort of thing. My other main role, apart from coming up with money to pay the bills, was that of hypemaster.

David's approach to selling records was about as low-key as you could get: a couple of cute, clever ads in *MRR* and Southern California's *Flipside* that said in essence: "Um, we put out some records, so if you want to buy them, here's what they cost and how to order them."

I, on the other hand, would say or do almost anything to get people to pay attention to us. These weren't just records, I'd insist, they represented a paradigmatic shift in punk rock history, and perhaps in the entire course of Western civilization.

It wasn't only hot air I was spouting. There was a tongue-in-cheek aspect to my blather, but I sincerely and passionately believed in what we were doing.

I had also learned a lesson from *Lookout* magazine, back when it was still a xeroxed newsletter emanating from Spy Rock. Mostly for fun, but also as an experiment, I'd written musical and political articles with the breathless awe-verging-on-reverence you'd find in high society gossip columns.

I might be describing a show or get-together attended by 20 people in someone's backyard, but I'd talk about it as if it were the event of the season, as if anyone who was anyone was there. If you didn't recognize the names I tossed around, the implication was clear: you must be completely, hopelessly out of it.

I was amazed at how seriously people took these stories, at how I could turn obscure nobodies into mini-celebrities simply by dangling their names in front of the public often enough. The same went for the club. When I talked about it, it was no longer just plain "Gilman Street." Nothing short of "the world famous" Gilman Street would do.

David wasn't as impressed by this approach as I was. He seldom said anything, but he had a way of cocking his eyebrow, curling his lip, and screwing up his forehead when I got carried away with the overblown rhetoric.

I chose not to notice. With our limited cash and connections, we had to rely on imagination and creativity to get our message to the public. If David found some of my tactics crass, so be it. I felt like I owed it to our bands to give them best shot I could at being heard.

Deeper and fuller conversation might have revealed the fault lines already destined to divide us, might even have prevented the label from happening in the first place. But all great enterprises, it seems, whether in the realm of commerce or art, require a certain mutual suspension of disbelief.

3.
A Broken-Toed Kickoff

I was sorry to see 1987 go. It had been one of the most exciting years of my life, and it was hard to imagine what 1988 could do for an encore.

True, the first month of the new year would mark the official launch of Lookout Records, but that slightly annoyed me. I'd wanted 1987 to be our startup date.

Why? No particular reason, just that I liked the sound and feel of it. All the bands were done recording by November, so if we busted our asses and pressured our manufacturers, I was sure we could get the records out before Christmas.

David pointed out, correctly of course, that even if we got everything done, it made no sense to bring out our first releases at the peak of the holiday season, when nobody would be paying attention. Not being big on holidays myself, I assumed we could operate as if no one else cared, but David insisted that we wait till January, so 1988 it would be.

In the meantime, we had an anniversary to celebrate: December 31, 1987 would mark one year since Gilman had opened its doors. There was a sharp chill in the midwinter air that night, but inside, the club was awash with the soft, warm glow of accomplishment.

For once everything seemed perfect. There was a crowd, but it wasn't crowded. The energy level was high, but not the nerve-wracking, stressful kind of high. No one was starting fights. Everywhere you looked you saw happy faces and togetherness.

It was a low-key event with only three bands, all Gilman regulars: Stikky, Isocracy, and Operation Ivy. It made a pleasant change from the habit we'd gotten into of letting five or sometimes even six bands play, causing shows to drag on to a bleary-eyed two or three in the morning.

If there was one thing detracting from my enjoyment, it was a slight grievance I'd been nursing since my birthday in October. It was aimed more at Tim Yohannan than at the club, but it wasn't always easy to tell the two apart.

I'd been planning to celebrate my birthday onstage with the Lookouts, so I'd set up a show that included us, Isocracy, and MDC. It was a lineup I was sure would pack the place, but at the last minute, Tim pulled the plug. Gilman, he said, had been given the "rare opportunity" to present an "important" DC band called Scream.

I'd heard of Scream, and I figured Tim was entitled to his opinion about how important they were. But I didn't see why they had to ruin my birthday.

"Not that many people are going to come see some obscure DC band," I told Tim. "But if you think they should play, we'll just add them onto our bill."

"It wouldn't be a good match-up," he said. "Scream is a serious band. You guys and Isocracy and MDC? C'mon, you gotta admit that's kind of a clown show. We owe Scream more respect."

Gilman in those days worked the same way *MRR* did: you could discuss and argue all you wanted, but Tim's decision was final. My show was canceled and Scream played to a half-full house. I hung around for a while on the sidewalk out front, but didn't go in.

If Tim had wanted to clue me in about Scream, he'd picked the wrong way to go about it. I already had a chip on my shoulder about what I saw as the excessively austere and ponderous DC sound.

Ironically, Dischord Records, which epitomized that sound, was one of my chief models for how a punk label should be run. Nearly everything about Lookout owed something to Dischord in terms of inspiration and example. Everything, that is, except the music.

I'll admit I'd become pretty narrow-minded about listening to anything from outside our immediate scene. Because of that, I missed out on all sorts of great music, both mainstream and underground. Even David marveled at my almost-willful ignorance of anything that wasn't produced within a 50-mile radius of Berkeley.

But our anniversary celebration was no time for grudges and resentments. Once Lookout Records was up and running, I vowed, Tim would see I was capable of more than a "clown show." Meanwhile, I was going to enjoy the party.

I'd had a couple of beers, typically my limit on Gilman nights. Although I had a history of heavy, sometimes excessive drinking, I was seldom if ever drunk at the club.

That was only partly because of the "two blocks away" rule (immortalized in song by Isocracy) that in theory banned Gilman members from drinking in the immediate vicinity. Over-21s could head to Picante, the Mexican bar and burrito joint down on 6th Street. The underaged and adventurous retreated to nearby bushes to do their drinking.

But as one of the more visible regulars, especially as one who was always harping on about doing things "the Gilman way," I had to set a good example. We'd been having less trouble since the night the punks, with False Prophets guitarist George Tabb and Jane Guskin of the Yeastie Girlz leading the charge, stood up to a gang of skinheads and sent them running. But there were still occasional problems with people who wanted to start fights or just be a pain in the ass.

Since alcohol typically figured in these incidents, I felt it was my responsibility to at least stay more sober than the people causing them. Beers or no beers, I felt especially clear-headed and positive on that anniversary night. If only every show could be like this, I remember thinking.

Midway through the Operation Ivy set, I took a break and climbed on stage, where, crouched on all fours in front of the bass amp, I watched the action as if from the eye of a hurricane. A kid twice my size came sailing out of the crowd in what can only be described as a reverse stage dive. He landed on top of me, which caused my right foot to bend sharply backward, snapping my big toe.

I'd suffered many sprains and strains over the years, and had always dealt with them by "walking it off." I tried to do the same this time, even though I kind of knew I was dealing with a broken bone.

Just standing up was hard enough, let alone walking, but I forced myself to anyway, as if I could make my toe better by sheer will power. It wasn't simply a matter of me being an idiot, though that played a part in it. I also, through some bit of convoluted punk logic, saw it as a protest against the American health care system.

A few months earlier, at the On Broadway in San Francisco, I'd been kicked between the eyes—deliberately, as near as I could tell—by a stage diver. Spewing blood everywhere, I somehow made it to San Francisco General, the local "charity" hospital, where I sat for ten hours waiting to get stitched up.

Every time it looked like they were finally about to get to me, a new gunshot or stabbing victim would be rolled in. I sat there seething at the barbarism of it all. It might not make sense to you (nor to me, looking back on it), but until America offered the universal health care that other civilized nations did, I vowed never to go through an emergency room ordeal like that again.

Limping around in agony for the next several months gave me carte blanche to gripe and fulminate to my heart's content, but it would prove to be one of the dumber decisions of my life. My toe never healed properly; despite thousands of dollars worth of surgery and corrective footwear, it still gives me problems today.

But what, you ask, does my broken toe have to do with the story of Lookout Records? Just that I was in a lot of pain the first month or two we were in business. It might also provide some insight into my headstrong-to-the-point-of-stupid attitude that certain people—say David, for example—found it hard to deal with.

Apart from my aching foot, the opening months of 1988 went smoothly. Records arrived from the pressing plant; the covers, produced with typical David

Hayes efficiency, were ready and waiting (except for Isocracy, based on a concept by yours truly and run off in a last-minute, all-night copy shop frenzy).

We held the first of several stuffing parties, which consisted of David and me sitting on the floor inserting records, lyric booklets, and covers into thousands of plastic bags. I was surprised when David produced a sequential stamper: his idea was that each record would be numbered from 1 to 1,000. I didn't see the point of it, (or anything else that created extra work), but David explained that little touches like these were important to people.

David wasn't obsessive about such things—a few years later, his new label would release a compilation whose title, *Make The Collector Nerd Sweat*, poked fun at those who were—but he was far more aware of and attentive to formats and packaging than I was.

To me the music itself was all that mattered. I didn't care how it was transmitted to the listener as long as it got there. As I saw it, our first releases came out on 7" vinyl not as some sort of aesthetic statement, but because that was what we could afford, and what people seemed to want. When, a year or so later, we started making cassettes, it was for the same reason.

The idea of doing CDs barely came up. This was partly for financial reasons, but also because the mere existence of CDs was a hot-button topic among punks. Some believed any band that released music in this new format automatically forfeited all credibility.

The debate wasn't as irrational or pointless as it might sound today. Many people felt consumers were being forced or tricked into buying for a second time— and at a much higher price—the same music they already owned on records. And there were the audio purists, who insisted CDs lacked the "warmth," or some similarly intangible quality, of vinyl. Personally, I couldn't hear the difference.

Anyway, as long as *Maximum Rocknroll* refused to review or even acknowledge the existence of CDs, we weren't likely to sell enough of them to justify the flak we'd take for making them.

There are probably people who can tell you the exact day David and I brought boxes of our first four 7"s to sell at Gilman. I'm not one of them. It was somewhere near the end of January, as best as I can recall.

There's usually a burst of excitement about any new record. I'd sold a hundred copies of the Lookouts LP at Gilman the weekend it came out.

But interest in that record had quickly tapered off. With our new 7"s, the opposite happened. Operation Ivy and Isocracy were the best sellers, but Crimpshrine and Corrupted Morals didn't lag far behind. Having to do second

pressings for all four started to seem like a real possibility.

Selling records solely at shows and through the mail would only take us so far, though. To reach a larger audience, we needed to get them into stores. A few local shops were willing to take some on consignment, and, if we were lucky, even pay us for them.

To make our records readily available outside Berkeley and San Francisco, however, we'd have to deal with distributors. This can be a tricky business, and it's the hurdle at which many independent labels fall. We nearly did ourselves.

At the risk of over-simplifying, a distributor is like a record label for record labels. And we were like the new, unknown band hoping to convince someone to take a chance on us.

The large, well-established distributors weren't interested because we were too small and nobody had heard of our bands. Besides, most of them were partially or wholly owned by major labels, which meant we wouldn't want to work with them, either.

Punks—at least our kind of punks—didn't do that. So our only choice was to deal with independent, DIY distributors that operated—hopefully—along the same lines we did.

Some of them did a decent job, and most meant well, but independent distributors had an unfortunate habit of going broke or closing up shop, often while owing a ton of money to labels. Luckily there was one shining exception to this rule.

San Francisco-based Mordam (pronounced "more damn") Records had enjoyed considerable success as a label—its first release was by a then-unknown Faith No More—but the company hit its stride when it branched out into distribution.

Totally independent, adamantly refusing major label-connected deals, Mordam was the reason a magazine like *Maximum Rocknroll* and records like *Turn It Around* could be found in shops all over the USA.

Mordam handled over a dozen punk rock labels, chief among them Jello Biafra's Alternative Tentacles, home to the Dead Kennedys. That connection was the linchpin of a highly effective strategy. Simply put, if you were selling punk records in the 1980s, you had to carry the Dead Kennedys. And if you wanted the Dead Kennedys, you had to deal with Mordam.

That in turn meant you paid your bills on time, not just for your Dead Kennedys records, but for anything and everything Mordam handled, no matter what tiny, obscure label it might be on. This gave Mordam the ability, almost unique among independent distributors, to pay its labels in full every month, like clockwork.

It didn't matter if you were Jello Biafra, sitting on a warehouse packed with highly marketable Dead Kennedys LPs, or a kid cranking out the occasional 7" from your bedroom: you got the same respect and reliably honest treatment.

Mordam was the brainchild of Ruth Schwartz, a smart and savvy young woman who'd been involved with *Maximum Rocknroll* since its earliest days. Warm-hearted and endlessly helpful, she also had a reputation for being a little sharp-tongued. Which was understandable: while extremely hard working and conscientious herself, she constantly had to deal with punks who, to put it mildly, weren't.

Spend a few minutes in her office as she fielded phone calls and contended with excuses on the level of "the dog ate my record covers," and it would become obvious why she sometimes seemed to lack patience. The day would come when I, too, would be the object of her withering sarcasm or a peremptory "I don't need to hear the story of your life; just tell me if the record's going to be here on time."

lookout records
PROFIT MOTIVE CHART

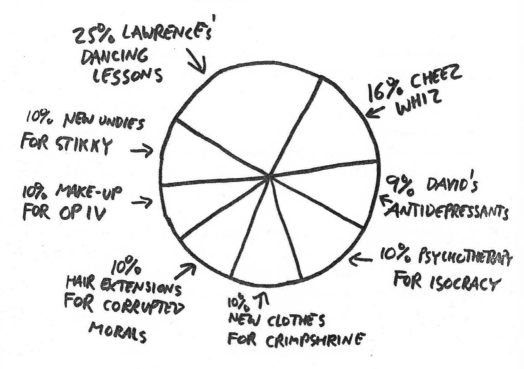

25% LAWRENCE'S DANCING LESSONS

16% CHEEZ WHIZ

10% NEW UNDIES FOR STIKKY →

10% MAKE-UP FOR OP IV →

9% DAVID'S ANTIDEPRESSANTS

10% PSYCHOTHERAPY FOR ISOCRACY

10% HAIR EXTENSIONS FOR CORRUPTED MORALS

10% NEW CLOTHES FOR CRIMPSHRINE

IF YOU HAVE ANY QUESTIONS OR COMMENTS, CONTACT LAWRENCE LIVERMORE. (IF HE ISNT PRACTICING THE CHA-CHA).

Lookout may have been a chaotic, shoestring operation, but we had a solid business plan, as outlined here by Walter Glaser. (Drawing by Walter Glaser)

But that day had not yet arrived, because she politely but firmly refused to take Lookout on as a client. Her reasoning was hard to argue with, though I tried. She couldn't afford, she said, to take chances on another tiny startup label that might not even be around a year from now.

It did no good to point out that we'd have a far better chance of surviving if we got decent distribution. It was like the classic situation young jobseekers find themselves in: "They'll only hire me if I have experience, but how do I get experience if no one will hire me?"

Not long after getting the thumbs-down from Mordam, the news got a lot worse. Systematic, one of our next best options as an indie distributor, had gone out of business, just after we'd given them hundreds of copies of our new releases. The chances of getting paid for those records, or even seeing them again, stood somewhere between slim and nonexistent.

So it looked like the dream might be over before it had a chance to begin. True, if we sold all our remaining copies, we might still break even, but that was a pretty big if. And though there was enough demand for our records to justify a second pressing, without the Systematic money, it was hard to say if or when that would be possible.

I hobbled around on my still-aching foot, cursing our luck and, like a good punk, blaming everything on "society." David, equally disappointed, stayed relatively unfazed and kept on with the business of selling the 7"s we had. For a month or two, the future of Lookout Records hung in an uncertain and precarious balance.

4.
Life At The Maxipad

The Systematic debacle didn't set us back as long or as badly as I'd feared. On the first weekend of March, four-fifths of the Lookout roster—Operation Ivy, Isocracy, Crimpshrine, and the Lookouts—headed up to Arcata in Humboldt County for what I called our "Gilman in exile" show.

A Humboldt State University student had written to ask if I could bring some of our bands to play at his school. Despite being over a hundred miles north of Spy Rock, Arcata sat within the boundaries of the somewhat lawless and exotic region known as the Emerald Triangle, making it almost a hometown show for the Lookouts.

None of the East Bay bands had ventured this far from Berkeley before, and I was nervous about whether they would live up to the nonstop praise I'd heaped on them in *Lookout* and *MRR*. At least once in a while I wondered if I'd ingested too much of my own propaganda.

The bands weren't always comfortable with the way I talked them up. Punks weren't supposed to make a big deal of themselves, let alone show any sign that they craved recognition or success.

Don't worry, I told them, just concentrate on your music and let me take care of the bragging. But it was important, I argued, not to wallow in false modesty. If you don't have some faith in your own significance, why expect anyone else to?

Ultimately, I believed in these bands, as much as I'd ever believed in anything. My ongoing nightmare was that they or I would screw something up, miss a crucial opportunity, and see them lost in the shuffle and forgotten.

I'd watched it happen to some friends of mine. Their band, the Pushups, had briefly been the darlings of San Francisco's New Wave scene at the tail end of the 1970s. Combining power pop and quirky synths with Beatles-esque harmonies, they could and probably should have been stars. Maybe even superstars.

Instead they squabbled about how to get signed, dithered when they should have been dashing forward, and acrimoniously dissolved just as everything was starting to come their way.

I'd been friends with Al, their drummer, ever since my hippie days. Shortly after the Pushups imploded in 1980, I drove him and his equipment out to a warehouse in Hunter's Point for an audition.

Before joining the Pushups, Al had spent several years with a Colorado band called the Ravers. The Ravers' roadie, a young kid by the name of Eric Boucher, eventually showed up on Al's doorstep in San Francisco, looking for a place to stay while he transformed himself into Jello Biafra and started what would become Northern California's biggest punk rock band, the Dead Kennedys.

Now it was Al who needed a favor, or more specifically, a job. Since the Dead Kennedys were looking for a new drummer, Biafra offered him a tryout.

It was my first time meeting Biafra. He exuded the same sort of quasi-didactic bombast that he did onstage, but in a lower key, and was actually quite pleasant to talk to. Having barely slept for the previous 72 hours—I was still in my hard partying days—I flopped down behind the bass amp and fell asleep while Al ran through some numbers with the band.

I must not have been fully asleep, because I remember being vaguely aware of the music, and finding it strangely restful. The Dead Kennedys were often disparaged as being little more than a wall of noise for Biafra to shout over, but as I drifted in and out of consciousness I realized that these guys were actually really good musicians. Al, a solid drummer in the Ringo Starr tradition, could keep up with them, but that was about it.

Then Darren walked in. He was a regular on the SF punk scene, and had been spending a lot of time with my on-again, off-again girlfriend, to the point where I suspected they might be doing more than just hanging out. But he was such a nice, friendly guy that I'd never been able to get too upset about it.

Until that point, I'd assumed Al's "tryout" was a mere formality, that he was all but guaranteed to be the DKs' new drummer. But with Darren's first kick and snare hit, it was obvious Al was out of the running.

Though only a few years apart in age, Al and Darren represented wildly differing generations. Al continued to dabble in music until his premature death in the 1990s, but his moment, like that of the Pushups, had passed.

Experiences like that left me spooked by the missed opportunity, the chance not taken, and made me all the more determined not to allow a similar fate to befall the bands I'd promised to, pardon the pun, look out for.

But there was nothing to worry about. The Arcata show was every bit as great as I'd hoped. People would be talking about it far into the future, especially the couple who wandered off into the bushes during Isocracy's set and wound up conceiving a child.

Midway through the evening David Hayes and I took a walk with Operation Ivy to get burritos at Hey Juan, Arcata's hippie-flavored and distinctly un-Mexican version of a taqueria. Sitting on the sidewalk out front, bits of spilled beans and salsa collecting on the pavement around us, we talked about what should come next for the band.

"How about doing another 7"?" said David.

"Sounds good to me," I agreed, quietly wondering how we were going to pay for it.

"Yeah, we talked about that, but we decided we wanna make an album," said Lint.

An album? I almost choked on what was left of my burrito.

"It might be too soon to be thinking about albums," David said.

"Yeah, maybe. But that's what we wanna do."

We kicked this back and forth, but it was pointless. Lint claims I always used to say, "You can tell Operation Ivy, but you can't tell 'em much."

Some bands were so happy to be making a record that they'd follow any suggestion I offered. Others took it further, afraid to change the settings on their guitar amps without asking my opinion. But Operation Ivy would listen politely to whatever I said, then, just as politely, tell me, "Yeah, we already decided what we're gonna do."

At first I found this aggravating, but once I accepted that there was no use arguing with them, life became a lot simpler. Besides, I had to admit, they were usually right.

Two weeks later, Operation Ivy left on their first and only tour. "3,000 miles in a four-door car," Lint would one day sing about it, though by my math it looked more like 10,000. David rode along with them, and I was left to hold down the Lookout fort on my own.

Well, not completely on my own. As we'd driven away from the Arcata show, a young kid had run out in front of our truck, yelling "Stop!"

I thought he was going to tell us we'd left some cables or an amp behind, but he just wanted to introduce himself. Chris Appelgren, 14 years old at the time, had recently begun hosting the punk rock show on KMUD, Southern Humboldt's new community radio station. I stopped by for an interview the following Saturday, and wound up sticking around as Chris's co-host for the next several years.

Chris, in turn, became Lookout's first employee, folding record covers and packaging mail orders for a few hours a week. He earned minimum wage, if that, and the job was only meant to last as long as David was away.

Then I got a call from Ruth Schwartz. She'd changed her mind. Lookout was going to be a Mordam label after all.

I don't know if she'd heard rumors about how well our first releases were doing, or if Tim Yohannan had put in a good word for us. Whatever the reason, once Ruth took charge, selling records was no longer going to be a problem.

Our entire inventory, even the several hundred unsold Lookouts albums that had languished in my kitchen for the past year, vanished into the cavernous Mordam warehouse. It felt like only days had passed when Ruth called to say she was out of stock. How soon, she wanted to know, could we re-press everything?

Sales doubled and doubled again. Because there was a three-month lag between when records sold and when we got paid, I had to do some creative account juggling at first. But once we got caught up, and for as long as I stayed with the label, covering our bills would never again be an issue.

Until then, David had literally been able to do our accounting on the back of an envelope. His system, straightforward and simple, worked well for the first couple of years. I tried to teach myself how to do bookkeeping on my new computer, a 512k (yes, *kilo*bytes) Macintosh, but until at least 1990, paper and pen remained faster and more efficient.

David phoned me after the first night of the Operation Ivy tour, practically gushing. "It was amazing! Everyone already knew all the words!" Six weeks later, Op Ivy were welcomed back by a packed Gilman. It reminded me of that Supremes show I'd seen as a teenager, when Detroit turned out to honor its hometown girls made good. I began to think both the band and our label might be on the brink of something far bigger than we'd bargained for.

At the beginning of the year I'd given up my room at the Rathouse and relocated to the *Maximum Rocknroll* house at 484 Clipper Street, near the top of a steep hill overlooking San Francisco's Noe Valley. It had seemed like a dream move at the time, but things hadn't worked out so well.

People living at the Maxipad, as it was often called, got cheap(ish) rent in exchange for working on the magazine. The trouble with this deal was that the amount of work expected of us was never specified, not to mention where it began or ended.

Most of us thought we were doing an adequate job as long as the magazine came out on time, which it always did. But Tim Yohannan, who presided over us like a crotchety counselor at sleepaway camp, couldn't stand to see anyone sitting idle. He'd point out that there were still scene reports and record reviews to be typed for next month's issue, or the month's after that.

Isocracy's Jason Beebout (with mic) joins Operation Ivy on stage. It wasn't unusual for half the audience to do likewise. (Photo by Murray Bowles)

The only time we could relax was weekday mornings, when Tim was at his part-time job in Berkeley. For a few hours the "shitworkers," as we were known, could lounge around the living room, cracking jokes and goofing off.

But somewhere between 12 and 1, Walter Glaser would spot Tim's car turning into the driveway and shout, "Oh shit, Dad's home!" By the time Tim walked in we'd be parked in front of our computers inputting data so assiduously that he might even encourage us to take a break and relax. For five or ten minutes, anyway.

I don't mean to imply the place was some sort of gulag or sweatshop. Even when Tim was around, there was plenty of laughter and fun. But a certain level of earnestness and seriousness was expected. You needed to know which things could be joked about and which were out of bounds.

It was sometimes hard to keep a straight face about the letters that filled *MRR's* first several pages. Some were thoughtful and insightful, but others were mind-bogglingly dumb. Fed up with typing one too many of the latter, Walter and I put together a parody letter and slipped it into the pasteups for the next issue, thinking Tim would never notice:

Dear Maximum Roc end Role,

My name is Spike. Im in @ punk group called the Fucken Shitz. We halfent bean together for two long, butt you can still tottalie slam to us, we play hard thrash wiht intelijunt lerriks about anerkie and kiling yer parrunts. I wus wunderring if yoo gis cood intervoo us four yer maggazine. Our best toon is cald "Fuk You, Mom". It's hour fastestt song it really thrashes like crasie. Ane way how is your seen? My seen is coole. We plaed a gigg lazzed weak and their wuz sum heevy slaming. It was cowel. I no sum peepol r luzing fath in the punck seene, but as longe ass their's intelijunt fulks like me and yu gize, i thinke the zene has a brite fyutoor.

> Kep up the goode werk,
> Spike @narkie

P.S. Skinz comed & rekked a show. Wat nutzis!

We were wrong. Tim checked every word of the magazine, before and after it was laid out. He admitted Spike Anarkie wasn't far removed from certain punks we knew, but didn't think our little joke was funny. It showed a lack of respect for the scene, he said.

He might be right, I admitted. That was before I started noticing that words in my own column had mysteriously been changed or eliminated. It didn't happen often, and usually involved fairly trivial stuff, but it felt Orwellian enough to kind of creep me out.

Individual egos or opinions mattered little to Tim. He believed anything published in the magazine should reflect official policy, which, ultimately, was whatever he'd decided it should be. *MRR*, in Tim's view, was more than a fanzine or entertainment guide; ideally he thought it should serve as a focal point and springboard for political and cultural revolution.

Like me, Tim was a product of the 60s. Unlike me, he still clung unswervingly to the Marxist principles of his youth, jazzed up with more than a dollop of Machiavelli. People's feelings weren't important. Getting things done was.

If you were friends with him, working toward a common purpose, you couldn't ask for a more devoted ally. On all but a handful of subjects, he had a wicked sense of humor. His laugh—somewhere between a cackle and a bray—was as infectious as it was unmistakable.

Arguments, especially about politics or punk rock, were one of Tim's favorite pastimes. Although he could get loud and abrasive, those of us who lived with him knew no real malice was involved. Visitors didn't always understand that.

When three militant straight edge bands—Youth Of Today, No For An Answer, and Insted—spent the weekend with us, Tim picked a fight, accusing them of looking and acting like "a bunch of jocks."

To be fair, they kind of did, but the straight edgers didn't appreciate having it pointed out. They argued long and angrily into the night.

Tim outshouted them all. He sounded as mad as they were, but whenever he paused for breath I could see his face relaxing into an almost beatific smile.

Another epic dispute had Tim and I screaming our heads off about whether the new Seattle bands like Nirvana, Soundgarden, and Mudhoney qualified as "punk."

I said no; Tim surprised me by claiming at least some of them did. I don't know if he really believed it, or just wanted to fight. In any event, when someone from Nirvana phoned to ask if they could play a Sunday matinee at Gilman, he was told to forget about it, on the grounds that "nobody would come."

By far my favorite thing about the Maxipad was the people I met there. It felt like every punk rock-related person in the world would eventually show up at our door. I talked LSD and spiritual experiences with Youth Of Today singer and budding Hare Krishna Ray Cappo, got a detailed tutorial in the history of European punk from German fanzine editor Dolf Hermannstädter, and traded gossip and rumors with columnists and contributors from places I'd never known existed.

What wasn't so cool was when *MRR* began to feel a little like a cross between a job and a cult. Living there demanded a level of commitment few people could sustain for long, so there was a constant turnover of kids moving in, often straight from school or their parents' houses, and out again within a matter of months.

MRR itself didn't seem to be the problem; many volunteers remained involved for decades. The people succumbing to rapid burnout syndrome were mainly those who lived there.

"I thought maybe Lookout could use a San Francisco base of operations," Tim had said when he offered me a room at the Maxipad, but there was never time to work on either the record label or my magazine, at least not while Tim was around. Any non-*MRR* work typically got done between 2 and 6 in the morning, when he was asleep.

Just when I thought I was used to Tim's quirks and foibles, he announced a ban on romantic relationships among those of us living at the Maxipad. It reminded me a little too much of the Moonies, whose leader had recently been in the news for personally assigning brides and grooms to his followers.

Tim's edict failed to stop one pair of Maxipadders from falling in love, and we

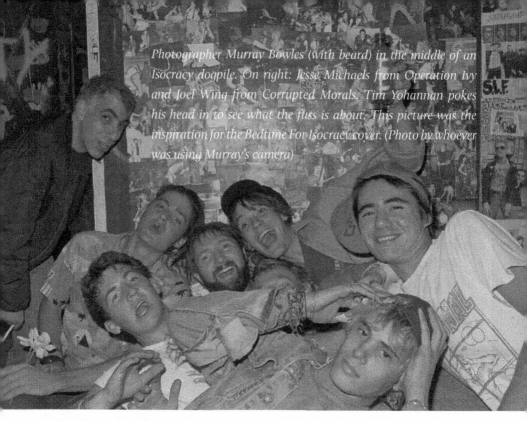
Photographer Murray Bowles (with beard) in the middle of an Isocracy dogpile. On right: Jesse Michaels from Operation Ivy and Joel Wing from Corrupted Morals. Tim Yohannan pokes his head in to see what the fuss is about. This picture was the inspiration for the Bedtime For Isocracy cover. (Photo by whoever was using Murray's camera)

all had to pitch in to cover for them. The ensuing shenanigans would have made for a hilarious romantic comedy, but in real life it was more than a little pathetic.

There was no point in questioning Tim about policies like this. He'd give you an exasperated, pitying look that implied you must be an idiot for failing to grasp his reasoning. Unable to challenge him on important issues, I sniped at him about trivial ones—musical styles, or his unhealthy diet, in which greasy ribs and cigarettes were the two most important food groups. An undercurrent of meanness crept into what had once been good-natured bickering.

"Wait till Ian gets here," Tim kept saying. "You need to have a talk with him."

He meant Ian MacKaye, former singer for Minor Threat and co-founder of Dischord Records. His new band, Fugazi, was coming to Gilman to play their first California show, and they'd be staying with us.

I wasn't looking forward to it. Ian's reputation as the straightest straight edger ever, combined with Tim's obvious hope that meeting him might help sort out my bad attitude, made it feel like I was getting sent to the principal's office.

But the Ian who wandered into our living room one morning wearing striped pajamas, cracking jokes and asking friendly questions, bore no resemblance to the avenging angel I'd expected. He felt more like everybody's favorite uncle.

I liked and admired him, and wished he could "have a talk" with Tim, and maybe exert some of his benign, calming influence in that direction. I felt bad that I couldn't really get into Ian's music. It was a bit too angular and mathematical for my pop-punk heart.

But once Fugazi said their goodbyes and set out for Southern California, life at the Maxipad returned to normal. In other words, not so good.

I knew I'd have to leave, probably sooner rather than later, but hung on, hoping things might improve. One afternoon I came home to find a note from Tim taped to my door:

"The upstairs bathtub and sink need scrubbing. Take care of it."

I went right to work, but midway though the job had an epiphany.

It wasn't that the bathroom didn't need cleaning. Nor did I mind doing it. In an earlier incarnation, after all, I'd been a half-decent janitor.

What bothered me was how I'd been asked. Not asked, told. Even more troubling was the way I'd reflexively followed Tim's order without giving it a second thought.

In the early 1970s, I'd gotten involved with another music-and-politics collective, the Rainbow People's Party, also known as the White Panthers. Their version of Tim Yohannan had been John Sinclair, onetime manager of the MC5 and outspoken advocate of marijuana-fueled revolution.

White Panther "shitworkers" were called "cadre," to distinguish them from the "Central Committee," which determined policy and assigned duties. I happily did whatever job I was asked to, assuming that "the cause" was more important than my feelings or ego.

But one day I innocently asked John Sinclair how he could give speeches denouncing "honky death drugs" like heroin or cocaine, then come home and do cocaine in the back room with fellow members of the Central Committee.

"My statements are perfectly correct," he said. "It's just a matter of bringing my private practice into line with my public policy."

This Nixonian reply jolted me out of my previously unquestioned loyalty to John and the Panthers. Soon afterward I left, never to return.

I hadn't grown quite that disillusioned with Tim, but I suspected that if I kept living at the Maxipad, I might. I went downstairs to tell him, but before I could open my mouth, he said, "I think you need to move out."

It worked out for the best. We never became close friends again, but were able to get along reasonably well for quite a few more years. After giving some thought to my options, I packed up my truck and went back to living fulltime on Spy Rock.

Not, of course, until I'd finished scrubbing out the bathtub.

5.
1988, Stand Up And Take A Look Around

Living on a mountain 180 miles away from Berkeley, with no phone and only as much electricity as my solar panels could generate, left me with a scattershot perspective on what came next.

I can reconstruct some of it from memory and conversations with friends, but I also need to rely on old *Lookout* magazines and the one or two-page catalogs we assembled during those days.

Memories are tricky things, with their own agendas. I recall those last two years on Spy Rock as some sort of fleeting golden age, but it's like examining the past through a series of cracked and faded photographs, or a herky-jerky old time film with yawning gaps between the frames.

So it's hard to describe exactly where, when, and in what order events unfolded. One of the few things I know for certain is that by the time 1988 was over we had twice as many releases, twice as much money, and Lookout Records was on the verge of falling apart.

David was the prime mover behind our sixth, seventh, and eighth releases, though when it came to Sacramento's erratic yet irresistible Sewer Trout, I would have done my best to bring them to Lookout if he hadn't. The Stikky LP, though, was all David's doing.

As much as I enjoyed Stikky's manic hybrid of comedy, crunching metal, and hyperactive hardcore, it hadn't occurred to me to do a record with them. I didn't really "get" the style of music they simultaneously loved and lampooned. It played well on stage, but I wasn't sure if it could be captured on vinyl.

The Stikky kids—brothers Chris and Todd Wilder, and Chris Dodge, who also played with No Use For A Name—were astonishingly gifted musicians, with a repertoire of songs that could have filled two or three albums. But the quality of their Lookout recording didn't do the band justice. In my opinion, it didn't even measure up to some of their self-released cassettes.

I'm still not sure why. David had been there for the whole session ("6 hours including a pizza break," the liner notes bragged), and most records he worked on came out sounding pretty good. I suspected the problem might have been his tendency to value speed and efficiency over getting the "perfect" sound.

Part of this was economics; our recording budgets in those days were laughably tiny. But it was an attitude as well. David had little patience with bands who took themselves or their music too seriously.

With him around there'd be no agonizing over all but inaudible differences between various takes and mixes. David was notorious for cutting short any such debates with a "Sounds great! What's next?"

This is not necessarily a bad approach. The near-limitless possibilities afforded by multi-track recording can leave you trapped in the audio equivalent of a hall of mirrors, endlessly reaching for that one elusive tweak that will fulfill your artistic vision.

Sooner or later, though, you stop being creative and start crawling up your own ass. That's when there needs to be someone willing to call time and say, "Sounds great, what's next?" It's especially true when dealing with punk rock. Take too long fussing over it, and you can produce it to death.

It's also possible to go to the opposite extreme. Bands are sometimes so determined to be "punk" that they create something deliberately slapdash and shabby. That's not something Stikky would have done, though. Wacky antics notwithstanding, they were as serious about their music as they were about their silliness.

Being young and eager to please, however, they may have been taking cues from David's nonchalance. If he seemed happy, they'd be unlikely to argue with him. David, meanwhile, wouldn't have wanted to interrupt the band when they appeared to be on a roll.

What marred the record most was its trebly tone. Neither the band nor David could have done much about that without help from Kevin Army.

Kevin engineered and produced most of our early releases. He was good at his work, enormously supportive with our young bands, and deservedly became a vital part of Lookout history.

But during his own career as a musician, he'd suffered some significant hearing loss, especially in the upper ranges. Later on he'd learn to compensate for it, but his first efforts for Lookout often over-emphasized the treble frequencies. In some cases, the imbalance wasn't that noticeable, but with Stikky it was, almost painfully so.

That's my theory, anyway. Much of Kevin's subsequent work could stand shoulder to shoulder with that produced in studios costing ten or a hundred times more than the rudimentary setups he used. But in 1987 and 1988, he, like all of us, was still finding his way.

I spent many hours in the studio with him. He could be a little thin-skinned at times, but this was usually a reaction to know-it-alls like myself who kept trying to tell him how to do his job. Kevin's arched eyebrows and waspish sarcasm could quickly bring over-ambitious musicians back to earth, but occasionally might have intimidated them into keeping their mouths shut even when something needed to be said.

The Stikky album was far from a failure. We sold every copy we pressed, and probably could have sold more. But its shortcomings highlighted the differences beginning to surface between David and me. His attitude seemed to be, "It's only punk rock, it's good enough."

That rubbed me the wrong way. I didn't see why we should confine ourselves to some subcultural ghetto by putting out haphazardly made records. If the music we were releasing was as good as I believed it was, didn't it make sense to do whatever we could to let it shine?

Many records David subsequently worked on were excellently done. But he seemed to harbor an almost deliberately anti-commercial instinct that became more evident as the year passed.

He never brought a band to Lookout that I actively disliked, but his tastes were headed in a different direction from my own. People were already saying it was easy to tell which records were David's doing and which were Larry's.

Certain bands—Op Ivy and Sewer Trout, for example—we totally agreed on. But David's love for noisy, abrasive, metal-tinged hardcore was something I never fully understood or appreciated.

Even when it came to music we both liked, we found things to disagree about. He didn't want to hear me speculate about bands becoming popular even on an underground—let alone a mainstream—level. It almost felt as if he thought it was our job to stop that from happening, or at least delay it as much as possible.

That might sound crazy today, but in 1988, especially on the *MRR*-dominated Northern California punk scene, there was an inbuilt hostility to anything that looked or sounded like "success." Even if you secretly dreamed of bigger things, you'd be wise not to admit it.

This confused me. I saw no logical reason why some of our bands shouldn't sell hundreds of thousands, even millions of records. I was convinced, after all, that they were just as good as, if not better than, most bands who did. But the minute I said anything like that, I risked incurring the wrath of *MRR*, "the punks," and, most of all, my partner.

It wasn't just that topic. It began to seem like everything I said got on David's nerves.

Now that I was living back on Spy Rock, we saw less of each other, but when we did meet up, I was constantly walking on eggshells to avoid upsetting him. If I asked what was wrong, he'd say there was no point in trying to explain. In the middle of a conversation, he'd jump up and run out of the room, shouting, "You don't understand anything I say!" or simply, "AAAAAAAAAAAAAAURGHHHH!"

Having spent most of my adult life in touchy-feely California, I thought everything was resolvable if you just "talked about it." I'd chase him down, trying to do just that, but David wasn't a "talking about it" kind of guy.

With my attempts at communication only exasperating him further, I had to accept that his real problem was me. Still, it came as a shock when he said he was quitting Lookout and starting his own label. The next thing I knew, he was passing out a flyer asking for bands to be on his first release, a compilation called *Floyd*.

In the meantime, he finished a couple more records for our label. One was an EP by Plaid Retina, who practiced in an abandoned boxcar in the Central Valley, and played a loud, frantic, adventurous variety of hardcore that you could almost call jazz-thrash.

The other was Sewer Trout's *Songs About Drinking*, which I've always regarded as a Lookout classic. My main project at the time was *Ovary Action*, an EP by the Yeastie Girlz, one of those groups that almost literally came to life on the sidewalk in front of Gilman.

Pre-geek, pre-graffiti Gilman.
(Photo by Murray Bowles)

"Political all-girl a cappella rap" might not sound like the most marketable of concepts, but I wanted them for our label even if they never sold a single record. If nothing else, our overwhelmingly male roster needed some balance. More to the point, the Yeastie Girlz were delivering a message that needed to be heard.

Their recording sounded a little dry to me, though. I urged them to add some rhythm tracks. "You'll reach way more people," I promised.

I might as well have asked Operation Ivy to rewrite their songs without the ska parts. My suggestion wasn't so much rejected as ignored. The Yeasties had started out a cappella, and were staying that way.

I didn't push it. I knew *Ovary Action* would do far better if it sounded more like a conventional rap record, but I didn't want to replay the tired music industry trope of a male label boss telling women performers how to present themselves.

Despite my reservations, the record went on to become Lookout's third or fourth best-selling EP ever. Years later, one of the songs, "You Suck," did get a backing track, in a remix by the political rap group Consolidated, and became a much bigger hit. Not that I'm one to say "I told you so" or anything.

All through 1988, Lookout led a charmed life. Every record we put out did somewhere between very well and great. But what would happen if David went ahead with his plan to quit?

Launching and running the label had been so much a joint operation that I couldn't imagine continuing without him. This became all the more obvious as I recruited bands for the compilation I was planning. By mid-autumn I'd enlisted enough of my favorites to fill an LP, but had nothing in the way of artwork, recording, or even a title.

David's record, meanwhile, was well on its way to completion, but he was struggling with a lack of resources and distribution. Somehow we wound up agreeing that it made no sense to do two separate Bay Area compilations, and joined forces to turn our two records into a 34-track double LP called *The Thing That Ate Floyd*.

It was arguably our best compilation ever, and at least for a while there was no more talk of David leaving. Our attention shifted to the long-awaited but repeatedly delayed Operation Ivy album.

It had been in the works ever since that sidewalk meeting in Arcata, but for months nothing happened. I'd always assumed they'd go into the studio with Kevin Army, but Operation Ivy weren't about to do anything that conventional. They were determined to record at Gilman Street.

I think they were hoping to capture the electricity and excitement of their live shows, a nice trick if you could manage it. But without an audience, Gilman was just a barnlike structure with mediocre acoustics. It lacked soundproofing, isolation booths, a control room, and all those other features that professional recording studios use to create the illusion that your favorite band is playing right there in your living room.

It wouldn't be impossible to make a good record at Gilman, but it also wouldn't be easy. All the equipment would have to be trucked in, and there'd be other aggravations. Without a crowd of warm bodies, for example, the club could get uncomfortably cold and damp, even with the ancient heater that roared like a jet engine overhead.

The Gilman plan had one huge asset, however. His name was Radley Hirsch. Radley had first showed up when the club was struggling with the expensive but dysfunctional sound system we'd been misled into buying, and rebuilt that system into a thing of beauty for a fraction of the original cost.

No one, not even Tim Yohannan, was at more shows than Radley. Even on those dispiriting nights when band members outnumbered the audience, Radley would be there working his ass off to make the best of it.

"How do you get the patience to sit through some of those shows?" I once asked him.

"It's not about the individual shows," he answered, with his sheepish, toothy grin. "It's about the club. Anyway," he added as an afterthought, "if I didn't do it, who would?"

Radley loved Op Ivy, and the feeling was mutual. My one reservation was that he might be too much of a fan, too reluctant to let them know if some of their ideas turned out to be unrealistic.

But the band had earned the right to do things their own way. They'd barely put a foot wrong since they'd started, so I backed off and left them to it. I might have stopped by the club once while they were working, but that was about it.

Crimpshrine was another band that seldom asked for or listened to advice. If Op Ivy was an explosive skyrocket, Crimpshrine was a smoldering Roman candle. Viewed superficially, the two bands had little in common, but both were about as East Bay as you could get.

Like Operation Ivy, Crimpshrine set out to tour the US in 1988. After only six days, however, half the band bailed out and drove back to California, leaving drummer Aaron Cometbus and singer-guitarist Jeff Ott stranded on the side of the road.

Instead of skulking back to the Bay Area, Aaron and Jeff made frantic phone calls in search of anyone who could play bass and/or had a car. Paul Curran, from the Benicia band Poultry Magic, qualified on both counts. He hopped into his Ford Pinto and headed east to become the third member of a reconstituted Crimpshrine.

Zigzagging across the country, using borrowed equipment and playing anywhere people would have them, they made up their tour as they went along, with help from Kamala back in Berkeley. What would have been a fatal setback to almost any other band became fundamental to the Crimpshrine legend.

I'd been sensible enough to put out their first 7", *Sleep, What's That?*, but I totally blew it by not releasing the Crimpshrine album.

My excuse—a flimsy one at best—is that when Aaron handed me a cassette of what would become the *Lame Gig Contest* LP, I thought he was just asking my opinion of the band's latest demo.

Granted, Aaron had an oblique, sometimes impenetrable way of communicating. He seldom came right out and said what he wanted; you were supposed to intuitively ferret out his intentions.

At the time, Crimpshrine had just added a second guitarist, Idon, who played in a more traditional rock style than I was used to. I suggested it might be best to wait until the new guy settled in before trying to make a record.

But the band had already laid out its own money to do this recording. They couldn't afford to toss it aside as a premature demo and go back to re-record it later. Somehow I failed to figure that out.

So I was both shocked and upset when I heard it was being released on another label. "Why the hell didn't you ask me to put it out?" I asked Aaron.

"I did," he shrugged.

It was neither the first nor the last time Aaron and I would find ourselves communicating at cross purposes. His attitude seemed to be, "Oh well, as long as somebody's putting it out," while I hated the idea that such an iconic East Bay band was working with any label other than Lookout.

There was a problem here, and it was bigger than missing out on the Crimpshrine LP. I was in danger of thinking I—or at least Lookout—had first dibs on anything that came out of the East Bay. You might say I was getting a little big-headed.

Luckily, big-headedness was not something Gilman let you get away with. The minute your band, fanzine, or label showed signs of getting popular, there'd be a crowd of critics and hecklers eager to help cut you back down to size.

Operation Ivy got the worst of it. As soon as they started attracting fans from outside the usual punk circles, a small but vociferous posse began harassing them with shouts of "ska-boys!" and "sellouts!" Most vocal among the wrecking crew was that nice Jake Sayles from The Stoar, who was now working on the bellicose, paint-blistering scream he'd later put to use as Filth's lead singer.

Op Ivy didn't see the humor in it, no matter how many times I tried to explain that the hecklers were just goofing around. Lint took it especially badly; he didn't understand how people, especially people he'd considered friends, could be so disrespectful. I tried asking Jake and the gang to ease up a little. As I should have expected, it only made matters worse.

Op Ivy weren't the only ones stung by Gilman's snarky attitude. There was that one band whose manager strolled in wearing a Greatest Clichés Of the Prog-Rock 70s buckskin-fringed jacket.

"Where are the dressing rooms?" he demanded. We pointed to the legendarily rank men's toilet, which, to be fair, was the closest thing Gilman had to a "dressing room."

Slapshot were a Boston hardcore crew with matching varsity jackets and a rep for violently assaulting anyone they saw as insufficiently straight edge. A big deal on the East Coast, they'd so far acquired only a small following on our side of the country.

Their singer, a charming fellow by the name of Choke, brandished the broken end of a hockey stick as he half barked, half grunted out his menacing, violence-celebrating lyrics.

Gilman geeks in full effect. From left: Chris Wilder and Chris Dodge of Stikky, Steve von Till of Neurosis, Robert Eggplant, and Jesse Michaels. You can see my Detroit shirt, but my face is obscured by fists. (Photo by Murray Bowles)

A handful of wannabe tough-guy teenagers stood up front punching the air in time to his rantings, but most of what normally would have been the pit was filled with Gilman kids—"Gilman geeks," as they'd become known—making a mockery of Choke's chest-thumping machismo by playing leapfrog and doing monkey imitations.

The more they clowned around, the madder Choke got. At one point he shouted, "I'll play any club, basement, garage, or shithole, big or small, I don't care! But I'm not going to play for a bunch of kindergartners! This place is fucking punk rock Romper Room!"

We slipped a joke about Slapshot into the following month's *Flipside* ad and were rewarded with a note from the band that read in part: "All we have to say is when you guys have one decent, credible release under your emaciated vegetarian fag natural fiber cotton belts, then you can call us names. Love, Slapshot." It made a perfect centerpiece for our next *MRR* ad.

As the autumn days grew shorter, I began wondering, then worrying, about the Operation Ivy album. The band had been holed up with Radley for months, with little to show for it.

If I pestered them enough, I'd get a cassette mix of a song or two, with the caution that it was "nowhere near finished." Eventually I collected enough fragments to get an idea of what songs were going to be on the album, but not a hint of when it might be done.

I was also worried that the individual songs didn't match up sonically or thematically the way you'd expect an album to. It was as if each had been created as a separate work, meant to stand on its own.

Conversations with the band and Radley revealed this was not an accident, but part of Radley's vision. The band weren't sure if they liked it or not, but felt they had no choice but to keep going.

As winter settled in, I made jokes about how they'd have to re-record the song "Freeze Up" because its chorus, "It's 1988, stand up and take a look around," would soon be out of date. I began hearing rumbles of discontent from the band.

"We don't know what Radley's trying to do anymore, and when we ask, he won't tell us."

"He's mixing in this heavy bass sound, like it was a disco record."

They asked me to talk to Radley, to see if I could get some answers about where the project was headed.

Normally as sweet and easy-going a guy as you could hope to meet, Radley seemed frazzled and touchy. He suggested the problem might be that Operation

Ivy hadn't worked at this level before, that they didn't know what a professional quality recording was supposed to sound like.

That could be true, I conceded, but though I didn't come right out and say so, the recordings didn't sound quite right to me, either. Some were as good as or better than anything Lookout had done, but others just felt . . . weird. Ultimately, though, it didn't matter what I thought. My responsibility was to the band, and if they weren't happy, neither was I.

This dragged on for a couple more weeks. Then I got one of my least favorite phone calls ever. The band wanted me to tell Radley they were giving up on the project, and that he was, for want of a better word, fired.

"Can't you tell him yourself?" I pleaded.

No, they'd decided it would be easier if Radley heard the news from me. Easier for who, they didn't say.

It was one of the hardest things I had to do during my entire time at Lookout. I would have rather gone out kicking puppies and setting kittens on fire. Radley left me in no doubt about how painful this was for him, but he knew I was only the messenger—an unwilling one at that—and didn't take it out on me.

That experience cast a pall over the final days of 1988, a year that, apart from the broken toe, the missing Op Ivy album, and the unhappy dealings with Radley, had given me little to complain about.

And there was plenty to look forward to. Now that he'd re-committed himself to Lookout, David was hard at work on several projects. One of them was an EP we were doing with an exciting new band called Sweet Children.

6.
Enter The Weasel

Ben Weasel was still a teenager when he started sending letters and scene reports to *Maximum Rocknroll* lambasting bands like Hüsker Dü, Sonic Youth, and the Replacements—almost any band, really, who'd been around longer than he had or had made some kind of name for itself.

Sounding at times like an educated Spike Anarkie, he made his points viciously but hilariously. For every old school punk who threatened to cancel his *MRR* subscription if we didn't stop printing stuff by "that Weasel asshole," there were two or three new fans who thought he was one of the best things about the magazine.

Given Tim Yohannan's caustic sense of humor and unrelenting sympathy for underdogs and upstarts, Ben's place at the magazine was secure no matter how many readers complained. Eventually Tim offered him his own column, giving him an even larger audience to piss off.

I liked Ben's writing from the start. His in-your-face, take-no-prisoners attitude reminded me of what I'd tried to do with *Lookout* magazine, and his mockery of the complacent, self-satisfied punk rockers of Chicago's yesteryear mirrored the abuse we heaped on the "West Bay," our derisory term for San Francisco.

"The City," as it smugly described itself, had long disparaged the East Bay as a colorless, cultureless wasteland. Renowned *Chronicle* columnist Herb Caen referred to it as "East Berlin."

Lately we'd been returning the favor, and Frisco folks didn't appreciate it (calling their town "Frisco" made them even madder). This Ben Weasel guy, with his unfailing knack for getting under people's skin, seemed cut from the same cloth. It was a case, I assumed, of great minds thinking alike.

Because of that, I was sure I would like Ben's band, Screeching Weasel, long before I'd actually heard them. In May of 1988 they came to California for the first time, and played at Gilman with Operation Ivy. They were staying with Lint and Op Ivy bassist Matt Freeman, so I went over to meet them.

Ben was tall, but with a bit of a slouch, possibly from his habit of hunching over the always-lit cigarette that seemed to be the center point of his existence. His dark hair, slightly sallow skin, and sharp, piercing eyes framed a confused but

Screeching Weasel's first Gilman show, 1988.
(Photo by Murray Bowles)

undeniable charisma. I hadn't made it through the front door before he hit me with a barrage of sarcastic insults.

There'd been no introduction or greeting, but he obviously knew who I was, and launched into a tirade about wimpy Californians, vegetarians, politically correct commies, and chicks who didn't shave their legs, all obviously aimed at getting a rise out of me. I could barely stop laughing. He was even funnier in person than in print.

What Ben didn't know was that beneath my groovy California peace punk image lived a kid from Detroit with an attitude at least as aggrieved and pugnacious as any Chicago city slicker could muster. I could dish the un-PC dirt with the best—or worst—of them.

It looked like the start of a beautiful friendship. Though we seldom stopped arguing or insulting each other, we agreed about most things. Even when we didn't, neither of us took our disputes so seriously that there was any danger of them turning ugly.

There was another side to Ben Weasel, one he didn't let most people see. Despite his curmudgeonly image, he was deeply idealistic. Older, more jaded scene veterans might even have written him off as a hopeless romantic. Preoccupied with trading barbs and quips, I failed to notice this at first.

Years later, I found a battered, unlabeled cassette under the back seat of an old car I was sending to the junkyard. Popping it into the tape deck, I discovered it was an interview I'd done for *MRR*, but had never got around to transcribing. An impossibly young-sounding Ben Weasel bubbled excitedly about DIY spaces, the importance of independent music, and how sad it was to see the punk scene overtaken by negativity and backbiting.

What shocked me was how different the 1988 Ben-and-Larry dynamic had been from the way I remembered it. In my mind, I'd been the idealist and Ben the embittered cynic, but the tape told a different tale. There was no shortage of sardonic shit-talking in this interview, but most of it had been coming from me.

It was especially embarrassing to hear young Ben say he understood why I felt disillusioned, but that he wasn't going to give up on his hopes and dreams just because the previous generation—i.e., mine—had blown it so badly.

I'd never thought of Ben and myself as coming from different generations, but some quick math revealed that at the time of the interview, I'd been roughly twice Ben's age, old enough, in other words, to be his dad. And at 20, he himself was already older than many Gilman kids.

I wondered why I'd never felt self-conscious about that. Did it have something to do with the years I'd spent in isolation on Spy Rock? Did being off the grid make me think I was also beyond the reach of the aging process?

A couple Gilman regulars were older than me, most notably Tim Yohannan. Unlike me, however, Tim bore no illusions about still being a teenager. If anything, he seemed older than he was, probably because of his constant and often futile attempts to impose order on a warehouse full of rambunctious kids.

By the fall of 1988 Tim was getting fed up with Gilman. He felt—not without reason—that a handful of dedicated volunteers did all the work, while everyone else treated the club as a place to hang out and party.

Considering the time, money, and effort *MRR* had put into Gilman, you could hardly blame him. Especially since no one else was stepping up to make sure the bills got paid and the doors stayed open.

"Things can't keep going like this," Tim warned darkly. And they didn't. He abruptly canceled all upcoming shows and announced that Gilman Street was shutting down.

"We gave it our best," he editorialized in *MRR*. But it was time, he insisted, to let it go. This flew in the face of what most of us thought. If anything, the fun was barely getting started. But without Tim's money and organizing skills, I didn't see how the club could survive.

Luckily, there were other people who did. A small group of them began meeting to discuss how Gilman could be reopened. Nobody took them seriously at first, but within a few weeks, the club was back in business.

I think Tim was genuinely shocked, maybe even a little offended, that Gilman was able to carry on so easily without him. He still came around when there were bands he wanted to see, but never again took a direct role in running the place. He helped out in less visible ways, though, such as never asking to be paid back a penny of the money *MRR* had invested in it.

With Tim gone, Gilman became less ideologically driven, more chaotic, and, some claimed, more fun. I liked it both with and without him. Mostly I was relieved that the club was going to stay open.

Lookout kept growing in 1989, at least doubling in size again. We released six EPs and four full-length albums by bands including Neurosis, Crimpshrine, Kamala and the Karnivores, Surrogate Brains, Eyeball, Corrupted Morals, and Plaid Retina.

We were also going to release a Sweet Children EP, only to be told at the last minute that the band was changing its name to Green Day. I yelled, screamed, and pleaded with them not to do such a stupid thing, then went to the all-night copy shop and xeroxed a thousand covers with the new name and logo.

People are often surprised to hear that the Green Day EP didn't sell well at first. Part of the problem was that while Sweet Children had built up a little bit of a reputation, almost nobody had a clue who or what this "Green Day" was supposed to be.

There were also those who thought the record was *too* poppy. Tim Yohannan wouldn't let them play Gilman at first, claiming they weren't punk enough. And when they did start getting shows, not everyone was thrilled about it.

The Spike Anarkie types complained about the "Concord chicks" (Concord being a Los Angeles-style suburb on the wrong side of the East Bay hills) who flocked to see Sweet Children/Green Day. They'd plant themselves in front of the stage, flouncing back and forth in what became known as the "trout dance," obstructing the sweaty maelstrom of overwhelmingly male adolescents whose hyperactive bashing and slamming normally occupied that space.

I didn't see any harm in it, but the boys were outraged at this breach of punk rock etiquette. "Are you mad because the girls are interested in the band and not you?" I asked one of them.

"Like I'd ever go out with a Concord chick!" he sneered.

In the 1970s I'd watched a young Tom Petty on one of his first tours. Pressed against the stage, faces turned raptly upward as if they were having a religious experience, were several tightly packed rows of high school and college-aged girls. I remembered the devotion Petty had inspired in those young women more than the show itself.

A year or two later, Petty was selling out arenas and stadiums. It occurred to me that attracting a crowd of passionate female fans might be one of the surest signs a band was headed for bigger things. It's hard to say that without the risk of sounding a little sexist, but I watched a similar phenomenon unfold with Operation Ivy and Green Day.

Speaking of Operation Ivy, 1989's first drama was the same as 1988's last one: when, or if, their album would ever materialize. Not even the band themselves seemed to know. Worse, telltale signs were emerging that all was not well in the Op Ivy camp.

The differences were subtle, barely noticeable unless you were paying close attention, which, of course, I was. The unbridled exuberance they'd once brought to every show, no matter how tiny or thankless, seemed to be trickling away. It was still rare for them to pass up a chance to play, but I felt a sense of weariness setting in.

I tried to cheer them up by reminding them of how popular they were getting, but that was the last thing they needed to hear. "Larry, man, we just wanna concentrate on playing our music," Lint told me. "It's like everybody expects something from us."

Whether they realized it or not, Operation Ivy were reaching a crossroads: they'd soon be in a position—especially if they ever got their album out—to make a decent living playing music. For most musicians, this would be a dream come true. For those who were part of the Northern California punk scene, it could also be a problem.

Many scenesters—Tim Yohannan foremost among them—were deeply suspicious of bands who made more than enough money to cover the costs of drum heads, guitar strings, and putting gas in the tour van. When it came to paying rent or buying food, musicians were supposed to get day jobs like everyone else, even if it meant flipping burgers or working for corporations whose principles were utterly antithetical to punk.

It was a ridiculous philosophy, one that had more in common with religious fundamentalism than rational thought. But it was pervasive enough to have at least some effect, even on me.

That ambivalence might explain why Operation Ivy and other Lookout bands remained largely invisible in the mainstream media, who already operated on the assumption that punk rock had been dead and buried since 1979. That made it hard enough to get them to pay attention to us, but wary of being called a sellout—or feeling like one—most of the time I didn't bother trying.

Even Bay Area media like the alterna-weekly *East Bay Express* showed little interest. Gina Arnold, their music critic (and inspiration for the Mr. T Experience's "I Wrote A Book About Rock and Roll"), though paid to cover the local music scene, was too busy gushing over Nirvana and the Replacements to notice we had one.

The San Francisco papers were worse, with music coverage focusing mostly on the tattered remnants of the hippie era. Cutting edge 80s music to them meant Eddie Money or Journey. Maybe, on an especially adventurous day, Huey Lewis and the News.

It wasn't often that our bands got good gigs in the city, so when Op Ivy told me they were playing a South of Market saloon called the Covered Wagon, I convinced some SF journalists to come check them out. At last, I thought, the East Bay would get some recognition.

Unfortunately, Lint turned up for the show blind drunk. I had never seen Operation Ivy play a bad show before, but this wasn't just bad, it was a disaster.

None of the writers I'd invited spoke to me afterward, but I saw one rolling his eyes as he headed for the exit. When the onstage fiasco limped to a merciful conclusion, I all but dragged Lint out onto the sidewalk.

"How dare you?" I shouted. "You've got more talent and opportunities than most people get in a lifetime, and you piss it away like some bum in the gutter!"

It was a little dramatic, maybe, but not totally uncalled for. True, I was furious about how he'd embarrassed both his band and me, but more than that, I was concerned about him as a friend. I knew someone didn't get that drunk if he was feeling good about his life.

Lint's drinking would get worse before it got better. In a 2001 interview for *Hit List*, he surprised me by vividly recalling our conversation. "That was an amazing thing to have someone be that honest with me," he said. "I still think about it sometimes." I was astonished that he could remember it at all.

It might have been ironic for me to be lecturing him, considering I was no slouch at hitting the bottle myself. But there were things I hadn't yet learned about alcohol, one being that for certain people—I would turn out to be one of them—self-control by itself was of no use.

So I assumed Lint just needed to acquire some discipline and limit his drinking for at least as long as it took to finish the album. Another tour might help, too; maybe it would introduce some structure into his life.

The tour never happened, but the album finally did. Lint recalls David Hayes asking him, with characteristic bluntness, "Are you guys gonna make a record or not?"

The band called a meeting, and the consensus was, "Uh . . . okay, we will." A six-day studio marathon ensued, with Kevin Army producing.

Like some of Kevin's other early work, the record, *Energy*, sounded a little trebly. But it captured the power and intensity of Operation Ivy at their peak.

It took a couple more months to cajole and wheedle the cover art out of Jesse Michaels, their gifted but mercurial lead singer. All that was missing now was the lyric sheet.

The plan was for Jesse to take care of that, too, but just before it was due at the printer, he crept up David's stairs at midnight to leave a despairing note outside the door saying he couldn't do it. David took over, and at last the pieces were in place for what promised to be the biggest release in Lookout's history.

We scheduled a show at Gilman for May 28, featuring Op Ivy, the Lookouts (we had an album coming out, too), and three bands with new 7"s: Surrogate Brains, Green Day, and, supposedly, Crimpshrine.

I say supposedly because Aaron Cometbus was out of town, touring with another band, Sweet Baby. Without him, at least in most people's opinion, there was no Crimpshrine.

No racists allowed. Ninnies, goofballs, and nincompoops always welcome. (Photo by Murray Bowles)

While waiting to see how that mystery would resolve itself, I booked another show for Op Ivy and the Lookouts in the tiny Humboldt County town of Garberville. It was meant to be a benefit for KMUD, home of the *Wild In The Streets* program that Chris Appelgren and I co-hosted.

By now the Lookouts had a decent fan base in Humboldt County, and with Operation Ivy headlining, I knew we'd pack the Vets Hall and raise a ton of money for the radio station. To round out the lineup, I added Screeching Weasel and Green Day. Neither band was well known that far north, but I was sure people would love them.

Screeching Weasel were making their second trip to California, Ben and I having kept in touch since his 1988 visit. I'd offered them a place on Lookout, but Ben had already made arrangements to release their second album on Roadkill Records, a label he and a friend were starting in Chicago.

The partnership hadn't worked out. Although *Boogadaboogadaboogada* sold thousands of copies, Ben claimed he'd barely seen a penny from it. Sounding more burnt out and disillusioned than the year before, he complained it was impossible to make money playing punk rock.

"If you'd put that record out on Lookout," I told him, "you'd be making money."

"Yeah, well, I didn't. So what am I supposed to do now?"

"Tour some more. Build up your reputation around the country, then do your next record with us." I also encouraged him to bring the band back to California as soon as possible, which was part of the reason Screeching Weasel ended up on the Garberville bill.

"Living Behind Bars," one of my favorite songs on the new Lookouts LP, was about visiting the Ashtray, one of Oakland's first, and definitely most notorious punkhouses. It was home to Jesse Michaels, Jake Sayles, and Lenny from Isocracy.

I'd once taken Ben there for a visit, and will never forget the appalled expression on his face as he sat there amid the ruins of what passed for a living room. Midway through the evening, Jesse started dancing like some lithe aquatic creature on the headrest of an easy chair.

Not to be outdone, I jumped onto the back of the sofa and did likewise. Knowing my dance moves were no match for Jesse's, I jazzed up my routine by stuffing a raw potato in my mouth. When Ben asked what the hell I was doing, I told him this was the traditional East Bay "potato dance," for which I later found myself immortalized in the Screeching Weasel song, "Punkhouse."

Not far from the Ashtray, in Emeryville, was a studio called Dancing Dog, where many Lookout bands had worked. The owner, Dave Bryson, also practiced and recorded there, and a few years later his band, Counting Crows, landed a major label deal and a multi-million selling record.

"It's your fault," people would mutter every time "Mr. Jones" came on the radio. "Lookout money paid for their demo."

David Hayes lived nearby, and when I worked late at the studio, I often stayed at his place. On one such night, just as I was going to sleep, Matt and Lint showed up at the door, looking utterly shell-shocked.

Before I could ask what was going on, Lint blurted out, "Jesse doesn't want to be in Operation Ivy anymore. We're breaking up."

We walked around the deserted, mostly industrial neighborhood, trying to make sense of what had happened, but there was no sense to be made.

Normally I tried not to take band fights or breakups too seriously. Some bands broke up every time there was a disagreement about a song arrangement or whose turn it was to pay rent on the practice space. It would typically be forgotten about by the time the next gig or recording session rolled around.

Operation Ivy was not that kind of band. I can't remember a single time they told me, "This is how it's gonna be," only to later say, "We changed our minds."

"Maybe Jesse didn't mean what he said," I suggested. "Or you guys just need a little time off." But I knew in my heart neither of these things was true. It was the end of Operation Ivy, and nothing would ever be the same again.

"No matter what," I told them, "you'll always have a home at Lookout." They nodded numbly. Their musical future was the last thing they were thinking about.

Our triumphant record release party had been transformed into a wake. The same bands would play, but the tone would be oh so different.

Would it also be a requiem for our East Bay scene? Many great bands remained, and the club was going stronger than ever, but Operation Ivy had stood out and towered over everything so completely. It was hard to imagine what it would be like going on without them.

7.
The Rodeo

Delicate egos and easily bruised feelings are an occupational hazard of dealing with musicians and artists. Record label owners, too, it must be said.

Luckily most people involved with Lookout were good-natured and agreeable. There were, however, exceptions. We didn't have any full-fledged prima donnas, but whenever you get that many creative people operating in close proximity, there's a potential for conflict.

It didn't help that I was not exactly a master of diplomacy. I tended to shoot my mouth off first, then wonder why everyone was mad at me. I suffered from the dual liability of being thin-skinned myself, yet oblivious to the effects my words had on others.

Both Operation Ivy and (especially) Isocracy complained about the way I tried to pit them against each other, teasing them about who was selling more records or playing bigger shows. It was all in fun, I claimed, but privately I thought that if it prompted them to work a little harder or turn their cover art in on time, so much the better.

This theory had its flaws. Some bands respond well to a little ribbing. Others are annoyed and offended. Running a label gave me a crash course in figuring out which was which.

Certain issues, though, were so fraught and baffling that even I knew to stay clear of them. For example, the question of "Crimpshrine," or, as some put it, "the fake Crimpshrine," playing Op Ivy's farewell show.

One or more members of Crimpshrine might want to murder me for saying this, but the band had at least one thing in common with the Grateful Dead, about whom Bay Area rock impresario Bill Graham once said, "They're not the best at what they do, they're the only ones who do what they do."

At the core of what Crimpshrine did was the long-time partnership between Jeff Ott, their gravel-voiced singer-guitarist, and drummer-songwriter Aaron Cometbus, who combined a uniquely ramshackle sense of rhythm with poignant, poetic lyrics that remain tattooed on many a punk rock heart.

I met Jeff when he was a 16-year-old runaway, barefoot in the streets of Berkeley,

Crimpshrine at Gilman, December, 1987.
(Photo by Murray Bowles)

blitzed out of his mind on LSD. He was tall, with a striking, charismatic presence, but what I remember most was how incomprehensibly dirty his feet were. His eyes, too, left an impression, with pupils so dilated they threatened to eclipse the rest of his face.

Although I had many conversations with Jeff over the years, I never got to know him as well as I did Aaron. Of course there was some question about how well you could "know" Aaron, who made something of an art form out of being casually inscrutable.

Despite his disheveled appearance and a life that oscillated unpredictably between the pragmatic and the visionary, I saw Aaron as the primary driving force behind Crimpshrine, and the glue that held it together.

I'd known Aaron even before hearing of Crimpshrine, thanks to the quirky but highly regarded magazine he'd founded when he was 13 ("before *MRR*," he liked to remind you), and had been publishing ever since. Its name changed with each issue, but usually contained the word "Cometbus" (e.g., *Ride The Wohl Whip Cometbus*, *Pleasures Of The Cometbus Harbour*, *Shelter From Form Farm Cometbus*). Eventually both the magazine and Aaron himself would become just plain *Cometbus*.

Aaron had an elaborate set of values and unwritten rules about how things were supposed to be done, especially when it came to bands, fanzines, and punk rock. Some of those rules made perfect sense, others felt slightly idiosyncratic, and every so often he'd bust out with one that seemed to have been plucked from a parallel universe.

Arguing with him about this stuff was useless. Believe me, I tried. Once I gave up on the notion that I could persuade or browbeat him into changing his opinion, we got along a lot better.

Even that rapprochement might not have happened if Aaron and I didn't agree on the basics. Loyalty, honesty, and responsibility were as fundamental to a band as they were to a record label, and it was on those rocks that Crimpshrine ultimately foundered.

I could tell something had gone awry when Jeff booked "Crimpshrine" to play the Op Ivy show even though Aaron wouldn't be there. There were rumors—unverified, to be fair—that this was Jeff's way of getting even with Aaron for going on tour with Sweet Baby. Other people claimed Jeff just really wanted to play the show and was refusing to let Aaron's absence stop him.

Sweet Baby, originally known as Sweet Baby Jesus, had been one of my favorite bands since the first time I saw them. Singer Dallas Denery looked and dressed like the professor from *Gilligan's Island* (later in life he'd become an actual professor), and his harmonies with guitarist Matt Buenostro owed more to the Everly Brothers than the Ramones, but their songs, while they didn't fit neatly into any particular genre, were among the standouts on *Turn It Around*.

I never pictured them on any label but Lookout. Instead, in a deal engineered by Kevin Army, they'd signed to Ruby Records, a subsidiary of Slash Records, which was in turn owned by London Records and distributed by Warner Brothers. In its early days Slash had released classic LPs by bands like the Germs and X, and had continued to release successful, if slightly more mainstream, records throughout the 1980s. Most of us, however, had never heard of Ruby.

Kevin had a good head on his shoulders, and I agreed with him about 90% of the time, but in this case I thought he and the band were making a big mistake. While Ruby could offer major label distribution and a recording budget 10 or 20 times greater than we could, what they didn't have—and Lookout did—was a devoted fan base who already knew about Sweet Baby, and who were willing to check out almost anything our label released.

It's not always true, of course, that bands will do better on indie labels. But small, essentially unknown bands have the odds stacked against them if they sign with a major—or a label that's run and distributed like one—too early in their career. For example, a band that sells a couple thousand copies of its first release on an indie is off to a bright and promising start. Deliver numbers like that for a major and you're a miserable flop, an embarrassment, the sooner forgotten, the better.

It's often thought that once you sign to a major label—even if it's only the subsidiary of a semi-subsidiary—you've got it made. Your struggle to break into the music business is over. You've "arrived."

In reality—whether in 1989 or today—your struggle is just beginning. The overwhelming odds are that within a couple years you'll have been dropped or downsized into a tax write-off.

I wasn't one of those purists who believed you should never, under any circumstances, work with a major label. But counting on the corporate machinery to magically transform you into a star is going about it backwards.

The bands who did best, no matter what kind of label they were on, were those who had laid a solid foundation, built up a following, and charted a clear direction for where they wanted to go and what they wanted to accomplish. Sweet Baby had yet to do any of those things.

But Matt Wallace, Kevin Army's friend and former business partner, had recently helped propel Faith No More to major label success. I got the impression Kevin was hoping to follow a similar trajectory with Sweet Baby. He poured his heart and soul into recording their album, *It's A Girl*, which came out sounding infinitely slicker and more professional than anything Lookout had ever done.

But with Sweet Baby's audience, which was still largely limited to punk rockers, that could be a liability as much as an asset. Accustomed as we were to second and third-generation copies of their demo tape, the new, more polished sound took some getting used to.

A far greater obstacle was Ruby's bizarre, almost incomprehensible marketing strategy. Apparently unable to decide—or just not having a clue—as to who might want to buy a Sweet Baby record, they pressed it on vinyl only.

That might have worked if the record was on Lookout. In 1989, labels like ours could still get away—though just barely—without issuing our stuff in CD form.

But a label like Ruby would have to sell many more records than we would to recoup its costs. That wouldn't happen unless Sweet Baby broke through to a more mainstream audience. The kind of audience, in other words, that bought its music almost exclusively on CD.

If they'd followed in the footsteps of Operation Ivy or Green Day, releasing records on Lookout and doing the DIY tour circuit, would things have worked out better for Sweet Baby? I think so. But their Ruby release sold poorly, and they were dropped before finishing their second LP.

It must have been hard on Kevin, because he loved and believed in Sweet Baby. And though money wasn't his prime concern, he could have used some better luck in that department, too. Working with bands and labels like ours, he'd been eking out a marginal existence at best.

Mindful of this, I offered him what I thought might be a better deal when Operation Ivy went in to re-record their album. Instead of paying him his usual hourly rate, I said, we'd give him a percentage of any profit the album might eventually make.

"I can't afford to take that kind of chance," he said flatly.

Professor Dallas Denery with Sweet Baby Jesus at Club Foot, 1986. (Photo by Murray Bowles)

Sweet Baby's deal with Ruby never aroused the hostile reaction some bands had to contend with. When Hüsker Dü signed to Warner, for example, a group of punks picketed their San Francisco show. Maybe it was because Sweet Baby had never specifically cast themselves in the role of "punks." Or that they were such nice guys it was hard to imagine getting mad at them.

It might also have explained why Aaron Cometbus, normally an outspoken advocate of the DIY ethic, was willing to tour with Sweet Baby despite the major label connection. As a result, however, he wasn't around to object when Jeff Ott arranged for a version of Crimpshrine—in which he'd be the only original member—to play the last Op Ivy show. Shortly afterward, this lineup would morph into a new band called Fifteen.

Neither Aaron nor Jeff has ever been willing to talk much about it, but this would mark an unhappy end to their long friendship and musical partnership. There were other issues, too, but at the time I was only vaguely aware of them, being preoccupied with record releases and the fact that the Lookouts were about to play our biggest show ever. It would turn out to be Gilman's biggest as well.

The club had a legal capacity of 299 when it opened, but for some reason the city had reduced it to 249. Both numbers were routinely ignored, but I don't think there'd ever been a crowd bigger than 350 or 400. On May 28, 1989, more people than that were lined up outside long before the doors opened.

Volunteers did their best to manage the overflow, which stretched down the block in both directions. Some people pushed their way in whenever the side door opened, but most waited patiently, in some cases for up to two hours, to pay their $5.

Supposedly about 600 people were in the club when Operation Ivy took the stage, but as one of the volunteers who helped count and disburse the money afterwards, I knew better. Approximately 800 people had paid, and maybe another 200 got in free. So, a thousand people in a room designated for one quarter that many? It was a little crowded.

Gilman regulars wandered around looking stunned. The first thing we'd be likely to say on running into each other was, "Who *are* all these people?"

It reminded me of being at Woodstock in 1969, surrounded by hippies asking the same question. But that had been on a vast open hillside. This was like Woodstock in a New York City subway car at rush hour.

The five-band lineup would have made for an amazing record release party, but once it got rebranded as "Operation Ivy's last show," it almost didn't matter who opened. We could have added a troupe of tap-dancing monkeys without most people noticing.

Green Day played first, followed by the Surrogate Brains and "Crimpshrine." Then it was the Lookouts' turn. Pushing my way toward the stage, dragging a guitar case that felt more like an anvil, I told myself there was no reason to be nervous. The vast majority of the crowd didn't care who we were or what we did as long as we hurried up and got out of the way so they could see Op Ivy.

I wasn't on drugs, and I don't think I'd even been drinking, but when I tuned up, plugged in, and looked at the crowd in front of me, all I could see was faces piled like so many billiard balls from floor to ceiling. And when I slipped a pick between my sweaty fingers and struck the first chord of "Living Behind Bars," it was like slamming an electronic cue ball down the middle of those racked faces and watching them explode into a multi-directional frenzy.

I barely remember anything after that. The biggest show of my life and I missed most of it. People tell me we played well, but I'll have to take their word for it, because my next conscious thought was that 30 minutes had gone by and it was time for us to get off the stage.

When Op Ivy finally came on, it felt almost anticlimactic. They seemed tired, disjointed, at loose ends. Much of the joy and excitement had been drained out of them. At times it almost looked as though they were going through the motions, like a divorcing couple trying to stay civil for the sake of the kids.

Even if that was the case, the crowd never noticed. They kept cheering wildly until the band had played pretty much every song they'd ever known, wrapping up with an extended dub version of "Hedgecore," their hymn to the peculiar East Bay sport of diving into hedges.

And with that, the Operation Ivy era was over. People trailed off into the night, lost in their thoughts and memories, most of them unaware that they hadn't actually seen the "last" Operation Ivy show: the band got together for one more impromptu gig in Eggplant's backyard the following afternoon.

Radley had put the previous winter's bad blood behind him and brought in his equipment to record the Gilman show for posterity. I had thought of releasing it as a live album, but listening to the tape afterward left me underwhelmed, and I never pursued it.

Soon afterward came the Garberville show, which until Operation Ivy dropped out, might have been the biggest punk rock event in Humboldt County history. I'd replaced Op Ivy with the Mr. T Experience, who'd been getting more popular in the Bay Area, but were relatively unknown up north. Even fewer people had heard of Screeching Weasel or Green Day.

This put the Lookouts in the unusual position of being the only real "name" on the bill. I still wasn't worried; the last time we'd played the Vets Hall, the place had been packed. Punk rock shows were rare enough in Southern Humboldt that kids would come no matter who was playing.

But they didn't this time. The Vets Hall was never more than half full. Adding insult to injury, I discovered that much of our potential audience had deserted us in favor of a Jerry Garcia show a few miles down the road.

If you know Humboldt County, you'll understand how that could happen, and if you don't, I could take up a lot of pages trying to explain it. Anywhere else you'd find little overlap between punk rockers and Jerry Garcia fans, but Humboldt is a world unto itself. Which was part of what I loved about the place.

It was pointless trying to explain that to Ben Weasel. His was not a world where punks and hippies happily coexisted, let alone put on shows and formed bands—or circle pits—together.

He was no fan of redwood trees, tie-dyed shirts, sleepy villages, or mountain wildernesses, either, but our cultural differences seemed to augment rather than diminish our friendship. He was one of the only people who could get away with ridiculing my supposed hippie-ness, to the point where I'd dial it up a few notches just to goad him into even more creative levels of abuse.

In reality, I hadn't been much of a hippie, certainly not by Humboldt or Mendocino standards, since the tail end of the 60s. I'd often gotten in trouble with my Spy Rock neighbors for dishing out the same sort of anti-hippie taunts Ben was now directing at me.

The Isocracy song "Rodeo"—which I'm almost positive had nothing to do with the annual Laytonville Rodeo that was happening that weekend—kept playing in my head as I dragged Ben to witness our local collection of cowboys, rednecks, circus clowns, and tie-dyed hill muffins straight out of *The Fabulous Furry Freak Brothers*.

He sat quietly fuming at the unfamiliar sights and sounds, but was mostly a good sport about it. Despite the taunts and insults that flew back and forth between us, I cherished Ben's friendship, and grew ever more certain that we were destined to do great things together.

8.
Too Much Golden Light

After the Garberville show, life settled into a long, idyllic summer. The new Lookouts record didn't sell as well as I'd hoped, but even that didn't bother me. It had accomplished what I'd set out to do in capturing the look, sound, and feel of Spy Rock.

The mountain provided both refuge and sustenance for me that year. I'd never been so happy there, and never dreamed I would soon be leaving. Running Lookout from a telephone and computer-free wilderness was a challenge, but as long as David took care of the city end of business, it was manageable.

But David was talking about quitting Lookout again, and this time it sounded like he really meant it. I tried not to take him seriously, told myself he was just going through one of his moods. But as the months rolled past, he grew steadily more insistent about it.

I knew he found it hard to get along with me, even if I didn't always understand why. Hell, I found it hard getting along with myself sometimes. But was I that difficult to work with? For David, it seemed, the answer was yes.

He was determined, he said, to start his own label. I tried convincing him there was nothing he could do on a separate label that he couldn't do just as easily on Lookout. Even if he and I didn't always like the same bands, I had never tried to stop him from putting out whatever records he wanted to.

None of my arguments had the slightest effect. My complacency began to dissolve into panic. I couldn't imagine running Lookout on my own.

Chris Appelgren could help out, but he was still in high school and lived 60 miles away, with no means of getting to Spy Rock unless I drove up and got him. His drawing was improving, and he'd put together some rudimentary ads and flyers, but he knew next to nothing about the kind of graphic design David did.

He'd be of no use at all when it came to bookkeeping, and I couldn't picture him laying down the law to bands when necessary, something David could accomplish with a terse word or pained grimace. At 16, Chris was not only younger than most of our musicians; he was still a little too much in awe of them.

Desperate to keep David on board, I offered him a deal where he'd act as the official face of Lookout, signing checks and filing legal papers while I took care of the day-to-day work behind the scenes. In exchange, he'd still get half the profits.

It would have been a crazy and wildly unequal arrangement, but that's how much I wanted him to stick around. He turned it down flat.

"There's too much golden light around Lookout right now," he said. It was an oddly archaic, almost hippie-esque way of putting it. David was about as much of a hippie as Ben Weasel, but I knew what he meant. For quite a while now, it had seemed like we could do no wrong, as if anything we touched was guaranteed to flourish.

What I didn't understand was why he saw this as a problem. Most of my life had been a case study in failure. What, I asked, was so terrible about finally enjoying a little success?

"It feels too much like a job," David said.

I didn't see what was wrong with that, either. Like it or not, most of us have to have jobs. Wasn't it better to do something fun and exciting instead of something boring and stupid? He brushed that argument aside, too.

"As of January first, I'm done," he said. "I don't want anything more to do with Lookout, and I don't want anything more from Lookout."

David Hayes, shortly after leaving Lookout, with Lint, now known as Tim again. (Photo by Murray Bowles)

He didn't say it in a loud or angry way, but with a quiet, steely determination that left me stunned and momentarily speechless. I finally had to accept that David wouldn't be changing his mind this time.

I told everyone Lookout would carry on as always, but I was like a kid whistling past the graveyard. Of course there would be changes—considering the huge role David had played, how could there not be? As for what they would be and how—or if—they would work, I had no idea.

I'd made a mess of so many things in my life—education, jobs, relationships— that I'd come to implicitly accept one of my parents' favorite sayings: "You can't win for losing." Lookout was one of the only things I'd ever done that had worked better instead of worse than expected, yet I couldn't shake the feeling that somehow, eventually, it would all go wrong.

I powered ahead anyway, propelled by inertia, and perhaps by a conviction that if I kept moving fast enough, I might outrun the failures of my past. Green Day were ready to make an album, so I urged them to get started on it. That same week, I told Neurosis I wanted to do their album, too.

The Green Day LP was an obvious choice. They were attracting bigger and bigger crowds, had written some great new songs, and were so excited to be playing music and making records that working with them was almost effortless.

Neurosis represented a step in a new direction. They'd been around longer than most Gilman bands and played a darker, harsher, more complex style of music. David had brought them to Lookout the previous spring, helping them produce a 7" EP called *Aberration*. Its cover featured a portrait of serial killer Richard Ramirez, aka the "Night Stalker."

I'd seen Neurosis many times, had a copy of their first album on Victor Hayden's ill-fated Alchemy Records, and the Lookouts had shared a bill with them once or twice, but I'd never listened to them that carefully. I'd always thought of them as being a little too metal. A "David band," in other words.

I started rethinking that assumption after a front-porch conversation with singer-guitarist Scott Kelly. He told me one of his biggest influences was King Crimson, the British prog-rockers I'd spent half the 1970s tripping my brains out to.

So my interest was piqued even before I delved deeper into their music. In any event, I felt Lookout owed Neurosis the chance to do an LP. We'd never done multi-record deals, but there was an unspoken understanding that once you were part of the Lookout family, you could keep making records with us for as long as you wanted.

My only hesitation about working with Neurosis was the possibility that I'd be stepping on David's toes. I felt sure they'd be one of the bands he'd want for his new label.

Whether he did or not, Neurosis made it clear they preferred to stick with Lookout. What they were after in terms of recording budgets, packaging, and distribution was far beyond anything Very Small Records, David's new label, could offer.

I wondered if it might also be more than Lookout could offer, especially when the band informed me they were planning a full-color cover, something Lookout had never done before. The film charges alone—this was before color separations could be easily and cheaply done on computers—meant we'd be spending at least double what we normally did on printing.

But Neurosis insisted their cover art, a painting of a giant nail being driven through some unfortunate person's tongue, would lose much of its effectiveness in anything less than full color. And they were right.

They laid down one other condition: "Before you decide to do our record, you need to come listen to us play the songs."

"I've already decided," I said. "I trust you guys. I'm sure whatever you're planning will be great."

"Nah. You'd better come hear us."

I'd been in the Bay Area only a couple days earlier and had no desire to leave Spy Rock again any time soon. But Neurosis were turning out to be another of those bands that it made no sense to argue with. I agreed to meet them at their studio on the night of October 18.

On October 17, the Bay Area was struck by its worst earthquake since the great San Francisco quake of 1906. Just down the road from Neurosis's studio, the Cypress Freeway collapsed, killing 42 people. Many nearby cities were without electricity or running water, but the studio had come through unscathed. The band set me up on a three-legged bar stool at one end of the room, then struck the oracular opening chords of *The Word As Law*.

There was once an advertisement for Maxell cassette tapes that showed a guy pinned to his chair, his hair being blown straight back by waves of sound. It's how I pictured myself as Neurosis blasted through their entire album without interruption or comment.

It was more like a symphony than a punk rock show. Give Wagner some electric guitars, and the *Götterdämmerung* might have sounded like this. Forty minutes later, as the hypnotic cacophony dissolved into silence, someone shouted: "Let's go look at the ruins!"

NEUROSIS

IN MY HORROR I FOREVER TRY THE THINGS I CANNOT DO★AND I CLAW WITH BLEEDING FINGERS BUT THE STONES WILL NEVER MOVE

Dave Ed and Scott Kelly of Neurosis at Own's Pizza, 1986. (Photo by Murray Bowles)

It was nearly midnight when we piled into a van and drove toward the wrecked freeway. We got as close as we could, then stepped out to gape at the devastation.

The remains of the overpass, floodlit from multiple directions, stood silhouetted against an iridescent sky. Bulldozers muscled their way though the debris with a great, grinding roar, while rescue workers clambered over piles of concrete in search of the dead.

Apart from the rumble of the machinery and the distant cry of police and fire sirens echoing off the hills, the night was eerily silent. But in my head I couldn't stop hearing the rising guitar crescendo, sounding like the air raid warning for the apocalypse, that introduces the song "To What End?"

There was something else that we all must have noticed but nobody saw fit to mention: the unspeakable stench of rotting corpses. Writing a description of *The Word As Law* for the Lookout catalog, I likened it to the sound of falling buildings and collapsing civilizations. I've never been able to hear it any other way.

Warm, sunny weather lingered another week or two, but that was the moment summer ended for me. The calm, unruffled sense of having all the time in the world vanished, and wouldn't return. With David's departure looming, Lookout felt like a runaway train with no one at the controls except—possibly—me.

Officially, David would be part of the label until the end of the year, but I saw little of him during those last few months. His final two projects, the Corrupted

Morals and Plaid Retina LPs, dragged on well past their deadlines, and didn't display the attention to detail usually evident in his work. It seemed strange, because those were two of his favorite bands.

Otherwise, the split-up produced no new hostility between the two of us. Though I'd originally felt resentful about David's new label, and maybe a little fearful that it might outshine Lookout, I soon realized it would pose no threat. Perhaps we could peacefully, maybe even cooperatively, co-exist.

Most of the bands David liked weren't ones I wanted for Lookout, and even when they were, it was seldom a problem. Making a point of living up—or, depending how you looked at it, down—to his label's name, he specialized in compilations, limited editions, and odd formats.

While I wasn't interested only in big bands and big releases, neither did I want Lookout to stay deliberately small. David's first compilation, *Make The Collector Nerd Sweat*, illustrated the contrast. With a lineup that included Crimpshrine, the Mr. T Experience, Jawbreaker, the Offspring, Samiam, and the Lookouts, the record should have been a perennial best-seller. But as a limited edition, pressed only on 10" vinyl? Maybe not so much.

I missed David's skills and insights, and the conversations we'd once had, but I didn't miss the arguments or sudden inexplicable rages. Despite the new challenges I was facing, running Lookout became, at least for a while, less stressful than before, when I'd always had to worry about saying the wrong thing or straying onto an unmentionable topic.

I had no trouble taking over the bookkeeping—it was just adding and subtracting, and making sure I didn't spend money I didn't have—but art and design were never something I'd be able to manage on my own.

Thankfully, I didn't have to. Others stepped in, often without my needing to ask. Neurosis handled every detail of their artwork as well as their recording. Green Day took two days and $675 to record and mix an album that would eventually sell over a million copies. Jesse Michaels put together the cover art, and Chris Appelgren, in one of the first fully-fledged examples of his own developing style, created the insert.

While I could barely draw a recognizable stick figure, I discovered I could come up with concepts that an actual artist could bring to life. Using this approach, I collaborated with Chris on many covers, catalogs, and ads. His technique might have lacked David's cool, effortless professionalism, but it had an uproarious, anarchic feel that appealed to the young audience we already had, and perhaps a new, even younger one.

There were papers to sign with the state and county, giving me sole responsibility for paying taxes and filing legal forms, but apart from that there was no specific event marking the dissolution of the David and Larry partnership. Rather than a short, sharp break, it felt more like David had just faded away.

And in the blink of an eye it was 1990, another of those years where so much would happen, in so many different directions, that it would be impossible to sum up in a chapter, or even a book.

The biggest, most obvious change saw me leaving the mountain and moving to Berkeley. Quitting Spy Rock wasn't something I'd planned on. I didn't even see it coming as the year began. It was more a case of destiny grabbing me by the scruff of the neck and dragging me away.

When it came to running a label, the mountain had its drawbacks, the most obvious being the lack of telephones and its limited supply of electricity. But a few more solar panels would give me all the power I needed, and I was already researching the cost of having a phone line put in.

Yet by summer I was gone. I meant it to be only a temporary departure, but Lookout quickly took root in its new surroundings, and the idea of returning to Spy Rock slowly receded. Eventually I hardly thought about it at all.

1990 was also the year I finally convinced the Mr. T Experience to join Lookout, something I'd been trying to do ever since starting the label.

I'd met singer-songwriter-guitarist "Dr. Frank" Portman back in 1984, before the band existed, when he was a smart-aleck Berkeley undergrad hosting one of the best shows on KALX, the campus radio station. The melodic, upbeat stuff he played stood out like a beacon in the night amid the sludgy, artsy pap favored by most of the station's DJs.

So did Frank's attitude, which ranged from profoundly silly—his rap version of "Green Eggs and Ham," for example—to casually, even callously acerbic. His deadpan comments oozed with the self-conscious ennui of late adolescence.

Fellow DJs Jon von Zelowitz and Kenny Kaos joined in promoting and keeping alive the kind of music that would become the foundation of the Lookout sound. When Frank and Jon Von formed the Mr. T Experience in 1985, Gilman and Lookout weren't even a glimmer on the horizon, so MTX, as they were often known, had to create their own scene.

In 1986 they put out their first record, *Everyone's Entitled To Their Own Opinion* (a title taken verbatim from bassist Byron's reply to a question I asked while interviewing them for *Cometbus*). In doing so, they inadvertently helped create the DIY template—Kevin Army recording, John Golden mastering, the

Alberti pressing plant in Southern California—that Lookout would use when we started making records.

But despite the common ground we shared and my longstanding fandom, the Mr. T Experience wouldn't let Lookout release their next record, nor the one after that. "We like what you're doing, but we'd rather work with a real label," was how they put it.

So *Night Shift At The Thrill Factory*, featuring Frank's punk rock distillation of his senior thesis, "The Complicated History of the Concept of the Soul," and *Big Black Bugs Bleed Blue Blood*, which included "At Gilman Street," the club's unofficial anthem, came out on an American subsidiary of Britain's Rough Trade Records.

If I was annoyed at missing out on *Night Shift*, I was angry and frustrated at seeing *Big Black Bugs* and its song about Gilman Street on a label with zero ties or connections to the East Bay. Frank listened to me make that case, and gently but firmly refuted it.

"At Gilman Street," he maintained, was not the anthem I'd made it out to be. If anything, it was a throwaway, a trifle, meant to tweak the club's exaggerated self-regard as much as celebrate it. I still bristled at having to buy another label's record

*"Dr." Frank Portman and Jon Von Zelowitz
of the Mr. T Experience at Club Foot, 1986.
(Photo by Murray Bowles)*

to hear my favorite East Bay song.

Not long afterward, Rough Trade went bankrupt, leaving the Mr. T Experience stranded and label-less. At last, the band conceded, it might be worth giving Lookout a try.

We scheduled an album for later that year, but threw together a quick 7" single so we could add MTX to the March record release show we'd planned for the Green Day and Neurosis albums.

Samiam had just done a Lookout single, too, so they'd be the fourth band on the bill. Two of Samiam's members, Jason Beebout and Martin Brohm, had been in Isocracy with Green Day's Al Sobrante. While this didn't necessarily have to lead to a rivalry between the two bands, Al made sure it did.

When Samiam were starting out, one of their members offhandedly told an interviewer that they saw their band as more serious than Isocracy had been. That was all it took to send Al on a full-fledged crusade, printing flyers denouncing Samiam as "sellouts," even staging one-man picket lines to discourage people from attending their shows.

Samiam laughed off Al's antics for the most part, but they weren't laughing when they realized they'd be opening for his band at the release party. Even though Green Day's new album was one of the main reasons 400 people were lined up outside Gilman that night, Samiam complained bitterly that they shouldn't have to play first.

I had decided the band order weeks in advance: Neurosis and Green Day would headline, since both had LPs coming out. Because Neurosis had a couple years' seniority on Green Day, they would play last.

Using the same logic for the 7" bands, Samiam had to play before the Mr. T Experience, who'd been around five years longer. They finally agreed to the opening slot—the alternative I offered was not to play at all—but a couple of them barely spoke to me for the next year or so. It was the only semi-sour note on an otherwise astounding night.

All four bands were greeted like superstars—and deserved it. While some thought groups as radically different as Neurosis and Green Day would make for a weird combination, the lovestruck teenage anthems of *39/Smooth* flowed seamlessly into the stark, subsuming majesty of *The Word As Law*.

There'd been moments scattered throughout the first couple of years when I'd caught myself thinking, "Whoa, Lookout is kind of turning into a big deal." In the wake of that March 16, 1990 show, there was no longer any doubt of it.

David's departure, it seemed, had not even slightly derailed the Lookout juggernaut. After two years of fearing I couldn't do anything without his help, I found myself managing better than ever. A lifetime of self-doubt began to be replaced by a quiet belief that if I could dream it, it was well on its way to being done.

9.
The Berkeley Way

One of the most iconic features of the early Lookout releases was the address on the sleeve: PO Box 1000, Laytonville, California.

I'd been randomly assigned that box number when the new post office opened, years before I knew I'd be running a magazine or record label. When I came down off the mountain in May of 1990, I continued using the address, assuming it wouldn't be long before I returned to Spy Rock.

The label was receiving hundreds of letters every week now. The Laytonville post office would forward them to me, but eventually a clerk told me they couldn't do that indefinitely. Unless I planned on coming back to Laytonville soon, I'd need to get a new PO box.

Would the Berkeley Post Office provide Lookout with anywhere near as memorable an address? In a word, no. The number they stuck us with—11374—was as bland as it was forgettable.

My main reason for moving to Berkeley had little to do with Lookout. As well as the label was doing, I didn't see it providing me with a full-time living, so I'd hit upon the idea of substitute teaching a couple days a week to augment my income. That required a college degree, something I'd been a couple years short of when I bailed out on education back in the 1970s.

At first I'd planned to attend Humboldt State in Arcata; it was closer to Spy Rock and had a reputation for being pretty easy academically. But transferring my credits there proved problematic, whereas UC Berkeley, the last school I'd attended, told me I was welcome to re-enroll.

The only remaining obstacle was finding somewhere to live. That piece fell into place when my brother, who built windsurfing boards for a living, offered me the room on Berkeley Way that he'd been using as a workshop.

Just three blocks from campus, it was one of several rooms and apartments tucked into a complex of houses that, in the 1960s, had functioned as a semi-communal (and semi-notorious) counterculture haven. Two big houses out front, two smaller cottages in back, not unlike the typical Berkeley setup described by Jack Kerouac in *The Dharma Bums*, where he talks about living with Alvah Goldbook (aka Allen Ginsberg) in "his little rose-covered cottage in the backyard of a bigger house on Milvia Street."

My room would be upstairs at the front of the big house; the cottage out back was covered not by roses but with a tangled morass of ivy, weeds, and trash. Reputed to have once been a major LSD lab, the cottage had since been occupied by squatters who had turned it into a crack house. If I came home late at night, I'd often have to thread my way past prostitutes and junkies going about their dreary business.

I had some history with the Berkeley Way house. In the early 1970s, my room had been home to a strange young man known as Jayel, who had served as my Dantean spirit guide to the Berkeley underworld. Jayel had arrived in California as a starry-eyed hippie kid in 1966, but by the time I met him he was locked into a downward spiral that ended with him being beaten and kicked to death in an alleyway during an alcoholic stupor.

Berkeley Way had been his last stop before slipping off into the shadows of SRO hotels and skid row desolation. Another young man from the Telegraph Avenue hippie scene had been shot dead on the back stairs of the house next door. No one ever explained exactly why.

Berkeley acquired the biggest part of its reputation in the 1960s, a decade it's never completely shaken off. Some parts of the city are incredibly beautiful, but neighborhoods like mine could feel like nondescript wastelands, with the ghosts of Owsley and the Grateful Dead brushing uneasily past aging activists, aspiring artists, and bohemian homeowners. And always the students, rolling into town and back out again as inexorably as the seasons and the tides.

My new home was badly in need of paint, a new roof, and a host of other repairs. It was what real estate agents disparaged as a "rent control special." Berkeley's law, among the strictest in the state, kept rents low, but it also handed landlords an excuse to neglect or even abandon their properties.

They were allowed to raise rents by a small percentage each year, but only if they registered with the city, filed the proper forms, and kept the premises fit for human habitation. Our landlord didn't see why he should have to do any of this.

Convinced that the City of Berkeley, aided by a cabal of "Mexicans and Communists," was out to rob him of his property, he stopped communicating or cooperating with the Rent Board. As a result, our rent remained perpetually frozen somewhere in the 1970s.

My room, roughly 12 by 15 feet, cost $98 a month. Students down the block were paying five or even ten times as much. In theory, that $98 included utilities, but our landlord seldom bothered to pay the bills, so having the water or electricity abruptly shut off was one downside to life on Berkeley Way.

The room had no kitchen, not even a hot plate or mini-fridge. Nor did it have any heat. But when the weather was decent, and a gentle breeze stirred the cedar boughs that brushed against the front windows, and the bells of the Campanile echoed off the hills and came floating down from campus, it felt like my own little piece of heaven.

By the time I put together some improvised furniture, stacked up some boxes of records, and rolled out the futon I'd been carrying around in the back of my truck, just about enough space remained for a path from the front door to the bathroom. Once I started bringing in employees, the futon had to go, too. For several years, I slept on, or in, a pile of blankets I kept wadded up in the corner.

As I was getting ready to leave Spy Rock the previous spring, I'd decided to release EPs by 10 different bands—among them, Green Day, the Lookouts, Fifteen, Cringer, Filth, and Blatz—in a single month. I don't remember what made me think that would be a good idea, let alone how I managed to make it happen.

Maybe I was trying to prove something—to David, myself, or both. I'd never heard of a small indie label putting out that many records at once. Much of my summer was spent slipping 7"s into sleeves, packing them into boxes, and shipping them off to Mordam in San Francisco.

Before moving to Berkeley I'd arranged to do another 7", this one for Brent's TV, a semi-acoustic, only-in-Arcata sort of group I'd become a huge fan of. When the vinyl arrived, I drove up north for a record-stuffing party at guitarist Chris Imlay's apartment.

With the band and their friends pitching in, the work was done in no time. Just as we finished, a blood-curdling howl came echoing up from the street.

It was Al Sobrante, cutting a wide swath through the hordes of HSU freshmen who had crowded into downtown Arcata on the first Friday night of the new semester. He was drunker than I'd ever seen him—come to think of it, I'd barely ever seen him drunk at all—and came across like a jovial grizzly bear trying to give everyone a well-intentioned hug.

It was strange encountering him outside his normal East Bay habitat, and stranger still to see him without the rest of Green Day in tow. Al had moved to Arcata and enrolled at HSU, declaring that he wanted to have "a real college experience" (prior to this he'd been attending community college in the Bay Area).

Billie Joe Armstrong and Mike Dirnt, Green Day's two younger members, had been expecting to do some serious touring now that they'd finished high school.

Instead they were suddenly short one drummer, a fact they'd only become aware of when a friend casually blurted out what she thought they already knew: Al was planning to put the band "on hiatus" for two years while he finished college.

Al seemed to think that was perfectly reasonable. After all, he pointed out, they'd still be able to do occasional shows on weekends or holiday breaks. I got the impression he was genuinely shocked when Mike and Billie took a different view.

For the first couple of years, Al had been the "adult" of the band, doing most of the planning, talking, and driving, and "the kids" had generally gone along with whatever he decided. Not this time, however.

"We were way too young and full of energy to wait six months or a year for someone to play gigs," Billie told me in a 2001 interview for *Hit List* magazine. "At the age of 18 that's like half a lifetime."

At the same time, he added, "I had this romantic thing in my head about how the gang doesn't split up, that a band never splits up. I didn't want to look for a new member. It was too cheesy, too lame."

In the end, though, they didn't have to look. Earlier that year, when the Lookouts were recording some new songs, Billie had come in with us to add some lead guitar and backing vocals. It was our first time working at Andy Ernst's Art Of Ears studio, where Green Day had done most of their recording. It would also be the first time Billie played music with our drummer, Tre Cool.

As a producer, Andy was almost the polar opposite of Kevin Army. While Kevin seldom hesitated to offer suggestions or criticism, Andy, a near-doppelganger for Jefferson Airplane bassist Jack Cassady, was so easy-going and laid-back that you practically had to drag an opinion out of him.

Kevin was the ideal producer if you were looking for someone to help mold and shape your sound. Andy was who you went to when you already knew what you wanted to sound like.

Andy's light but masterful touch on the mixing board combined with Billie's guitar riffs and vocals to help the Lookouts come up with our best-sounding record ever. Then we headed over to Jake and Jesse's new house in Oakland for a basement show featuring ourselves, Green Day, and Filth. It would be one of the last things we ever did as a band.

Not long afterward, Tre, still only 17, left home and moved to the East Bay. By September he was practicing regularly with Green Day, and in October the new lineup played its first show at a student co-op in North Berkeley.

Al Sobrante was a perfectly adequate drummer, but you had to wonder whether he'd have been able to keep up with Green Day indefinitely. Music was only part of his life, and maybe not even the most important part. Tre, on the other hand, was cut from the same cloth as Mike and Billie: music *was* his life.

Having played with Tre since the day he'd picked up his first drumstick, I had no doubt he was good enough to be in Green Day. My only question was how his style and attitude—he was as headstrong and rambunctious as he was gifted and powerful—would mesh with theirs.

It turned out to be a perfect fit. Tre's hyperactive antics barely fazed Mike and Billie—it might have helped that all three of them were the same age—and his drumming, more dynamic and nuanced than Al's, kicked Green Day's sound up to a whole new level, almost like going from black and white to technicolor.

The first time I saw this version of Green Day, I knew the Lookouts wouldn't be getting our drummer back. Though in theory Tre was only a temporary replacement, Mike and Billie must have quickly realized they'd be nuts to let him go.

That meant the Lookouts' five and a half year run was over. We never considered trying to find a new drummer. As important a part of my life as the band had been, I don't remember feeling that troubled about its demise, possibly because I was too busy with school and the record label to give it much thought.

Besides, I reminded myself, Tre would never have been able to reach his full potential with the Lookouts. Between my own responsibilities and our bassist Kain Kong spending much of his time studying in Germany, there was no telling when—

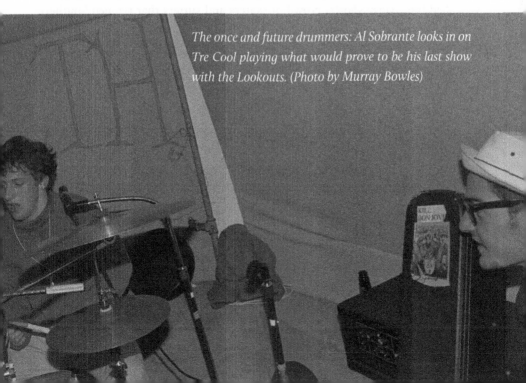

The once and future drummers: Al Sobrante looks in on Tre Cool playing what would prove to be his last show with the Lookouts. (Photo by Murray Bowles)

or if—we might start practicing or playing gigs again.

Al, so remarkably casual about leaving Green Day at first, suddenly showed signs of wanting to reclaim his throne. He started coming to the Bay Area more often, sometimes turning up at Green Day shows at the last minute to tell Tre his services wouldn't be needed that night.

I was there the last time he did this, at a sold-out Phoenix Theater in Petaluma, where Green Day were opening for Bad Religion. "I'm sure Tre'll never tell me that it bothered him," Billie reflected in the 2001 interview, "but that was a pretty awful thing we did, letting Al play that last big gig." Soon afterward, the band named Tre as their permanent drummer.

I'd been listening to Bad Religion for years, but that night was the first time I'd met them. Greg Graffin, their singer, was standoffish, showing little interest in discussing his band or his legendarily polysyllabic lyrics, but guitarist Brett Gurewitz was the opposite: friendly, outgoing, ready to talk about anything and everything.

He confided that his main influences were "Simon and Garfunkel and the Beatles"—a bold admission for a punk rocker. I thought he might be joking with me, but a closer examination of my favorite Bad Religion records revealed bits of lyric and melody lifted from both those groups.

Brett also ran Epitaph Records, which was on its way to becoming—if it wasn't already—the biggest punk rock label in the world. Apart from Bad Religion, I wasn't familiar with most of their bands, having tended to lump them in with what we called the "baggy shorts" crowd of skaters and surfers that typified Southern California punk.

Brett, on the other hand, knew a lot about the East Bay. He was full of compliments for our label and our bands. He was especially curious about Downfall, the short-lived project (they played only three shows) spearheaded by the three remaining Op Ivy members after Jesse Michaels left.

I told Brett how I'd promised Matt and Lint I'd put out anything they might do in the future. A couple years later I'd learn that he'd told them the same thing.

That autumn Lookout made its first foray into the digital age, releasing the Mr. T Experience's album, *Making Things With Light*, on CD as well as vinyl and cassette. I thought of it as an experiment, but within months the CD was outselling both the older formats.

I wasn't totally enthusiastic about the new technology, but could no longer afford to ignore it. *Maximum Rocknroll* still clung steadfastly to their anti-CD policy, but the rest of the world had moved on.

It was around that time I first heard whispers accusing Lookout of "selling out" or "going commercial." Even if charges like that came only from the most fanatical punker-than-punk set, they still stung, especially since our guiding principles were the same as they'd always been.

We remained completely independent, and our prices were a couple bucks cheaper than most indies, several bucks cheaper than the majors. We split all profits with the bands, 60% for them and 40% for us, a formula David and I had devised, and which I saw no reason to change.

Our system made no sense to anyone with a more traditional view of the music business. "How can you guys possibly make any money like that?" would be the first question I'd hear on meeting someone from "the industry."

"Simple," I'd flippantly reply. "We don't waste money on stupid stuff." But there was truth to this. Despite our rock-bottom prices, the profit-sharing plan provided bands with a higher return per record than they were likely to get anywhere else,

Green Day's new lineup, early 1991. From left: Mike Dirnt, Billie Joe Armstrong, Tre Cool. (Photo by Murray Bowles)

indie or major.

So I didn't feel I had anything to apologize for. Besides, if people didn't like the way Lookout operated, they were free to start their own label and run it however they wanted.

Now that I was learning most of our fans preferred to buy their music on CD, I decided to re-release the Operation Ivy and Green Day albums in that format. Green Day raised no objection. "Sure, man, whatever," was about as much as they had to say. But it took almost a year for the four members of Op Ivy to give the go-ahead.

They might have been agonizing over the "are CDs punk?" issue, or debating how to shrink and rearrange the cover art, but I think they also saw Operation Ivy as something whose time—great as it was—had come and gone.

"We've already sold almost 3,000 records," they argued. "How many more people are gonna wanna buy it on CD?" Ruth at Mordam echoed that sentiment.

I told everyone to let me worry about that. It was one of my last bits of Lookout business before what was left of 1990 disappeared into a blur of late-night study sessions, bicycling down to Gilman, balancing record release budgets, and a strobe-like whirl of memories and impressions that would be with me for the rest of my life.

10.
My Brain Hurts

My parents had always harped on the importance of going to college. If I didn't, my dad warned, I'd end up working on the assembly line or, as he had, at the Post Office.

I'd been sick of school since third grade, but I tried college anyway, partly to please my parents, partly to get away from home. I lasted two months before I was kicked out for getting drunk in the dorm. Dad's prediction came true: I went to work putting together brake drums for General Motors.

That turned out to be even less fun than college. For the next few years I bounced back and forth between failed attempts at education and failed attempts at having a job. Eventually I gave up on both.

By 1990 I'd studied at four different colleges on and (mostly) off for 25 years, with a grand total of 2.5 years worth of credit to show for it. I'd all but given up on the idea of ever graduating, especially now that Lookout had taken over my life.

Yet here I was, re-enrolling at Berkeley. This time, much to my surprise, I actually enjoyed it. I'd even show up early for my 8 am classes to grab a seat in the front row, much as I'd stake out a choice spot at a show.

"Our job is to teach you to think; everything else is just vocational training," my academic adviser was fond of saying. Professor Cavanaugh, a brilliant old school champion of the liberal arts, helped me set up a program that allowed me to study pretty much whatever I wanted. When the punks asked what I was majoring in, I told them "General Smartness."

That gave rise to the Smart Punks Club, my short-lived and futile attempt to counter the notion that to be truly "punk" you had to be—or at least act like you were—kind of dumb.

The nihilism and willful idiocy of the 1970s punk scene made a certain perverse sense. If nothing else, it annoyed the hippies. But it wasn't of much use when it came to more constructive things: building a club like Gilman, for example, or a label like Lookout.

But now dumb was creeping back into the scene (more likely, it had never gone away). An early harbinger was *Absolutely Zippo*, the brainchild—to use the term

Chris Appelgren's take on the smart punks-dumb punks culture clash, with special guest appearance by Spike Anarkie.

loosely—of Robert Eggplant. If *Maximum Rocknroll* and *Lookout* were the *Rolling Stone* and *New York Times* of the underground, *Zippo* was the mutant lovechild of *Cracked* and the *National Enquirer*.

Robert, an insightful kid with little formal education, attracted contributions from the likes of Aaron Cometbus, Jesse Michaels, Billie Joe Armstrong, and myself. Complain as I might about the New Dumb, I found it deeply satisfying to take a break from budget balancing and textual exegesis to dash off something "punk as fuk" for *Zippo*.

Deliberate misspellings and grammar-mangling assaults on taste, logic, and common sense were fundamental to the *Zippo* aesthetic. It was alarming how easily I could slip into that mode, especially when I discovered that many readers preferred my lunatic rants in *Zippo* to the "serious" stuff I wrote for *Lookout* and *MRR*.

Eggplant was also one of the prime movers of Blatz, a new band with tunes like "Fuk Shit Up," "Homemade Speed," and "Berkeley Is My Baby (But I Should've Aborted It)." Lead singer and lyricist Jesse Luscious, newly arrived from the East Coast, introduced himself with his fanzine, *Berkeley Sucks*. He would later become an elected city official who could barely stop singing Berkeley's praises.

There was never any doubt that Blatz were going to be on Lookout. They did an EP, *Cheaper Than The Beer*, before teaming up with Filth, their spiritual cousins, for the *Shit Split* LP.

On the surface, the two bands weren't that similar. Blatz never played a song the same way twice, walking a fine line between chaos and collapse. Filth, while they *sang* about chaos, did it in a structured and well-rehearsed way.

Regardless of differences and similarities, it was obvious that the two bands belonged together. But whereas Filth turned themselves into a near-caricature of traditional, old school punk, there was almost an element of—dare I say it?— hippieness to Blatz.

I stopped by the studio while the band was working on its side of the *Shit Split*. I was greeted at the door by an ashen-faced Kevin Army, who informed me that Blatz planned to "keep it real" by recording in the nude. They were expecting Kevin to do likewise.

Kevin had endured many sights, sounds, and smells during his years of recording Lookout bands, but he had never struck me as the get-naked type. Blatz would have to make do with a fully clothed producer.

Meanwhile, though still enjoying my classes at Berkeley, I was finding this education business more demanding than I'd expected. "Spare time" faded into a meaningless memory. Reading assignments consumed 30 to 50 hours a week, more when there were papers to write. In between classes and homework, I had to find a similar number of hours for the record label.

It didn't help when Chris quit Lookout to focus on his own studies. It was a great stroke of luck, then, to meet Patrick Hynes, an 18-year-old Berkeley freshman and perhaps the smartest of all the smart punks.

He mentioned that he did "a little drawing," and I told him I could use some help at the label. During his first visit to the office, he produced an *MRR* ad and sketched out a design for our next catalog.

He wasn't looking for a job, nor, as an Electrical Engineering and Computer Science major, did he have time for one. But despite being enrolled in one of Berkeley's most competitive and demanding programs, he was soon spending more time at Lookout than on campus.

Patrick was a priceless addition to the Lookout roster. His artistic style became as indelibly linked with our image as Chris's already had, and his calm, reasoned manner was the perfect antidote to the basket-of-kittens-and-headless-chickens uproar that typically characterized our operations.

Some people found him a little Spock-like: his engineer's mindset and inexorably rational thought process made him reluctant to engage in chit-chat or small talk, which, if you didn't know him, could make him seem unapproachable, or even a little intimidating. But that had its advantages, too.

When, for example, people tried to sell me on some harebrained project and refused to take no for an answer, I could tell them, "Run it by Patrick. If he gives the okay, I'm fine with it, too." That would usually be the last I'd hear of it.

It wasn't that he'd automatically turn them down, more that they were afraid to ask him in the first place. "Patrick doesn't like me," they'd protest, but that was seldom true. He'd simply ask, in his casually brusque, unaffected manner, that they logically explain the merits of what they were proposing.

He never argued or quibbled, just listened attentively, occasionally shaking his head or quietly observing, "No, that wouldn't work." Only if you really taxed his patience would you hear something like, "It's not my fault if what you're saying doesn't make sense."

As one of the few who was fluent in Patrick-ese, I became his de facto translator. I constantly had to tell people, "What Patrick really means is . . . " but I myself had little trouble communicating with him. I also discovered that beneath his Vulcan exterior lived the soul of an artist.

Within months of my showing him a few chords, he was developing into one of the best bassists and guitarists I'd ever known. He became an avid reader—*Moby*

Dick being a particular favorite—and cultivated the most impressive pompadour this side of the 1950s.

Chris's academic career didn't work out so well. After one abortive semester, he returned to Berkeley Way, completing the triumvirate that I've always thought of as the "classic" Lookout lineup. Many of the label's essential elements emerged during the two years David and I were partners, but the Chris-Patrick-Larry combo oversaw Lookout's transformation from hobby label to countercultural behemoth.

It wouldn't have looked that way to an outsider. Our "office" more closely resembled an incredibly disorganized dorm room occupied by a frolicking litter of poorly trained puppies.

The door would pop open about 9 each morning, and Chris and Pat would come tumbling in. They'd fire up the coffee pot and our primitive computer while I lay on the floor in a disheveled skein of blankets, trying to wring the last few minutes of sleep out of a foreshortened night.

Dumping a pile of artwork and mail orders onto the "desk"—a cheap wooden door stretched across two sticker-adorned filing cabinets—they'd take turns peppering me with questions and gossip. Almost simultaneously the phone would ring. Chris and Pat would look at the phone, the clock, at me, then each other. "I wonder who that is," someone would say. "Do you think it might be . . . Ben Weasel?"

Ben had gotten into the habit of calling first thing every day. Unfortunately, his "first thing" was on Chicago time, which in California meant 6 or 7 o'clock in the morning.

Persuading him not to call before 9 am West Coast time was not easy, but we finally got him properly trained. The image of Ben pacing around his apartment or staring at the clock, tapping his fingers in exasperation as he waited for us lazy Californians to get up, remained a running joke around Lookout HQ.

It wasn't as if Ben and I had any real business to transact. Not yet, anyway. He mostly wanted to vent about what he saw as the pointlessness of pursuing a career as a musician.

Screeching Weasel no longer existed, at least not officially. Ben had broken up the band not long after the 1989 tour. But, I kept reminding him, he and co-founder John Jughead could resurrect it any time they chose.

Instead they'd embarked on a new project called the Gore Gore Girls, which Ben wanted me to release on Lookout. It sounded like a watered-down Screeching Weasel.

"Why make things hard on yourself?" I asked. "Thousands of people would love to hear a new Screeching Weasel record. What's the use of starting from scratch with a new band they've never heard of?"

"I'm done with that Weasel bullshit," Ben grumbled. "It's time to move on."

It took a year or so of my nagging, coupled with my refusal to sign the Gore Gore Girls, before Ben finally agreed to re-form Screeching Weasel. We began making plans to release their next album, and, much to my surprise, Ben asked me to produce it.

I booked time at Art Of Ears for the summer of 1991. Ben, in need of something new to argue about, told me, "Don't waste money putting out a CD version. Punks don't buy CDs."

"They'll buy this one," I said, letting him know this was one topic that was no longer up for discussion.

The Green Day and Operation Ivy CDs had finally made it into production, but not before I had to head off a crisis created by that one-man conceptual art project, Al Sobrante.

Al wasn't even in Green Day anymore, but his handiwork lived on. The *39/ Smooth* lyric sheet included a copy of a letter purportedly from I.R.S. Records, a pseudo-indie label founded by the manager of Wishbone Ash and The Police.

Typed on I.R.S. stationery that Al claimed to have found while dumpster diving, the letter invited Green Day to leave Lookout and sign with them. It was a crude and obvious forgery, but I.R.S. didn't think it was as funny as we did. Nor did they appreciate the equally fake reply, in which I said Green Day would never be interested in "your cheesy, washed-up label."

It would be the first, but far from the last time—punks not being great respecters of trademarks and copyrights—that I'd have to do some fast talking to avoid being sued out of existence. "We're just a tiny label run out of my bedroom," I pleaded. "We'll never do it again!"

I.R.S agreed to let it slide "just this once," provided I made an official apology. It wound up being reprinted in a couple of mainstream publications; I don't know whether or not it helped their reputation, but it didn't do ours any harm.

Still convinced there wouldn't be much demand for Green Day or Op Ivy CDs, Ruth Schwartz warned me not to press too many. I quietly ignored her, ordering 3,000 of the former and 5,000 of the latter.

They sold out by mid-afternoon the day they went on sale, and a frantic Ruth called to ask how soon I could get her several thousand more.

The runaway success of the CDs meant that by mid-1991, we weren't just paying our bills; we were making a substantial profit. It was time to give Pat and

ack to the Bay Area just as Screeching Weasel arrived to record their new
e you happy to be back in San Francisco?" I asked guitarist Dan Vapid.
it here," he said. "They have good cheese."

in Hurts would become one of a tiny handful of albums I considered
e., containing no skippable tracks. It was also one of my first producer
maybe the one I'm proudest of.

always felt ambivalent about claiming that credit, because, honestly, I
uch to earn it. I've rarely seen a band so well-rehearsed, able to charge
g after song, often without a single re-take.

t was mostly limited to "That sounds good" or "Maybe we should try
guitars." Of the ideas I did come up with, many were rejected not
were bad, but because they would take more time and money.

labels are thrilled when a band tries to keep recording costs down, but,
Weasel might have carried it a bit too far. Convinced the record stood
of making a profit, Ben shot down nearly every suggestion for beefing
or adding extra hooks with the mantra-like, "We can't afford it."

nistaken. I'd developed a knack for setting record budgets, and I knew
y spend double the thousand bucks Ben had established as his upper
luck convincing him of that, though. We wound up spending about
the songs themselves were all but perfect, another couple days devoted

Jesse Luscious, one of Blatz's three singers, is now an elected public official in the City of Berkeley. (Photo by Murray Bowles)

We remind our fans, via this Patrick Hynes-created ad, to send their orders to our new address. (Drawing by Patrick Hynes)

Chris a raise, and though they deserved far more than the $5 an hour they'd been getting, I couldn't be sure our current string of luck would last.

So instead of cash, I offered them profit shares: they'd each get 5% ownership of the company for every year they worked there, up to a maximum of five years. At that point the two of them would own half the company—49% to be precise—while I would control the rest.

I'm not sure how seriously they took my offer. They were still teenagers, after all, doing this mostly for fun and adventure. Five years must have seemed like a near-eternity. Who knew where they—or Lookout—might be by then?

After spring semester, I took a quick trip, starting in Minneapolis, where, at a Screeching Weasel house show, I met a young art student named Erika Grove. I was sure I'd seen her face before, and it turned out I had: she'd been the cover model for a 7" by a popular Twin Cities band called the Porcelain Boys.

Erika also helped organize shows, gave bands a place to stay, and often drew or painted their portraits. The following year she visited the Lookout office in California, where she met Patrick Hynes. Eventually, they'd be married.

The next day I hopped into the van with Screeching Weasel, who were headed to Sioux Falls, South Dakota. I'd heard stories about Weasel tours, but assumed people had been exaggerating.

They weren't.

Ben liked to run "a tight ship," as he put it. In one sense, that made touring easy. You knew where you were supposed to sit in the van, and what you were supposed to say: little or nothing, unless asked a direct question. If you were, the correct answer was to agree with Ben.

The peanut gallery, aka the rhythm section, sat in back. Ben drove, one hand on the steering wheel and the other gesturing and pointing with his ever-present cigarette. He seldom shut up; it was like having your own traveling talk show, only without an on-off switch.

Whoever occupied the shotgun seat played second banana. Normally that role was filled by Jughead, but on this trip the honor was mine.

Sitting up front conferred certain privileges, including access to the radio dial. That didn't mean I got to choose the station—let's not get carried away—but I was entrusted with tuning the dial to whatever channel Captain Weasel selected, as well as adjusting the volume up for his favorite songs and down when he had an important point to make.

The Sioux Falls show was great, but risked being overshadowed by our adventure at the local pizza parlor. "Parlor" feels like a woeful understatement; it was more like a pizza amusement park, its highlight being a junior-sized train that circled the room and delivered people's orders to their tables.

"Driving" the train was a bizarre clown puppet, which, thanks to a microphone and transmitter controlled by an employee in an overhead booth, could talk—and talk back—to customers.

"Cheer up!" the puppet told Ben Weasel as the train rolled past. "Turn that frown upside down and put a smile on that handsome face!"

"Shut the fuck up and bring me my pizza," said Ben.

"Ooh, someone got up on the wrong side of bed this morning!" smirked the puppet.

Ben was still glowering when the train came around again, which the puppet duly noted.

"Why so grumpy? We're here to have fun! Fun and pizza!"

"How about if I punch your stupid puppet head in?" Ben seethed. He started out of his chair to do just that, but the train rolled away in the nick of time.

Luckily our order arrived before matters could degenerate into a full-fledged Weasel-puppet donnybrook. We drove back to Chicago, where I was handed off to the boys from Scherzo, a new East Bay band who'd just done their first record for

Lookout, and who were going to take me the rest of t

Barely out of high school, the guys from Sch wonderfulness of traveling around the country pla van saw no arguments, was unsullied by cigarette fact, that it was easy to see how the band had earne punks.

"Fuck those Scherzo kids," one black-clad M "They're always *smiling*. What the hell is their prob

We finished that leg of the tour in Manchest I might never have heard of if it hadn't become o that periodically sprang up in obscure corners of

Some kid would see our *MRR* ad and order school friends, and they'd start ordering their ow be a dozen fanatical Lookout devotees in a town had barely been heard of.

Rock Hill, South Carolina was one such sc Kids formed bands, put on basement shows, bo they'd graduate and go off to college, or reach more "mature" music like emo or hardcore or

The Manchester kids had a band called I amalgam of every Lookout band there ever w who were headlining that night.

I sang a Lookouts cover with Maude, th lived up to its name in every possible way. sweating like pigs in a barrel, we tore dow cesspit of New York City.

Hours early for our show at ABC No search of shade or something resembling fr spot near St. Mark's Place, we fell out ont dying dogs.

In front of us was a stairway, and at it stepped out into the sunlight, squinting s one of the gods descending from Olymp

None of us said a word. Too starst think we were hallucinating. But I cou from belonged to an Indian restaurant. A Throw in some chicken vindaloo and y

I got album. "A

"I like *My B* "perfect," credits, an

Yet I'v didn't do n through so

My inp doubling t because the

Norma Screeching little chance up the soun

He was we could saf limit. I had $975, and wh

to recording and mixing could have made the sound quality so much better.

After the album was done, we stuck around to record three more songs for a 7" release on Shred Of Dignity, soon to morph into a queercore label called Outpunk. Two of the songs were near-throwaways, but the third was a Weasel classic: "I Wanna Be A Homosexual."

Ben had written it in response to an Indiana band's jokey but vaguely homophobic "I Don't Wanna Be A Homosexual." Although straight himself, he'd come up with one of the greatest gay anthems ever.

I'd always assumed that the song would be released on Lookout. I offered to pay all the the recording costs for the extra three songs in exchange for the rights to use "I Wanna Be A Homosexual" as a bonus track on the *My Brain Hurts* CD. Matt Wobensmith, the kid behind Outpunk, turned me down flat.

Taking a cue from our own early ads, Matt had been taunting us as "shiny happy smart punx," and made it clear he no more wanted to work or cooperate with Lookout than he would with Geffen or Warner Brothers. In his opinion, we were yesterday's news, the sort of corporate dinosaur his label was out to upend.

Bargaining, blustering, sweet-talking—none of it worked. This was an important song, I pointed out, one that kids in middle America needed to hear, something that would never happen if it appeared only on a limited-edition 7".

No dice. This guy was more stubborn and determined than I was. The argument got bitter, at one point leaving me on the verge of tears, but *My Brain Hurts* would be the first Lookout CD issued without bonus tracks, and Outpunk's *Pervo-Devo* 7", limited to about 3,000 copies, became a highly sought-after collector's item.

The confrontation was a rude awakening. It began to dawn on me that Lookout was no longer the upstart new kid on the block. Slowly but surely, we were turning into the punk rock establishment.

11.
Buffy And The Hanks

Until the fall of 1991, I'd enjoyed all my classes at Berkeley. Then, months before I was due to graduate, the university reminded me that I couldn't get my degree without passing a "quantitative reasoning" course.

They could call it whatever fancy name they wanted. What I heard was "math."

I wasn't bad at basic arithmetic, but anything more advanced than that looked like gobbledygook to me. My adviser suggested I might stand a better chance of getting through an Introduction to Statistics course, since it relied more on logic than straight-up math.

Apparently I wasn't too hot at logic, either. Sixteen weeks of hell and humiliation ensued. Until that semester I'd been breezing through Berkeley with almost straight A's, but now each morning found me reduced to blithering idiocy by a course aimed primarily at freshmen.

On the bright side, being forced to wrap my brain around standard deviations and discrete variables helped keep me from getting too big for my britches. Lookout was growing so rapidly that it was tempting to believe some really smart guy must be in charge. Statistics class reminded me on a daily basis that this was not quite true.

As much as I struggled with it, statistics would be the only subject I put to direct use in running Lookout. Other courses gave me a philosophical and sociological grounding, but when it came to things like keeping track of royalties and budgeting for releases, statistics proved far more valuable.

Hoping to get a better insight into Lookout's finances, I tried using our new computer to create something called a "spreadsheet." I didn't know what a spreadsheet was or what it did, but everybody said I needed one.

I might still be staring at my computer screen like a transfixed zombie if it weren't for the Mr. T Experience's Jon Von Zelowitz, an MIT graduate who had a day job with an up-and-coming little Silicon Valley startup called Adobe Systems.

It was like Einstein teaching a five-year old how to add and subtract, but Jon got me up and running with my first spreadsheet. Examining it, I could see we were in even better shape than I'd thought.

It became clear that with dozens of releases already in print and many more in the pipeline, it no longer made sense to think only in terms of individual projects. Lookout had become a multi-tentacled entity that had to be monitored and managed as a whole. It was also important to continually evaluate whether the company we were becoming was the company we wanted to be.

So far, so good, I thought. Without having to challenge or compromise our principles, we were not just holding our own; we were thriving. Screeching Weasel's *My Brain Hurts* sold even better than I had hoped, and far better than Ben had predicted. We re-released their Roadkill album, *Boogadaboogadaboogada*, and it was even more successful.

Both were great albums, but while *My Brain Hurts* was clearly superior, *Boogada* consistently outsold it. For years I wondered why, until the answer finally dawned on me. The *My Brain Hurts* cover art told you nothing about what was inside, while *Boogada* featured the trademark Weasel head that would one day adorn thousands of punk rock body parts.

That image could be counted on to jump-start the sales of any record. Strange, then, that Ben used it so sparingly. Five albums would come and go before it appeared on a front cover again. I sometimes wondered if he deliberately avoided using such a reliable marketing device as a way of proving that his music could stand on its own and didn't need to be "sold."

If so, Lookout was the perfect label for him, because that was our philosophy, too. We never felt we should have to talk anyone into buying our records. If what we were doing didn't appeal to people, there were plenty of other labels they could check out.

We had a similar attitude when it came to the bands now inundating our office with demo tapes and promo packets. While flattered that so many people wanted to be on Lookout, I soon realized there weren't enough hours in the day to give even a perfunctory listen to all of them. More to the point, at least 90% of what came in wouldn't have been right for Lookout anyway.

I don't necessarily mean it was bad. Some bands that approached us had strong followings and the potential to sell hundreds of thousands of records. A few went on to do just that—on other labels.

No Use For A Name, for example. They'd had a song on *Turn It Around*, and couldn't seem to understand why, unlike several other bands on that comp, they hadn't been asked to do a record for Lookout. A visibly rattled Patrick Hynes recounted how their bassist had chased him into the Gilman men's room trying to

Lookout's junior brain trust, 1991. From left: Patrick Hynes and Chris Appelgren. (Photo by Larry Livermore)

give him their latest demo.

I never actually met Good Riddance, a political punk band from Santa Cruz, but felt like I knew them because of all the stuff they sent us. I liked their values but their music didn't quite cut it for me. Like No Use For A Name, they went on to have a highly successful career, and people would sometimes say, "Wow, you really missed the boat on those guys, didn't you?" They never understood that I wasn't into signing bands just for the sake of selling records. I was looking for bands that I loved.

In the winter of 1991-92, I let Chris and Pat put together their first project on their own, a *Floyd*-style compilation called *Can Of Pork*. One band Chris contacted was the Offspring. They'd been around forever and seemed like nice guys, but had never managed to break through to a larger audience.

When Chris mentioned he'd been talking to Dexter, their singer, I said, "Maybe we should do their next album." But either we weren't enthusiastic enough about pursuing them, or they weren't enthusiastic enough about being pursued. Neither the comp track nor the album ever materialized, and the Offspring wound up making other arrangements.

My lackadaisical recruiting style may have cost us one band I very much did want to work with. Following through on the promise I'd made when Op Ivy broke up, I agreed to release the first single by Lint (he was actually back to being Tim now) and Matt's newest band, Rancid, before I'd even heard it.

I wasn't completely confident about Rancid's prospects. Tim and Matt's two previous bands, Downfall and Generator, had quickly come and gone, the latter leaving even less of a trace than the former. I didn't think the name would help, either.

"Tim," I said, as we stood out in front of Gilman, "you know what 'rancid' means, don't you? Rotten, foul, smelly, that kind of thing?"

"Yo, Larry, I know," said Tim, "but see, we're gonna give it a different meaning."

I went to see them play in the living room of a North Oakland punk house. It was pure hardcore, with barely a hint of Op Ivy-style ska, but their furious, nonstop energy allayed any doubts I might have had.

I assumed the single would be followed by an LP, so it came as a shock when Tim stopped by one day and let slip that their album would be coming out not on Lookout, but on Epitaph.

"Why would you do that?" I demanded. "Haven't we always taken good care of you?"

"Yeah, I know, Larry," said Tim, "but like, Brett's really into us, and we thought it would be cool to work with him."

"Then why'd you ask us to do the 7"?"

"Larry, man, you know we love Lookout. We wanted to do a record with you guys."

It was hard to argue with that logic, but I tried anyway, accusing Tim of using us to help promote their Epitaph album, and maybe saying some other stuff that wasn't too pleasant or smart. When Tim had heard enough, he said, "Hey man, I gotta go, we'll talk about it later, okay?"

He headed down the stairs, and I followed him into the street, where we stood shouting at each other in the middle of Berkeley Way until, with a final, exasperated shrug, he walked away. It took me a long time to calm down and accept that I couldn't force someone to be on Lookout if he didn't want to be.

Tim and I patched things up eventually, and I was able to understand that while Rancid would have done fine on Lookout, going to Epitaph made sense for them. Not just because Epitaph was a big label and about to become much bigger, but because it was where the band felt most at home.

That might have been because as much as I liked Rancid, Epitaph's Brett Gurewitz loved them. And didn't hesitate to tell them so. I brooded about what I could or should have done differently, but finally realized I had bumped up against one of my biggest weaknesses as a would-be record mogul: my lack of schmooze-ability.

Even when I thought a band was great, I couldn't express that view in the breathless, unrestrained parlance of the music industry. In that world, bands were never "okay" or "pretty good" or even "really good," they were "amazing," "awesome," or "incredible." Preferably all three.

Not all bands needed to hear that kind of praise. Many Lookout bands didn't, or at least gave that impression. But in dealing with bands that did, it helped to be able to deliver outrageously effusive compliments without sounding forced or phony. It was kind of like that old Hollywood saying: "The only thing you need to make it in this town is sincerity. Once you can fake that, you've got it made."

It might have been how I was raised, where you showed love and respect for people by "helpfully" pointing out their flaws. Or maybe it was my Detroit-shaped personality: in certain ways I'd never left the street corner, where it was the epitome of uncool to let someone catch you being impressed by anything.

Ultimately, as you'd expect a Northern Californian to do, I blamed it on Los Angeles. Labels down there, located at the geographic and cultural heart of the entertainment business, had a built-in advantage. They also weren't hamstrung by our scene's ambivalence—and sometimes outright antipathy—toward bands that became "popular."

Southern California punk tended to be more apolitical and nihilistic—and, to be fair, sometimes more fun—than its ideologically driven Bay Area counterpart. It was also more unapologetically commercial.

In Los Angeles a band could openly acknowledge that they were looking for a record deal and hoping to make some money. Say that in San Francisco and you'd be subjected to an *MRR*-led inquisition.

Lookout—partly because we were local, partly because we'd been so outspokenly independent—tended to be more rigorously scrutinized by the punk purists than labels like Epitaph were. That being said, I wouldn't have had it any other way. Lookout wouldn't have survived, let alone prospered, in a more conventional show business environment. I didn't have the temperament or the smarts for it.

Complain as I might about Southern California, I always enjoyed it when Lookout work took me there. My favorite job was having records mastered at John Golden's Sunset Boulevard studio, where I could count on hearing a never-ending string of Hollywood and music industry stories, delivered in John's sunny, upbeat twang that made it sound like he'd just strolled in from the beach.

During visits to the Southland, I'd often stay with Al Flipside, a devoted surfer who usually *had* just come from the beach. Al and his wife Hudley published *Flipside* magazine, the only punk rock fanzine to seriously rival *Maximum Rocknroll* in scope and influence.

Many people, myself included, enjoyed both magazines, but they occupied opposite ends of the spectrum. *MRR* made serious business out of everything, while *Flipside*'s most serious business was having a good time.

Bands interviewed for *MRR* could expect to be grilled about capitalism and punk rock's place in the socio-economic structure. When Operation Ivy and I showed up for a *Flipside* interview, Al took us to the beach and tried to give us surfing lessons.

The *Flipside* crew were familiar with Lookout and the East Bay, but most LA scenesters paid little attention to what went on up north. Even Green Day barely dented the SoCal consciousness until 1992, when we released their second album.

I'd been bugging Billie, Mike, and Tre about coming up with something new since the spring of 1991, when I all but ordered them into the studio to record some demos. It turned out they had only enough material for half an album, and while the songs were good, they were less than fully formed.

Summer rolled by with no sign of further progress. I didn't understand what the holdup was. The way I saw it, Green Day were so talented that they could crank out an album anytime they wanted to.

Luckily, I didn't get a chance to hound them about it—they were not a band that responded well to that kind of pressure—because they spent most of the year on the road. Then in the fall of 1991, almost without warning, I was handed a finished 12-song tape. "It's called *Kerplunk*," they told me.

I took it down to LA for mastering, and as usual asked John Golden to make me a cassette copy. I liked to evaluate records based on the way an average listener would hear them, not via the high-tech equipment at John's studio, which could make almost anything sound good.

I boarded my plane back to Oakland, and as it taxied down the runway, I slipped the tape into my Walkman and hit play. I shivered when that first chord came crashing through my headphones. I knew in that instant that my whole life was about to change. My goofy little punk rock label was putting out a record by what was probably the best band in the world.

As soon as I got back to Berkeley, we started on the artwork. The concept was to feature a cute girl with a smoking gun on the front cover, and a dead punk boy on the back. I had to make Chris re-draw the cover girl a couple of times; his first draft had her looking too punk, and, several people pointed out, a little too much like Sam Ott, his then-girlfriend.

What I wanted was a cutesy semi-poseur suburban girl, the archetypal "Concord chick" that the punk boys loved to hate. Chris got her perfect on his third try. The dead kid, modeled after Josh Indar, who worked at the late-night Kinko's and later fronted the band Black Fork, was flawless from the start.

Left with some blank space on the insert, I threw in a story I'd originally dashed off for Janelle Blarg's *Tales Of Blarg* zine, a light-hearted account of "Laurie L.," a 14-year-old fangirl who'd killed her parents and fed their bones to the neighbor's dog when they tried to stop her from going on tour with Green Day.

It was so ridiculously over the top that I never imagined anyone taking the story seriously, but I still sometimes get asked what became of Laurie after she got out of prison. It never occurred to me to ask Green Day what they thought about including it in the album, figuring they'd find it as funny as I did. I was surprised to learn, years after the fact, that they didn't.

We pressed 10,000 copies of *Kerplunk*, twice as many as we'd done for any previous release, and sold every one of them the day it came out. I picked up the phone to order 10,000 more, and sat staring out my window into the wan midwinter sunlight.

For the time being, even as *Kerplunk* doubled and tripled its original sales, life loped along at its usual pace. There'd be periodic crises, rounds of frantic phone calls, and late-night dashes to the 24-hour copy shop, but there were also languorous moments of just hanging out with nothing in particular to do.

It was during one such interval that Chris, Patrick, and I decided to start a band. The original plan was to play only Hank Williams covers, and call ourselves—what else?—The Hanks. Patrick had already created our album art before we'd learned a single song.

But during a trip to Chicago I had a burst of inspiration and wrote several new songs of my own. I showed them to Chris and Pat when I got back, and the Potatomen were born. Why the Potatomen? We just really liked potatoes, I guess.

An unusually quiet Friday afternoon turned into our first practice. We thought it was sounding great until an angry neighbor yelled, "Turn it down!"

I was playing acoustic guitar, Patrick was using a tiny 12-volt amp for the bass, and Chris was "drumming" on a cardboard box, so there wasn't much to turn down. Instead, we drove to a deserted street in West Berkeley and practiced there. An hour or two later, figuring we were ready for the big time, we moved our session over to Gilman, setting up on the sidewalk across from the club.

Kids gawked at us, but hesitated to come over. You could see them wondering: "Are these guys doing some cool, experimental punk thing? Or are they embarrassing hippie burnouts singing for spare change?"

Then the girls from Tiger Trap, the band most people were there to see, came running across the street and started dancing and singing along with us. Where Tiger Trap went, the rest of Gilman followed. Our first show—all four or five songs of it—was a smash.

Through that year and into 1993, the Potatomen regularly played outside Gilman, and, when the weather wasn't so great, inside as well. We played in The Stoar, the hallway, in the back corner by the women's restroom, anywhere, in fact, except on the stage. We hadn't planned it that way, but it became a tradition.

In May I handed in my senior thesis and became a college graduate. I went to tell my parents the news; Mom was excited, but Dad barely looked up from his newspaper.

"Bill," Mom said, "Didn't you hear? Larry graduated from Berkeley."

"That's fine and good," he harrumphed. "It would be a lot more impressive if

The original Hanks, er, Potatomen, peforming in the Gilman Stoar. (Photographer unknown)

he'd done it 20 years ago."

I couldn't blame him. Back in the 1960s, he'd taken out a loan he couldn't afford to help pay for my first attempt at college, which lasted a whole two months before I was expelled. From then on, he told me, I'd be paying for my own education. I respected him for that, and still do.

"So," he asked, "now that you've finally got your college diploma, what are you going to do with it?"

Good question. I'd been planning on teaching, but had no time for that now. Lookout had long since become a more than fulltime job.

When I told my dad that, he shrugged and went back to his paper. Although he'd been hearing about Lookout for a few years already, he'd never taken it seriously. When I first told him I was starting a record label, his response had been, "That's a stupid idea." As far as I could tell, his opinion hadn't changed.

But life for me, at least for the time being, became a lot easier. With college out of the way, my work load was cut in half, down to a mere 50 or 60 hours a week. I hadn't felt so free in years. What I appreciated most was having time just to hang out, to linger over a burrito at The Hat (non-Lookout people knew it as El Sombrero), or enjoy some caffeine-fueled philosophizing at the Cafe Firenze.

We'd made the Firenze "our" cafe because it was so nondescript and obscure that nobody else went there. That didn't last long. Eventually it become such a scenester haven that the Potatomen had to write a song about it:

> *Gotta go down to the Cafe Firenze*
> *That's where we mostly spend our time*
> *That's where we go for our chemical energy*
> *That's where we go to moan and whine*

I'm still bewildered, even today, by how much we accomplished while seeming to do so little. The days slipped away in waves of laughter, good-natured argument, and occasional bursts of frenetic but exuberant activity. It was the time when Lookout most resembled what I'd imagined a truly awesome record label would be like.

We didn't think much about the future, nor plan for it; if we had, we might have seen clouds beginning to gather. Not storm clouds, but clouds of light, the golden light that David had railed against back in 1989. Everything was coming up Lookout; even our dumb moves—some of them, at least—turned out smart.

We were still at a point where we could, on the spur of the moment, declare an

Official Lookout Holiday, shut down the office, and take off to the movies for the opening day of *Buffy The Vampire Slayer*. That's how it was deep in the summer of 1992, but not for much longer.

The party wasn't over yet. In many respects, it was just getting started. But the crowds were arriving, the noise was getting louder, the private, unguarded moments increasingly hard to come by.

Those relaxed, carefree, happy-go-lucky days didn't disappear all at once, but disappear they did. It would be a good long while before it sunk in that our lives would never, could never, be that way again.

12.
East Bay To The World

POTATO ME

During my years as a student, I'd seldom been able to get away from Berkeley for more than a few days. The one time I tried was a disaster.

In December, 1991, having finished the last of my classes, I decided I deserved a vacation before starting on my thesis. I came home to find three weeks' worth of unopened mail orders piled halfway to the ceiling. My office and living quarters resembled a post-apocalyptic day care center.

That was only the visible damage. Phone calls hadn't been answered or returned, artwork hadn't been sent to the printer, records that had sold out during the Christmas rush hadn't been re-ordered. Chris and Pat were sitting where I'd left them, drinking coffee and chattering happily amid the wreckage.

No permanent harm had been done, except to my ability to trust and rely on them. What made it worse was that they didn't seem to understand how many problems they'd caused for Lookout and the people and businesses who depended on us. Their attitude was more or less, "Well, duh, what did you expect? We're kids!"

That experience left me feeling chained to the office. Weekend jaunts to Los Angeles or Chicago or Spy Rock were manageable, but anything longer than that seemed out of the question.

I tried keeping a tighter rein on Chris and Pat, but that was difficult. While technically I was the boss and they were employees, they were also friends. And if there's one thing you don't want to constantly be saying to your friends, it's "Hey, quit goofing off and get to work!"

Fortunately, I didn't have to. Maybe December's three-week fiasco was a one-off, maybe Chris and Pat were doing a crash course in growing up, but as 1992 unfolded, work got done, and got done well. There were even times when they found it necessary to point out where I'd been slacking off.

So I began to feel it might be safe to give them another chance at running the show. I planned a European trip for early summer, partly to celebrate graduating from college, but also to pursue my goal of setting up a UK base for Lookout.

Christy Colcord and Mary Jane Weatherbee were two American girls in danger of overstaying their tourist visas, but not keen on returning to the USA. They shared a sprawling Victorian house in Walthamstow, North London, with, among others, Aidan Taylor, a mild-mannered vicar's son from the provinces, and Simon Williams, an *NME* writer who would go on to found Fierce Panda Records.

Christy, Mary Jane, and Aidan had an aging but serviceable van, which they used to set up tours for bands, including Green Day's first two visits to Europe and the UK. They also imported and sold records from labels like ours.

Bands were beginning to complain that our records weren't being widely sold in Europe, and for the most part, they were right. People like Christy, Mary Jane, and Aidan did what they could, but the cost of shipping and import duties, combined with their limited resources, left them unable to do much more than sell through mail order and at shows. They were in no position to supply all the record shops in London, let alone the rest of the country or the Continent.

But I liked what they were doing and the way they went about it. They seemed like ideal candidates to help start Lookout UK and build it into a Europe-wide operation.

It wasn't the worst idea in the world, but I hadn't thought it through well enough. Most American labels licensed their records to already established European companies. In theory, my new friends could set up their own pressing and distribution network in London, but that would require far more capital than we could come up with.

Selling imported records via mail order was better than nothing, but it was inefficient, costly, and unlikely to grow into a full-fledged counterpart to Lookout USA any time soon. I guess I was hoping—or wishfully believing—that Lookout's golden light would work the same sort of magic in the UK that it had at home.

It would be a crucial mistake on my part. Unwilling to get involved in a licensing deal, yet unable to make a big enough investment in Lookout UK, I all but guaranteed we'd never have the kind of European distribution achieved by labels like Epitaph and Dischord.

That was bad enough in 1992. It would become a much worse problem in future years, as overseas demand for our records drastically outstripped supply. In America, Lookout releases were readily available and affordable, but in Europe, they remained expensive and hard to find.

Unfortunately, it took me far too long to figure this out. I was assuming Lookout UK would grow quickly once they had more records to sell. Which is how, after a 12-hour overnight flight from San Francisco, I found myself blearily attempting to wheel 300 copies of *Kerplunk* past British customs.

It never occurred to me that what I was doing might be construed as some kind of "business." I was just bringing some records over for my friends, I told the bemused border guard.

"So none of these are to be sold, sir? Would you categorize them as merchandise samples, then?"

Oh no, I insisted, it was nothing like that. It was just that I knew these people who played in a band, and there were these other people who arranged tours for them, and it wasn't like we were a "company," we were just a couple of friends trying to help out some other friends by pressing some records for them, and, with that, I launched into a detailed explanation of the history and philosophy of Lookout.

I thought he was finding it all quite fascinating, but, with a weary gesture, he cut me off in mid-sentence and said, "Never mind, sir. Have a pleasant stay in the United Kingdom." I hadn't done it on purpose, but me and my big mouth had just saved us several hundred pounds in import duties.

I dropped off the records in Walthamstow, paid a few visits, and went through the complicated and expensive process of setting up a Lookout UK bank account. Then I took off for Germany, where I was going to meet up with the Mr. T Experience and ride along with them on the Eastern European leg of their tour.

Mary Jane Weatherbee, Dr. Frank, and Aaron Rubin somewhere in Poland. (Photo by Larry Livermore)

The first show, in Osnabrück, seemed to go on forever. Germans felt their five deutschmarks entitled them to several hours of music; tell them you'd already played every song you know, and they'd yell, "Then play them again!" In the morning we headed east, to Poland.

Poland had had its own punk scene since the 1970s, defying all government efforts to control or suppress it. But until the communist regime collapsed at the end of the 80s, few American bands bothered trying to tour there.

So we felt like we were venturing into uncharted territory. We did our first show in Lodz (pronounced, for reasons that baffled me, "Woodj"), then set out on a painfully slow cross-country journey to Bialystok, just 30 miles from what until recently had been the USSR.

It was an exciting but challenging time to be traveling in Eastern Europe. Although Poland was no longer a Soviet satellite, the aftermath of the 1989 revolution was still unfolding—and unraveling. Countryside and cities alike existed in varying degrees of chaos. Poland felt like a nation still trying to decide whether it was being born . . . or dying.

Roads alternated between modern Western-type expressways and cobblestone paths of medieval vintage. We'd be barreling down the highway California-style, singing along to Right Said Fred's "I'm Too Sexy For My Shirt," then suddenly find ourselves in a desperate brake-slamming swerve to avoid crashing into a horse-drawn hay wagon.

We never knew if a town would have petrol or food, so we stocked up on both whenever we could. When we did find shops or cafes that were open, we often had to guess at what they were selling, because almost no one, including the punks organizing shows for us, spoke English.

We did master the words for two staples never in short supply: *piwo* and *wódka*—beer and vodka. I'd been around some hard-drinking scenes, but none came close to what I encountered among those Polish punk rockers. If you didn't accept a drink fast enough, they'd pour it down your throat without bothering to ask a second time.

I mentioned this to one scrawny young man in Bydgoszcz as he swayed precariously on the edge of a canal, demanding I finish off the half-liter of *wódka* he had somehow procured out of nowhere.

"No, is not so true," he said. "Polish people, we drink, but for good times only. Russians . . . " He paused to spit contemptuously, as though his mouth had endured a grave insult by having that word pass through it. "Russians, they are always drunk and fighting. Like crazy animals."

Every young Pole had been forced to study Russian at school—it was why so few of them knew English—but it was hard to find anyone who would admit to understanding a word of it, even when it would have come in handy. The farther east—and closer to Russia—we got, the truer this became.

Remnants of the Red Army, which had occupied Poland since the 1940s, were still stationed in this part of the country. They were supposed to be leaving soon, but, the Poles complained, were taking their time about it.

Winding through miles of sub-boreal forest, punctuated by dark wooden houses with vivid green or red shutters, it was easy to imagine we'd inadvertently crossed over into Russia, or at least into what I'd always imagined Russia would look like. My fantasies transformed our van into a horse-drawn sleigh and our journey into something out of Tolstoy or *Doctor Zhivago*.

That illusion evaporated when we hit the outskirts of Bialystok. Slightly more picturesque than some Polish towns we'd seen, its skyline was still dominated by grim concrete slabs of state socialist architecture.

"I bet no East Bay band has ever made it this far east!" I exulted, as we rolled into a roundabout in the shabby city center. A familiar bit of graffiti scrawled across a cement water tower told us Green Day had been there first.

At previous stops we'd been put up in people's apartments, but in Bialystok, we were shown to a spooky concrete barracks, several stories high and containing a hundred rooms or more. We were the only occupants.

Depending who you asked, the barracks had housed either Russian soldiers or workers at the abandoned factory next door. Except for the fact that the doors didn't lock, it compared poorly to some jails in which I'd been a guest.

I roamed the deserted corridors in search of, well, anything, but found a vast, unyielding maze of nothingness. In all the rooms and hallways, there was just one attempt at decoration, a magazine page that had been torn out and taped to the faded blue wall of an otherwise barren cell.

It was an uncaptioned photo of a vaguely hippie-ish, 1970s-style couple. It looked so odd, so tacky yet poignant, that we debated whether to leave it where it hung or bring it with us as a souvenir. In the end we decided to take it, reasoning that it would ultimately wind up in the trash otherwise. It proved to be the right choice: the photo achieved an immortality of sorts when it served as the cover art for the following year's Mr. T Experience album, *Our Bodies, Our Selves*.

Our last night in Poland was an especially riotous one. Having been voted the most sober (least drunk would have been more accurate), I was given the job of driving the van across town after the show. "You must not be stopped by police," our Polish host warned me. "If they find you have drinking, they put you in prison. Maybe for long time."

This was in Bydgoszcz, where the government hadn't yet figured out how to make the streetlights work, or, for that matter, where or if they wanted there to be streets. Adding to the fun, our van was British, so I had to navigate past giant holes and sandpits while steering from the wrong side of the road.

Not that there was a "wrong" side. Highway anarchy was in full effect. People drove wherever they felt like, or, more to the point, wherever they could. It took half an hour of seat-gripping terror to cover the four miles to where we were staying. At least there were no cops in sight, as much a relief for me as it must have been for the looters who were digging up and carting away the paving stones I'd been hoping to drive on.

Then we were off to Prague, where the Mr. T Experience would be opening for Fugazi. We were excited about that, not just because there'd be a big crowd, but because the promoters would have brought in a generous supply of beer for the bands, as was the practice in Europe. We knew Fugazi wouldn't want theirs, and were happily looking forward to drinking it for them.

The drive to Prague took most of the day. We whiled away the time tormenting Jon Von with accusations that he was secretly a space alien. Then Frank and I got into a religious argument.

I was going through one of my loudmouthed atheist phases; Frank, while not exactly a devout believer, took his theology seriously. He patiently put up with me until I breezily dismissed most of the New Testament, adding, "You've got to admit St. Paul was a bit of a wanker."

That was more than the normally placid Frank could bear. Dark clouds roiled off his face as he bellowed, "ST. PAUL WAS NOT A WANKER!" In that same instant, we narrowly missed smashing head-on into a tree that had mysteriously planted itself in our path. I took it as a sign to shut up, or at least stop blaspheming.

The Prague show was massively sold out, and the refrigerator, stocked with high-powered Czech beer, was similarly massive. Fugazi, as we'd expected, invited us to help ourselves.

People who've never met Fugazi sometimes think of the band as being somewhat severe and humorless. Few things could be further from the truth. From the moment they greeted us, it was nonstop comedy, like a punk rock Monty Python skit.

The clowning around subsided when they got on stage, but resumed as soon as the show was done. Aaron Rubin, Mr. T's bassist, recalls me haranguing

Ian MacKaye unloading the Fugazi van in Prague.
(Photo by Larry Livermore)

Fugazi about eating their dinner out of plastic dishes instead of something more environmentally friendly.

Without missing a beat, a poker-faced Ian shot back, "It's tough being a hippie, isn't it?"

Aaron also reminded me that Fugazi—who'd headlined the show and had drawn 90% of the crowd—gave their entire share of the money to the Mr. T Experience to help us on our way back to Germany. From what I hear, this was pretty typical of them.

While we hung out backstage drinking the rest of Fugazi's beer, I watched a normally even-tempered Ian nearly lose his cool with a Polish kid who couldn't have been more than 15. The kid was trying to convince him that Fugazi's traditional $5 show price, while eminently fair in America and Western Europe, was not affordable for people in the East Bloc states.

"If you charge $5 worth of zlotys," the boy insisted, "Polish people can not come to shows. We are poor."

Ian pointed out that not only had Fugazi's Polish shows been packed, but that the kid himself was currently at a show in Czechoslovakia. "So it can't be *that* unaffordable," he said.

The kid wasn't buying it. He made his case over and over, while Ian, visibly losing his patience, kept repeating that Fugazi had thought long and hard about their pricing policy, and didn't see a reason to change it.

The two of them were talking past each other, really. Both had valid points. Poland was an economic basket case, true, but Fugazi were not exactly getting rich on these far-flung Eastern European tours. Especially when they insisted on giving away most of their money.

Having said our goodbyes, we headed for the border. It was hard not to notice the dozens of young and not-so-young women loitering along the highway, trying to catch the eye of BMW and Mercedes-driving German men who'd come over to take advantage of the derisory exchange rates. Prague, as yet barely touched by tourism or commercial development, had felt like a magical, Disney-esque toy town. The countryside's pervasive poverty wasn't so cute.

I was dropped off in Dresden, and took a train up to Berlin to visit some Humboldt County friends who were homesteading in the recently opened up, but still largely dysfunctional wilds of what had been the Communist East.

The last time I'd been there, Berlin had still been bisected by the Wall, with its hulking presence, as it snaked through streets, byways, and plazas, serving as an unfailing orientation point. Without it, I was constantly, hopelessly lost.

I would have loved to stick around and re-acquaint myself with Germany's once and future capital, but I'd been gone long enough. I stopped in London to collect the rest of my things, then headed back to California, where, I'd been told, my presence was urgently required.

For much of the year, Screeching Weasel had been trying—struggling wouldn't be too strong a way of putting it—to finish their new album, the widely anticipated follow-up to *My Brain Hurts*. I'd vaguely hoped they'd get it done while I was away, but no such luck. From the sound of it, things weren't going well.

13.
The Queers Are Here

If it had been up to me, every Screeching Weasel album would have been made like *My Brain Hurts*, except that we'd spend a little more money and take a little more time. Note that I said a *little*.

But it was not up to me. Not even slightly. So the making of *Wiggle*, Screeching Weasel's second Lookout LP, turned into the sort of endlessly dragged out, temper-tormenting saga you'd have expected from some 1970s dinosaur-rock band.

Ideally, I would have liked Screeching Weasel to record with Andy Ernst in California again, but they decided to work with up-and-coming producer-engineer Mass Giorgini in Lafayette, Indiana, just three hours down the road from Chicago.

I'd first heard of Mass (short for Massimiliano, a name I loved trying to pronounce when I'd been drinking) in 1988, when he booked a show for Operation Ivy at Spud Zero, the all-ages club he started and ran. In the years since, he'd developed a state-of-the-art recording studio in a red-brick Civil War-era building on the edge of Lafayette's slightly decrepit downtown.

One of the hardest, most enthusiastic workers I've ever met, Mass would stay up all night, whether he was being paid or not, to correct a three-second snippet of tape where the drums felt a little off (no one else, not even the drummer, would have noticed). He loved the kind of music Lookout specialized in, which would have made him the perfect producer for us if he didn't live 2,000 miles away.

But Screeching Weasel could hardly have asked for a more ideal situation, unless maybe Mass moved his studio into Ben's apartment. Which, come to think of it, Ben probably would have preferred.

As both a friend and a fan of Screeching Weasel, Mass was willing to work with them on almost any terms necessary. This attitude would prove invaluable, if not essential, in the months to come.

The initial recordings went well, but then Ben refused to go back to Lafayette for additional overdubs or mixing. Instead, Mass would send him a cassette of the latest work, and Ben would listen to it, decide what he did or didn't like about it, then mail a copy to me in California. (In that pre-email era, each of these go-rounds would take three or four days.) Then he'd call me to complain about it.

The number 15 was considered unlucky in East Bay lore.
(*Drawing by Patrick Hynes*)

Sometimes he wouldn't even wait until I'd heard the latest mix before telling me what was wrong with the guitar tones or the instrumental-vocal balance. Following these talks, it would be my job to call Mass and explain what Ben wanted him to fix.

There are many ways to mix a record, but over the phone probably shouldn't be one of them. Still more frustrating was the fact that there was nothing really wrong with the record to begin with. All the fussing and tweaking did little to improve it, and might even have hurt it.

In terms of both songwriting and performance, *Wiggle* never quite reached the heights of *My Brain Hurts*, but then few records could. When Ben finally threw up his hands and declared the record done, it was hard to tell what all the agonizing had accomplished.

It sold well, almost as well as *My Brain Hurts* and *Boogada*, and for the first time in his life, Ben was making a decent living from his music. You'd think he'd be ecstatic about that, and I believe he was. Briefly.

Still the early morning calls came like clockwork.

"Larry," he'd greet me on a good day. On mornings that didn't look so promising, "Livermore" would be the first word out of his mouth. But as often as not, he'd skip the greetings altogether and go straight to "This is hopeless" or "We're fucked."

Calming musicians down and encouraging them to look on the bright side was part of my job. Ben wasn't the only one who required this sort of psychic handholding, but his needs dwarfed those of all the others. He seemed to find success a greater burden than failure.

So I was happy when he found something to take his mind off his troubles, real or imagined. "There's this band from New Hampshire called the Queers," he told me. "You're nuts if you don't sign them."

I'd heard of the Queers, who'd been around since the early 80s, but for some reason I'd always pigeonholed them as one of those obscure bands scenesters and hipsters rave about but nobody else pays attention to. Then Ben sent me a demo containing most of the material that would end up on their *Love Songs For The Retarded* LP. Within minutes I knew it had to be on Lookout.

The songs were irresistibly melodic; a couple of the slower numbers, heavily influenced by doo-wop and the Beach Boys, were almost heartbreakingly beautiful. Singer, songwriter, and guitarist Joe King, aka Joe Queer, was ten years younger than me, but we'd obviously grown up listening to a lot of the same music. I was singing along to the tape, trying out some additional harmonies, when Ben called to ask what I thought.

"The demo's good enough to put out just as it is," I said. "But I think it's worth getting the band into the studio to re-record it. Maybe give it a little of the Phil Spector wall of sound treatment."

"Joe asked me to produce it," said Ben.

I bit my tongue to stop myself from asking why, after months of avoiding the studio during the making of *Wiggle*, he was ready to rush back in there with another band. I also didn't bother noting that if he approached the Queers record the way he had his own band's, there was no telling when or if it would ever be released.

My snarky attitude was not aimed entirely at Ben. After all, despite the problems he'd created with *Wiggle*, it had come out well in the end. And he'd done a masterful—and fast—job with *My Brain Hurts*. To be honest, my biggest grudge was that I wouldn't be producing the record myself.

I flew to Chicago to meet the Queers, and found them camped out in Ben's apartment. Joe, who did most of the talking, came across like an easier-going version of Ben, less cynical and acerbic, but equally fond of wisecracks and stories. I liked him immediately.

Joe's Jughead was Hugh O'Neill, a deceptively low-key but highly skilled drummer. While Joe was the band's only original member, Hugh had been with the Queers for more than half their 12-year history.

Rounding out the trio was a young-looking kid named Chris Barnard, who hadn't joined until 1990 ("His mom wouldn't let him out of the house before then," Joe was fond of saying), when he'd promptly been saddled with the nickname "B-Face."

Although he was an excellent bass player and wholeheartedly devoted to the band, poor B-Face didn't get a lot of respect. In that sense he was a counterpart to Dan Vapid, who at the time was living in a tiny room off the front hallway in Ben's apartment.

They were only a couple of years apart in age, but Ben talked to and about Vapid as if he were a dimwitted child. It must have been frustrating for Dan, who in reality was blessed with a keen and insightful intellect. But his shyness, combined with an inability to get a word in edgewise when Ben was holding forth, meant people didn't always realize that.

I got along great with Joe from the start, much as I had with Ben, only minus the arguments and insults. Unlike Ben, Joe had no obvious axes to grind. And also unlike Ben, who had a tendency to hammer any given subject into the ground, then dig it up and start hammering all over again, Joe had an attention span that hopped and jumped all over the place, like fireflies on speed.

With everyone, even Ben, on their best behavior, it was an enjoyable, almost relaxing weekend. I tried explaining to the Queers how the money end of things worked, but Joe cut me off, saying Ben had already told him how reliable Lookout was when it came to paying its bands. That seemed to be as much as he wanted to know about it.

The next time I'd see the Queers would be at Sonic Iguana, Mass's studio in Lafayette, where Ben was determined to crank out their LP in two days flat. He approached it the same way he had *My Brain Hurts*: one or two takes and done for nearly every song.

If you've seen the *Love Songs For The Retarded* cover photo—a bleary-eyed band surrounded by a staggering array of bottles—you'll have some idea what the recording session looked like. I was already learning that, whatever you might have heard or imagined about the rock and roll lifestyle, heavy drinking is not usually helpful when you're trying to get serious work done.

I was tempted to say something as I helped unload cases of Budweiser along with the band's signature bass cabinet with its spray-painted slogan, "THE QUEERS ARE HERE." But I kept my mouth shut. This was Ben's show, not mine.

Ben had the sense to go easy on his own drinking, and Mass didn't drink at all, but a couple band members were on their way to being completely blotto by the time we were done setting up the mics.

It didn't matter in the slightest. Song after song rolled out effortlessly, as if the Queers had been waiting all their lives to make this record. They were so well-rehearsed, I said afterward, that they could have recorded it even in an alcohol-induced coma. That might, in fact, be exactly what they had done.

It was my first time working with Mass and the experience was utterly exhilarating. Nothing fazed him; his energy and enthusiasm were almost unnerving. If a song came out perfect the first time, he was thrilled. If somebody screwed up, he was equally happy to try it again.

Mass had urged me to come in early so I could meet his father, who'd helped him design and build the studio. I made a point of coming late. Punk rockers weren't supposed to hang out with their dads, I thought. It wasn't natural.

But when I walked in, Aldo Giorgini, Mass's dad, was still there, puttering around with some wires. His face lit up when he saw me.

"A pleasure to meet you!" he shouted. "I was just reading your column in the new *Maximum Rocknroll*. May I ask you a question about it?"

It wasn't just my column he'd read; he'd been through the entire issue, more thoroughly than I had. A professor of engineering at Purdue University and a

world-renowned artist and sculptor, Aldo had recently embarked on his third Ph.D. for "fun." He had the insatiable curiosity and enthusiasm of a small child coupled with the sagacity and insight of an elder statesman.

Punk might not have been his favorite form of music, but when a teenaged Mass and his brother Flaviano started a band, Aldo, who, as a widower was raising the boys on his own, helped them outfit a tour van and chauffeured them to shows until they were old enough to drive themselves. He loved hanging out at the studio and meeting the various characters that passed through.

By the time Aldo took off and the Queers went to work, it was long past dark. And it was long past dawn when we took a few hours off to sleep. We repeated the process the following night, and bingo, a new Lookout classic was in the can.

Ben deserved a lot of credit for making everything come off as smoothly as it had. Although he milked his producer status for all it was worth—I joked about getting him a captain's hat so we could all salute him and say "Aye aye, sir!"—he stayed on the ball, taking notes, barking orders, and putting down his foot whenever goofing around threatened to degenerate into goofing off.

It helped immensely, too, that the band came in with a fully developed and rehearsed set of songs. In all my years working with the Queers, it was the only time that would happen.

Some of the most exuberant moments came when we all gathered around the mic to shout out gang vocals on songs like "You're Tripping" and "I Hate Everything." But I was bitterly disappointed when I couldn't quite nail the backing vocals on "Debra Jean," the song I'd most been looking forward to singing.

Ben let me try several retakes, but finally called a halt, saying we were spending too much time on one song. He was right. We were there to record the Queers, not the Larry Livermore harmony sessions.

Even so, I brooded about it all the way back to California, wondering how or why I could have frozen up at the crucial moment despite having practiced the song for weeks ahead of time. I was doubly mystified when, with no one else around, I found I could sing along perfectly with the finished master tape.

I was still pondering this one quiet afternoon when I had some unexpected visitors. A band by the name of Avail climbed the stairs and piled into my office. They'd sent a record to Lookout a few weeks earlier, they said. Why hadn't they heard anything back yet?

I didn't have the faintest idea who these guys were. Sporting long hair and dressed more like the Allman Brothers than a punk band, they seemed oddly out of place in the Lookout office, but showed no sign of wanting to leave.

"We get hundreds of records and tapes," I said, pointing to our ever-mounting demo pile. "If you sent us something, it's probably in there somewhere."

"You mean you haven't listened to it yet?" said Joe Banks, who I'd learn was their guitarist and chief spokesperson.

I thought I'd made that obvious, but these guys weren't taking the hint. I tried another tack.

"If you've already got a record out," I asked, "why send it to me? Are you looking to ditch your label?"

"Our label's okay," said Beau Beau, a slight, wiry guy with a long chin beard, who'd barely stopped bouncing around the room since he'd walked in. "But they can't give us the distribution we need. Lookout could get our record out to way more people."

"We've kind of got as many bands as we can handle," I started to say, only to be interrupted by their singer, Tim Barry, whose folksy, aw-shucks manner only partially concealed an unyielding single-mindedness.

"Would you just listen to the record?" he said. It didn't sound like a question.

I went rooting through the demo pile and found it. It was actually pretty good, though different from almost anything Lookout had done. More rock than punk, at some points it reminded me of the anthemic hippie music I'd loved back in the 60s.

I doubted it would appeal to Lookout's audience, but agreed to come watch them play a Sunday afternoon show with Rancid at a cafe in Santa Rosa. "Avail are amazing live," someone told me. "When they play back home in Richmond, there'll be like a thousand people singing along."

However big they might be in Virginia, they were more or less unknown in California. Sharing a bill with Rancid, one of the most intense and passionate live bands around, wasn't going to do Avail any favors, either. It would be, I feared, a hopeless mismatch.

The Santa Rosa venue didn't normally host punk shows. Set in a nondescript strip mall, it looked better suited for a leisurely midday kaffeeklatsch. The crowd was on the small side, too, maybe 30 or 40 people. Even Rancid, I suspected, might be hard-pressed to generate much excitement.

But Avail's set left me slackjawed and astounded. They weren't a flashy band, nor did they go in for gimmicks and histrionics, but from the instant they started playing, I couldn't keep my eyes off them.

"Of course I'll put your record out," I said. "Whatever made you think I wouldn't?"

A month later, while visiting Avail in Virginia, I got the chance to see one of their legendary hometown shows. It lived up to everything I'd heard: over a thousand people, jumping and stomping so furiously that the entire building reverberated like the inside of a giant kick drum.

I wasn't sure, though, if that feeling could be reproduced in the studio. As I watched them play I was already mulling over what approach to use and which engineer to hire, but I needn't have troubled myself. Avail turned out to be one of those bands who, like Neurosis, handled every aspect of recording, artwork, and packaging themselves. They didn't invite me into the studio with them and, in fact, never even bothered telling me where they were recording.

Not all of Avail's fans were thrilled with their move to Lookout. Our label had gained a reputation, especially among hardcore kids, as being too silly, too frivolous, and, thanks to our recent successes, too commercial. Some even dared to suggest Avail were "selling out."

I asked Joe Banks how he felt about that. The usually jovial, but always straight-to-the-point guitarist didn't mince words.

"Fuck 'em," he said.

Ben Weasel was not an Avail fan, and rarely passed up a chance to remind me of that. His opinion of them didn't improve even when I told him the new Avail record had become one of Lookout's top sellers.

But while Avail merely got on Ben's nerves, he couldn't stand our other newest signing, Pansy Division.

Pansy Division got their start as a concept, a gleam in the eye of a talented, ambitious musician named Jon Ginoli, who'd migrated west from Peoria, Illinois with the goal of forming an out-loud-and-proud gay punk rock band.

Gay musicians weren't unusual in punk rock—especially not during the first wave of 70s punk—but I'd never heard of a band that made being gay its principal calling card. I went to San Francisco's Klub Komotion to see them, only to discover there was no "them," just Jon singing and playing guitar along with a backing tape.

Jon's tunes were poppy and melodic, with lyrics ranging from scabrously funny to poignant and touching. Get yourself a band, I told him, and you've got a record deal. It didn't take him long to do just that.

Ben Weasel may not have appreciated them, and our printer raised a stink about the naked guy on their album cover, but other than that, Pansy Division were amazingly well received, especially—much to my surprise—by predominantly straight punk rock audiences. I'd had hopes—and I think Jon might have, too—of making inroads into the club and house music-dominated gay scene, but that never really happened.

By any other measure, though, *Undressed*, Pansy Division's first album, was a success. Lookout now had 70 records in print, and had broken even or made money on all but one (the exception being a Juke 7" that Chris had good-naturedly let go way over budget).

We'd reached a point where we could count on selling a few thousand copies of anything we released simply because it said "Lookout" on the cover. It was an enviable position to be in, and also meant we could afford to take chances on bands that ranged far afield from the style we'd become known for.

Nuisance hailed from Humboldt County, with words and music deeply rooted in the wild mountain culture of the Emerald Triangle. Most of the Gilman kids loved them, but as with Nirvana—who Nuisance slightly resembled—it would be stretching a point to call them a punk band.

In the back of my mind I harbored hopes that they might break through to the same mass audience Nirvana had, but though Nuisance fell a few million records short of that mark, they, along with Brent's TV, remain among the Lookout bands I'm proudest of. Songs like "Big Sky" or "Harvest Time" instantly transported me back to Spy Rock and gave a voice to the unique and fleeting culture I'd known there.

Caught up in the excitement of the moment, I didn't realize what a fortunate position I was in, what a rare and priceless asset it is for a label to attract the kind of devotion normally reserved for performers. I wouldn't fully appreciate or understand this until it began to slip away.

14.
Not Just Boys Fun

For our 1993 catalog, Patrick drew a poster-sized cartoon that's still my favorite Lookout graphic, a stylized portrait of "Lookout Records H.Q."

You can see me in the window, pounding away on the computer about pulp mills and pollution, a pet cause of mine at the time. Chris and Pat are gabbling over a giant pot of coffee, and our friend Thadicus, who didn't work there but was a frequent visitor, is unleashing a cacophonous barrage of guitar noise.

We didn't usually let Thadicus play guitar in the office, the flying saucer landing on the roof might have been an exaggeration, and the streetscape, with its dumpster-diving and passed-out punks was more metaphorical than literal. Otherwise it was a pretty accurate picture of life on Berkeley Way.

Except for one thing. Hollie Retzinger, Janelle Blarg's best friend, drew a parody of our poster pointing out that every single punk on it was male. That didn't reflect reality, nor was it the kind of image I wanted to project.

Molly and Phyllis from Raooul.
(Photo by Larry Livermore)

"We've gotta change it," I told Pat. Without batting an eye, he picked up his pen and transformed a couple of the boys into girls.

That solved the immediate problem, but not the larger one. I wanted Lookout to be a label for everyone. You don't accomplish that by, whether consciously or not, excluding half the human race.

I suppose we could have fallen back on the classic punk excuse: "Society made us this way!" Punk rock, like rock and roll in general, had always been predominantly a guy's game, so much so that it was all but taken for granted.

Women had been part of the scene, of course, but struggled against the double whammy of being judged by their gender and appearance as much as, if not more than, their ability and accomplishments.

Even when they achieved tremendous success—the Go-Go's, for example, or Blondie's Debbie Harry—it was common to hear them described as "girl bands" or "chick singers." I'd never, not even once, heard Operation Ivy or Green Day referred to as the "boy bands" they obviously were.

On learning a woman was in a band, men would typically leap to the clichéd assumption that she must be the bass player or singer. I lost track of how many times I heard some guy say, "Chicks can't hit hard enough to play drums," to which I'd reply that they obviously hadn't met Heather from Tiger Trap.

Men also seemed to feel no shame about discussing whether a woman had "the right looks" to be in a band. Granted, anyone who performs in public is opening themselves up to comments and criticism, but I'd seldom if ever heard it said that a guy was too old, young, fat, skinny, ugly, or beautiful to be on stage playing music. I heard it about women all the time.

Before I hop up onto too high a horse, I'd better admit that I'd been guilty of this myself. Aaron Cometbus called my attention to a *Lookout* review where, not content with trashing a band's musicianship, I'd made unkind remarks about a female member's appearance. Instead of admitting I'd been wrong, I argued—and continued to argue long afterward—that I was just doing my job as a journalist, reporting the facts as I saw them.

Anybody who knew me during those years will tell you I could be pigheadedly stubborn, but the problem went deeper than that. I genuinely didn't understand how or why I'd been out of line; casually dissecting a woman's appearance as though she were as much ornament as human being was so deeply ingrained in the social structure that it just seemed, well, normal.

Thankfully, that was starting to change. Gilman may not have been the first punk rock venue to explicitly ban sexist language and behavior, but it was probably the most influential. Women helped in every aspect of organizing, building, and running the club; seeing them in positions of authority and responsibility became the new "normal." So too did seeing them onstage, playing in many of the bands that flourished there.

Some of those bands, like Frightwig or L7, had been around before the club opened. Others, like San Francisco's Tribe 8 or Sacramento's Tiger Trap, got their start elsewhere, but found an enthusiastic new audience at Gilman.

Then there were the likes of the Yeastie Girlz, Kamala and the Karnivores, Spitboy, Raooul, and the Tourettes, all strictly homegrown, and touring bands like Bikini Kill, who helped bring the message of riot grrrl to the East Bay.

Though bands like Bikini Kill and Bratmobile had been around for a couple of years already, I was only vaguely aware of the riot grrrl movement until I paid a visit to Olympia in 1993. I was staying with friends at the Lucky 7 house, and while leafing through a pile of zines in the kitchen, came across a copy of *Girl Germs*.

I studied it, and liked the sound of it, but still managed to at least partially miss the point. Being old enough to have lived through the women's liberation movement of the late 60s and early 70s, I assumed riot grrrls would be eager for my insights, analyses, and advice. Call it my early 90s version of "mansplaining."

Patronizing and clueless as I might have been, at least I didn't stray into the realm of open hostility. In *We Owe You Nothing*, Dan Sinker writes: "The vehemence fanzines large and small reserved for riot grrrl—and Bikini Kill in particular—was shocking. The punk-zine editors' use of 'bitches,' 'cunts,' 'man-haters,' and 'dykes' was proof-positive that sexism was still strong in the punk scene."

I was appalled, too, by the troglodytic name-callers, but at the same time wondered aloud if the cry of "girls up front, boys to the rear" was a form of "reverse discrimination." It was gently but firmly pointed out to me that no such complaints had been heard during all the years when "boys to the front" was de facto reality.

Violent, aggressive guys had long made life in the pit a misery for anyone who didn't want to dodge flying fists and feet to watch their favorite band. But there was another way that men, often perfectly nice and well-intentioned men, colonized the space in front of the stage. Being, on average, taller than most women, they'd plant themselves in a piece of prime real estate, seemingly oblivious to the fact that they were making it impossible for anyone shorter to see.

A little self-awareness and consideration could have solved that problem, but until riot grrrl came along, it was not something most men even thought about. Male domination of the pit was just "the way it is."

It took a while before I realized that sounding off about riot grrrl in the *Lookout* or my *MRR* column was another way of occupying space without considering how it affected others. Even then I dodged the question of why the vast majority of zine writers and columnists were men. Wasn't that, too, "the way it is"?

Gradually, though not always easily, my thinking evolved. I came to accept that the value and validity of riot grrrl would not be determined by my ability to grasp or explain it. I never became a big fan of most riot grrrl music—Patrick and I were especially indignant about bands without bass players—but I remain in awe of what the movement accomplished.

The casual, unthinking sexism so commonplace in the 80s and early 90s punk scene no longer went unchallenged. The number of women involved at every level of punk rock—and music in general—multiplied almost, if not quite, to the point

Kamala Parks playing drums at Gilman, the club that probably never would have existed without her efforts. (Photo by Murray Bowles)

where people no longer felt the need to categorize or stereotype musicians, writers, or artists based on gender.

Women played a major part in running record labels, too, though they didn't always get credit for it. Quite often a label would be associated in the public mind with a charismatic male owner while a woman, or women, did much of the vital work behind the scenes.

Donna Dresch's all-female Chainsaw Records was an exception, but Kill Rock Stars and K Records, the other two labels most associated with riot grrrl, fit this pattern. So did more traditional punk labels like Epitaph and Fat Wreck Chords, the latter having recently been launched by NOFX singer "Fat Mike" Burkett and his wife Erin.

My introduction to Fat came when Mike called to ask where we got the plastic bags we used for 7" records. I gave him the name of our manufacturer, but warned him he might have to wait a few weeks, because we'd been buying bags as fast as the company could make them.

"Oh man," he sighed, "I need them right away. I've got this 7" coming out."

I offered to let him have some of ours, and took the train over to meet him at the Mordam warehouse. As I counted out bags, I asked Mike why he was starting a label. From what I'd heard, NOFX were doing great on Epitaph.

"Yeah, we are," said Mike. "But I seen how much money Brett was making, so I figured why not get in on some of that?"

It's not always easy to tell whether Mike is joking or serious. This was one of those times.

"Good luck with that," I said, then asked him for the five or ten bucks the plastic bags had cost.

"You want me to . . . pay for them?" He looked deeply offended.

Again I wasn't sure how seriously to take him. "Um, yeah. I had to pay for them. I came all the way from the East Bay to get them for you. It's not like you plan on giving them away, is it?"

He counted out the cash with a pained expression. I wondered if I was being unnecessarily petty, but reminded myself that Mike wasn't exactly a charity case. I never did find out if he really thought I was being a tightwad, or was just having a little fun with me.

People often ask how much competition there was between Lookout and Fat, and are surprised when I say not a lot.

"How could there not have been?" they'll insist. "You guys were signing the same kind of bands."

That wasn't exactly true. Someone who thinks all punk rock sounds alike might not be able to tell the difference between Good Riddance and Operation Ivy, or No Use For A Name and Green Day, but I could, and so could our fans. Mike and I liked similar stuff, but not usually the same stuff.

The only Fat-related thing I remember getting mildly annoyed about was when Mike promised—strongly implied, anyway—that NOFX would contribute a song to Chris and Pat's *Can Of Pork* compilation if they included a track by Lagwagon, who were about to release their first LP on Fat.

The Lagwagon song arrived, but not the NOFX one. "Whoa dude, we totally forgot to record that!" Mike said when I called to ask him about it. I never knew whether he'd genuinely forgotten, or had pulled a bait-and-switch on us. Not that it mattered; Mike had the kind of full-speed-ahead yet happy-go-lucky personality that made it hard to get mad at him.

Nearly a year passed before I ran into Mike again. I was at Andy Ernst's studio, where Ben Weasel and I were remixing *Anthem For A New Tomorrow*, the new Screeching Weasel album. Mike, at Ben's invitation, came in to do a guest vocal on the song "Peter Brady."

He nailed the track in one or two takes, then stuck around to tell us some tour stories and rave about his latest signing, a Canadian band called Propagandhi.

"They've already sold 30,000 of their first record," he said.

I don't know whose eyes opened wider, mine or Ben's. A band we'd barely heard of selling 30,000 records? Screeching Weasel had been around for six or seven years before they started racking up totals like that.

"He's probably exaggerating," I told Ben. But he wasn't. We listened in bewilderment to the cassette of *How To Clean Everything* that Mike left with us. It was good, but I didn't hear anything *that* special about it. Not 30,000 copies worth of special, anyway.

Propagandhi went on to sell hundreds of thousands of records, and while I wasn't a big fan myself, I could see their appeal. What I didn't understand was why Screeching Weasel, who I considered a better band, didn't do nearly as well.

The more I looked into it, the more obvious it became that we had a distribution problem. As great as our relationship with Mordam had been—and continued to be—it had some limitations.

The biggest single drawback was that there were certain companies Mordam wouldn't sell to. One in particular was RED (Relativity Entertainment Distribution), which had started out as an independent distributor, but had since become a Sony subsidiary. They did a highly effective job for Fat and Epitaph, but because of their corporate ownership, Ruth refused to deal with them.

I agreed that both Lookout and Mordam should remain steadfastly independent, but allowing RED to buy our records wouldn't give them any control over our operations. Regardless of who owned them, they'd be just another customer.

What made it doubly frustrating was that Mordam sold to other companies with major label connections. It was becoming almost impossible not to; as soon as the majors spotted an independent distributor or label doing well, they'd try to buy into the action.

That meant there were always judgment calls to make. What did you do, for example, when an independent distributor you'd had a long-standing relationship with was partially or wholly taken over by a major? Complicating things further, I suspected Ruth's objection to RED was as much personal as ideological, dating back to some bad experiences she'd had with the company years earlier, before, ironically, Sony acquired it.

Unfortunately for us, RED was the distributor best equipped to get records into the chain stores where, like it or not, the majority of Americans bought their music. While smaller Mordam labels might still sell most of their records in independent shops, our bands were attracting fans in parts of the country where stores like that didn't even exist.

Once a year all the Mordam labels would gather in San Francisco for a convention, where we'd talk about issues like this. Discussions could get quite heated, not unlike early Gilman Street meetings.

Everyone was free to express an opinion, but it often boiled down to Jello Biafra and I complaining that distribution standards needed to be adapted to modern realities, while Tim Yohannan shouted from the other end of the table that the two of us were turning into greedy capitalists.

Ruth occasionally injected a point of order or information, but mostly sat listening until we'd all had our say. Then she'd thank us for our input, bring the meeting to a close, and go on running Mordam more or less the way she always had. Which, complain as we might about RED and the like, had largely been brilliant.

I harbored nagging suspicions that we could be doing even better, but by 1993 we'd sold over 50,000 copies of each Green Day album, a once-unimaginable number for a label like ours. But when, people began to ask, was Green Day going to come out with something new?

The band had been on the road so much I hadn't had a chance to talk to them about their plans. But Kerplunk had only been out for a year; it had been almost two years between 39/Smooth and Kerplunk. So I didn't see a need to rush things.

Anna Joy and Annie from Blatz.
(Photographer unknown)

"Maybe they're not going to do their next record on Lookout," people suggested.

I scoffed. "They've got a great deal here," I said. "Where else would they go?"

"A bigger label? Maybe a major?"

I hadn't thought about that. Except for Sweet Baby's unhappy experience, none of the Gilman bands had seriously tried making the leap to a major. Green Day were now at a point where it might be possible, but it still didn't seem like it would make sense.

A few more months passed, and now even I was starting to wonder. When Tre stopped by the office, I asked what was going on.

"Well, um, we're talking about maybe working with a management team," he let slip.

Pressing him further, I learned they weren't just *talking* about a management team, they'd already signed with one. And they'd done so in hopes of landing a major label deal.

I convened an emergency band meeting at Cafe Hell, our semi-affectionate name for Au Coquelet (less politely known as the Cockring). Billie, Mike, and Tre looked ill at ease and uncomfortable, but I charged ahead, trying to convince them to do at least one more record with Lookout.

"Right now you'll have to sell yourselves to a major label, and you'll be doing it on their terms," I argued. "Plus you'll be staking everything on one roll of the dice. If your first record isn't a success, they'll drop you just like that. But sell 100,000 or more of your next record on Lookout—which you will—and the majors will come begging. You could write your own ticket."

It would have been good advice for most bands, and in some ways, maybe even for Green Day. But Billie, no longer the diffident teenager I'd once known, said quietly, "We're ready to go for it now."

I could tell it was time to shut up and accept what I was being told. Lookout had done a good job for Green Day, but we didn't own them. We'd kept their records in print, got them distributed, and made sure they got paid, but everything else about the band's success was their own doing. They deserved to reap the rewards any way—and anywhere—they chose.

A few days later the Lookout office played host to a surreal gathering. Chris, Pat, and I watched Green Day file in, followed by their new managers. The ludicrously cramped room contained only three chairs, so most of us stood around awkwardly while Elliot Cahn and Jeff Saltzman, the attorneys behind the dubiously named Cahn-Man Management, asked questions and explained what was likely to happen next.

Cahn and Saltzman had previously worked mainly with metal bands like Testament and Exodus, who apparently were semi-big, even if I'd never heard of them. Hell, I was barely aware the Bay Area had a metal scene. When I was riding around with Isocracy in 1987, they'd excitedly pointed out Metallica's house. "Metallica?" I'd asked. "What's that?"

Neither Cahn nor Saltzman sported the horns or devil tails I was halfway expecting. They were cordial, and assured us that "we'd never do anything to hurt Lookout," but it was clear their world and ours didn't share a lot of common ground.

Lookout had seldom bothered with written contracts before then, but during the Cafe Hell meeting, I asked Green Day if they'd sign one to cover the records we'd already released. "Sure," they said.

Working off the top of my head, I wrote a two-page statement of the understanding we had with all our bands. I felt like a kid playing lawyer as I tried to make everything sound official and legal while not straying from the original intent of our agreement. The last thing I wanted was something resembling the major label contracts I'd seen, which could run 75 pages or more, and were filled with what, to me at least, sounded mostly like gibberish.

A real lawyer could have driven a truck through the loopholes I left, but the basic idea was that Green Day were free to move on, and owed us nothing from any future releases. Their first two albums and first two EPs, as long as we kept the records in print and paid royalties on time, would stay on Lookout.

The final clause became standard in all our contracts: "Lookout Records and Green Day agree to treat each other with respect and openness at all times, and recognize that while this agreement provides specific guidelines as to what is expected of each other, the truest contract is one based on trust and friendship."

That language got a chuckle, if not a belly laugh, out of nearly every lawyer who saw it, but it held fast in the one court that truly mattered—that of Billie, Mike, and Tre. Unlike many bands who leave an indie for a major, they never so much as hinted at taking their records with them.

They barely glanced at our contract before signing it, with Billie adding a little guitar amp doodle next to his name for emphasis. A few weeks later, we got word that Green Day had agreed to a deal with Reprise Records, a division of Warner Brothers.

15.
Get Ready For Action

At first I feared—I think a lot of people did—that Green Day's departure would leave a giant hole in the East Bay scene. But as the weeks and months went by, it was hard to notice much difference.

For one thing, Green Day weren't really gone. They still played shows—though not, of course, at Gilman, where major label bands weren't allowed—and hung out whenever they were in town. And we sold plenty of their records. More than ever, in fact.

Still, I found the absence of any visible change a little unnerving. It reminded me of what historians called the "Phony War," the six months after World War II was declared, when not much of anything happened. Until, of course, all hell broke loose.

Okay, losing one of your bands to a major label wasn't quite the same thing as a world war. All the same, it seemed like *something* should be going on. It was, of course, just not where everyday East Bay punks like us could see. Managers, label reps, public relations agents, and marketing specialists were mapping out what they hoped would be Green Day's future. The band themselves were polishing up the songs that might take them there.

Out of sight, out of mind, I guess. Green Day had never been the kind of band who required a lot of attention, but I had other Lookout bands who did. Among them were the Queers, who'd done even better than I'd expected with *Love Songs For The Retarded*, and were now getting ready to re-release *Grow Up*, their out-of-print first LP.

But there was a problem. A couple of the songs featured lyrics that were a bit, well, questionable. Even making allowances for the band's rough-hewn working-class origins, I preferred not to hear lines like "We may be the Queers but we ain't no fags." The song "Gay Boy" didn't come off too well, either.

Joe and Hugh, the two older Queers, came from a different generation, both culturally and chronologically, than most Lookout punks. They'd grown up—as had I—during a time when the casual use of terms like "fags" was so common that most people barely even noticed, let alone thought about it.

I.R.S.

INTERNATIONAL RECORD SYNDICATE, INC.

Green Day
P.O. box 784
El Sobrante, CA.
94803

Billie, Mike, and John;
You may not know this, but we've been watching you and we think
you're the hottest punk band out of the bay area since the
Dead Kennedy's!
You unique sound and your excellent first e.p. <u>1000 Hours</u> has
made us sit up and take notice.
Even though we have several projects going right now, we are
willing to put some of them aside and get you guys into the
studio as soon as possible.
We would like to start out with an L.P. and follow that up with
a national, and possibly european, tour.
We will try to get into contact with your lawyer and possibly
buy out the rest of your contract with Lookout.
Keep up the good work and we'll look foward to working with
you soon.

Cheers; *Lori*

Lori Blumenthal
I.R.S. Records
(212) 841-8091

NEW YORK 1755 BROADWAY, 81H FLOOR, NEW YORK, NY 10019 · 212/841-8042
LOS ANGELES 3939 LANKERSHIM BLVC., UNIVERSAL CITY, CA 91604 · 818/508-3130
CHICAGO · DALLAS · ATLANTA · BOSTON · SAN FRANCISCO · LONDON · TORONTO

*Al Sobrante's handiwork: the forged letter that almost put the
kibosh on Green Day's first album. (Art by Al Sobrante)*

Having heard words like that all our lives, when the first wave of punk arrived, with its emphasis on offending and outraging people—Fried Abortions, anyone?—bands frequently resorted to insults that dated back to elementary school.

No doubt that's why they'd called themselves the Queers in the first place. Play punk rock in those days and you were going to get called "queer" anyway. Might as well beat your tormenters to the punch.

The name served as a first-class attention-getter, and led to some funny mix-ups, especially after word got around that we'd also signed an overtly gay band. Journalists regularly confused the Queers with Pansy Division, and to this day internet data bases often classify them under "gay and lesbian music."

There was nothing gay (or lesbian) about the Queers, but I wasn't sure a couple dodgy lyrics made them closet homophobes, either. It felt more like having to explain to your otherwise sweet grandma that while it might have been considered acceptable to talk about "colored people" or "Chinamen" when she was younger, we didn't do that anymore.

"Grandma," aka Joe Queer, looked bewildered when I brought up the issue. "We've gotta do something about the lyrics," I said. "That's not the kind of thing people expect from Lookout."

"Geez Louise," he said, "what is people's problem? Why don't they just get over it?" But when it sunk in that the *Grow Up* re-release might not happen unless there were some changes, his ears perked up enough to discuss how we might go about it.

Our choices were limited. We couldn't re-record the offending songs or edit out certain words, because that would sound like crap. If we took the songs off altogether, it would mean doing new artwork and changing the basic character of the record. Besides, *Grow Up* only had 12 songs to begin with. We couldn't really spare any.

The only idea I could come up with, besides not releasing the album, was to include a note from the band explaining that they would express themselves differently if they had it to do over. We settled on a halfhearted-sounding, "We know some of these lyrics are pretty insensitive but we didn't write these songs to hurt anybody's feelings. We are older now and even if we aren't any smarter, we're not as dumb either."

It wasn't ideal. Even with the disclaimer, I felt ambivalent about the record. But it had so many great songs—and only a couple troublesome ones—that it seemed a shame not to put it out. Certain people, of course, weren't going to be happy no matter what we did.

Some were offended that I released *Grow Up* at all; others were outraged that I was trying to "censor" the Queers. I found both viewpoints tiresome, not because I didn't think it was an important issue, but because wrestling with moral dilemmas wasn't what I'd signed up for. Running a record label was supposed to be fun, not an exercise in getting everybody mad at me.

Debates over freedom of expression vs. sexism and homophobia weren't the only source of controversy. Another question that kept coming up was how and where to draw the line between good business sense and crass commercialism.

When Gilman was new, it felt like everyone was on the same side. The idea of Lookout or its bands getting "too big" seemed so ridiculous that it was barely worth thinking about.

Even after Green Day's signing to Reprise, the East Bay scene still felt that way most of the time. But something in the chemistry was changing.

For as long as I could remember, people had played in punk bands mainly for fun, excitement, or idealism. But by 1993 a Fat and Lookout-sized elephant had entered the room. It was becoming obvious that, however we might feel about it, there was money to be made playing punk rock.

This didn't mean most bands were suddenly hoping to strike it rich. Some deliberately handled—or mishandled—their affairs almost as if to guarantee that wouldn't happen. But those in search of money, or who were hoping to play music professionally, began to see Lookout as a potential gateway.

That made me the chief gatekeeper. And it meant that bands who didn't make it onto our roster were no longer mad at me solely for failing to appreciate their art. In their minds, at least, I was also barring their way to fame and fortune.

I found it awkward enough turning down bands I only knew casually or who had introduced themselves by way of a demo tape. It was far worse when friends were involved.

Jeffrey and Cinder, the husband-and-wife team behind Cinder Block, the company that printed our t-shirts, started a band called Tilt, which also included former Crimpshrine bassist Pete Rypins. They were a good band, maybe even a very good band, so when they asked us to put out their first 7" and a subsequent LP, it was hard to think of a reason not to.

Still, I hesitated. There was something about Tilt that seemed to set them apart from most Lookout bands. The music itself wasn't so different; it was more their attitude. It was just that little bit more "professional" and businesslike than we were used to dealing with. Tilt felt, in some vague, not quite definable way, "un-Lookout."

It wasn't that I was afraid of losing money; if anything, I could see them selling quite a few records. So, good friends, good band, a chance to help them out and maybe make a profit for ourselves: what could go wrong?

Not a thing, as it happened. Both the 7" and the LP sold well, everybody seemed happy, and I found myself asking, "So what was the big deal anyway? Do I have to be madly in love with every record we put out?"

Tilt's music still didn't speak to me with the same intensity as that of other Lookout bands, but I liked it well enough, and was pleased with the way our relationship had developed. So when they were ready to record their second album, I let them know we'd be happy to put it out.

To my surprise, they said they were shopping it around to other labels. "We thought it would be a good idea to see what else is out there," was how Jeffrey put it.

I wished them luck, and figured that was that, but apparently what was "out there" hadn't looked as good as they'd hoped, because a month later they were back, saying they'd decided to stick with Lookout after all.

That's not how it works, I told them. We put out records by bands who *want* to be on Lookout, not bands that see us as a fallback position when no one else is interested.

Ruffled feathers notwithstanding, I still liked Tilt as people, and took no pleasure in dropping them from the label. But it felt like the right thing to do. Fortunately, they found a home at Fat, where, I believe, they did even better than they had on Lookout.

By my standards, that was a happy ending. Not everyone understood how I could think that way. Wasn't I sorry, they'd ask, about missing out on all those Tilt albums we could have sold? No, I said, not really. Where once I'd almost felt like I had to sign every reasonably decent East Bay band, that no longer seemed possible or wise.

Instead, I moved in the opposite direction, focusing on bands that had something more going for them than the ability or desire to sell records. Raooul, for example: five 14-year-old girls, some with classical music training, some with none at all, who kicked up more of a screech-laden ruckus than Blatz and Isocracy combined.

Then there were the Ne'er Do Wells and Judy and the Loadies, both offshoots of the ever-fertile Brent's TV axis. The Ne'er Do Wells were a garage-y 60s-style combo that Al Sobrante had joined after arriving in Arcata; the Loadies were more or less the same band plus Judy and a trombone, and minus Al.

Judy shared vocals with John Denery—who she'd later marry—and performed sitting down so she could knit as she sang. Neither band was well known outside Humboldt County, but putting the two of them together on a split CD meant a precious and unique piece of local history would be semi-immortalized.

That was one of the things I loved most about Lookout: giving a voice to bands who otherwise would barely have been heard, let alone remembered. It was less lucrative, but felt more rewarding than trying to sign every band that showed signs of becoming popular.

Not everyone saw it that way. There were those who thought Lookout shouldn't be run like a business or as a vehicle for my personal expression, but as a community-based institution answerable to the needs and desires of "the scene."

I didn't completely disagree. We would have been nothing without the support of the local punks, so it seemed reasonable to at least listen to their concerns. For the most part I found this helpful, but sometimes it felt like everyone who'd ever bought a record, attended a show, or read a fanzine thought they were entitled to a seat on our board of directors.

No one, however, offered criticism and advice as freely as *Maximum Rocknroll*'s Tim Yohannan. I was still, after six years, writing a monthly column for the magazine, and despite occasional disagreements, getting along reasonably well with him. But an ugly incident in the spring of 1993 made me wonder if things could stay that way.

It sounded like a funny idea at first. Tim organized a posse of *MRR* shitworkers to mount a cream pie attack on Screeching Weasel when they and the Queers played Gilman. Nobody said so out loud, but it was obvious that Ben—with his reputation as someone whose goat could be easily gotten—was the main target.

But Screeching Weasel weren't Isocracy or Blatz, and Ben's interactions with his audiences were not always comical or good-natured. Paul Think, a skinny, self-styled punk rapper had learned this the hard way when, at a Chicago show, he'd hit the singer with a Little Debbie snack cake (or fruit pie; stories varied).

Ben was never going to retaliate violently against Tim, who was twice his age and half his size, and no doubt Tim knew this. But as mad as I could get at Ben sometimes, it hurt to see him standing there with whipped cream dripping down his face, his anger underpinned by a deep, abiding sadness.

Tim defended the pie throwing as a blow for "fun" and spontaneity, but it was fun and spontaneity at someone else's expense. I knew he wouldn't dare pull the same stunt on, say, Fugazi. And I remembered how he'd yelled at us for being "disrespectful" when we'd ridiculed Slapshot's hockey stick-wielding antics.

What, I wondered, made those bands more deserving of respect than Screeching

Weasel? I questioned Tim about this, but got an evasive non-answer that seemed to imply he saw Screeching Weasel—and most Lookout bands—more or less as novelty acts.

It was an attitude that had dogged Lookout since the beginning, but which had grown more prevalent with the rise of emo, hardcore, and other more "serious" subgenres of punk. I grew used to hearing fresh-faced, barely-20-somethings dismissing our music with a world-weary, "Yeah, I used to like that stuff when I was younger."

Among those most likely to express such sentiments were the Romulan-haired, skinny-jeaned waifs who'd burst onto the scene around the same time as riot grrrl. I'd first encountered them in Olympia, but they'd migrated down the coast and into the East Bay. People often referred to them as the "North Oakland hipsters," but to Patrick they were the "sleazy mods."

I liked their clothes and hairstyles, but I wasn't so sure about their music, a blend of Olympia artsiness and the new style of Southern California screamo. It had a certain entertainment value, but I couldn't see the supposed genius my

Ben Weasel after the Tim Yohannan-organized pie attack at Gilman, 1993. (Photo by Larry Livermore)

younger friends were raving about.

Considering that the hipsters were typically half my age, maybe I should have accepted that time was catching up with me. Especially when I heard myself reacting to these new sounds the way my father had to the Beatles: "That's not music, it's just a bunch of noise."

Born Against were not hipsters—at least nothing like our local hipsters, anyway—but they enjoyed enormous credibility across the punk rock spectrum. They played a blistering brand of hardcore unlike anything from the East Bay, or, really, from anywhere.

At first glance they looked and sounded like the virtual antithesis of a Lookout band. But there was something about them I liked, something that distinguished them from every other hardcore band I'd seen. It might have been the way frontman Sam McPheeters leavened his confrontational howls with a hefty dose of self-deprecating humor.

I don't remember who came up with the idea of putting Screeching Weasel and Born Against together on a Lookout EP, or the even better idea of having each band perform songs the other had written, but that person was a genius.

We had Ben, whose attitude toward punk rock politics could be summed up by the lyric "I don't give a fuck about Nicaragua," delivering an impassioned protest against the war in El Salvador. Sam, whose fury and intensity made Ian MacKaye look like a light-hearted song-and-dance man, half crooned, half screamed a starry-eyed love song to Janelle Blarg.

The record became a must-have for both Screeching Weasel and Born Against fans, most of whom previously had little to do with each other. And it momentarily silenced the critics who claimed Lookout never did anything "serious." Which was ironic, since it was among the least serious releases we'd done.

Meanwhile, I got word that Green Day were finally recording their new album. I had thought they'd be working down in Los Angeles, but instead they'd set up shop in West Berkeley, at Fantasy Studios, often known as "the house that Creedence [Clearwater Revival] built." I stopped by for a visit and found Tre out front.

"Record done yet?" I asked.

"Nah, man, we're setting up drum sounds."

"What? You've been here for weeks. You haven't even started recording?"

"Not yet, but it'll go fast once everything's ready."

I knew they were operating in a different world now, but this was the first time it truly sunk in. If Lookout had been doing the record, it would already be recorded, mixed, mastered, and on its way to the pressing plant.

I only knew a few of their new songs, and one of them I hadn't liked much the first time I'd heard it at Gilman. It had what seemed like an unnecessarily long drum and bass intro, and, at least in my mind, didn't sound like a "normal" Green Day song.

A few weeks later, Rob Cavallo, their producer, handed me a test CD of the finished album and asked my opinion. I skipped randomly through a few tracks before landing on that drum and bass intro. I still wasn't wild about it, but it sounded infinitely tighter and more powerful than before. Then the guitars kicked in with the fire of a thousand suns, and I was hooked. This, the reference sheet told me, was called "Longview."

I went back and listened to the album straight through from the beginning. I don't know how much credit was due to Cavallo and how much to the band, but it was nearly perfect. So much so that my faith in the indie way of doing things felt sorely tested. It shouldn't be possible, I thought, for a major label to produce a punk record this good.

But the impossible had happened.

"You nailed it," I told Cavallo. "You caught the band at their best, and didn't lose a thing. The East Bay comes through loud and clear."

He seemed happy to hear that. Maybe I was being schmoozed, or maybe he really did value my opinion. It was hard to tell. If I'd learned anything from my forays into the mainstream music industry, it was that you could never be completely sure whether people meant what they were saying. Eventually I realized that they themselves didn't always know.

My gut feeling was that Green Day could have done a lot worse than hook up with Cavallo. He seemed to genuinely care about the band, and that's half the battle right there. I played the CD several more times, trying to figure out what it reminded me of. An artful amalgam of *39/Smooth* and *Kerplunk*, I finally decided, captured on tape by genius space engineers from the future.

Then everything hung suspended for a few more months. Richie Bucher was busy drawing the cover art, Patrick Hynes was hand lettering the liner notes and lyrics, and I went back to running Lookout and arguing with Ben Weasel.

16.
Welcome To Paradise

The final weeks of 1993 felt uncannily relaxed, as if the year's work were already done, and nothing remained but to tie up loose ends.

That was an illusion, of course. Even if we'd gotten the routine down to where records seemed to come out of their own accord, the end of the year also meant inventories, accounting, paying bands, and, last but far from least, taxes.

Prior to Lookout, my dealings with the Internal Revenue Service had been minimal. When I worked at the factory, they'd taken their cut out of my paycheck without bothering to ask. Then came the hippie years, when I earned so little that I didn't need to pay taxes at all.

But now that Lookout was turning a profit, it became my job not just to give the government their share, but to figure out what that share was.

Business taxes can be complicated—30, 40, or 50 pages worth of complicated. Worse, they tend to involve math. Sometimes quite a lot of it.

I could have hired an accountant, but that would have gone against my DIY principles—not to mention my cheapskate principles. Besides, an accountant wouldn't be of any use until I'd organized our financial data into a form he or she could make sense of. By then, I reasoned, most of the hard work would already be done.

Sales tax was the worst. Each of California's 58 counties set its own rate, so even if we'd only sold one or two records in some far-flung rural outpost, it required a separate calculation. The amounts owed could be truly trivial: $1.74 for Amador County, $2.12 for Yolo, that sort of thing. But the Franchise Tax Board had a reputation for being ruthless if you screwed up.

Income tax involved much larger sums, but was slightly more straightforward. Until 1993 we'd owed only minimal amounts, thanks to the perfectly legal strategy of spending as much as we could in December on things we'd need in January anyway, thus winding up—on paper, at least—with little or no profit.

But our cash flow had gotten too big for that technique to work anymore. Sales cracked the million-dollar mark, a mind-boggling milestone for someone who not too many years before had been wondering how he was going to pay his rent.

"Wasn't it scary having to deal with all that money?" people sometimes ask. Strangely enough, no. Lookout had grown so organically, so naturally, that it didn't seem that significant to add some extra zeroes to the balance sheet. Anyway, between poring over account books, bank records, royalty reports, and receipts, not to mention fielding Ben Weasel's phone calls and laying out a new issue of *Lookout* magazine, I had little time for idle thought or reflection.

To tell the truth, I found it comforting to bury myself in never-ending mountains of data. Well, maybe not comforting, but diverting. And I needed some diversion. Despite Lookout's success, my mental state was not so good.

I was fine as long I kept my mind on running the label. But give me a free hour or two to contemplate what it all meant or where my life might be going, and a vague, foreboding dread began playing around the edges of my consciousness. I couldn't put my finger on exactly where it came from, but something didn't feel right.

I don't know if it helped or hurt that I spent so little time alone. Technically the office shut down at 5 or 6 pm, but people were often coming and going until midnight. The few private hours I had before Chris and Pat showed up again in the morning were mostly taken up by work or sleep.

Judy and the Loadies, strumming, knitting, and singing.
(Photo by Larry Livermore)

The office still doubled as my bedroom, but it never felt like one, and not just because it lacked a bed. We'd added phones, a fax line, a printer, and digital audio equipment; machines and wires occupied as much space as people. When I lay down at night, the multicolored lights of encroaching technology stared and blinked back at me from every corner.

I wondered if I should look for another place to live, but because Berkeley was a college town, housing was scarce and expensive. I thought I'd lucked out when I found and rented an affordable apartment down the block, but when I came to pick up the keys, the landlord had changed his mind.

"I took a walk past that place you told me you worked," he said. "There's no way in hell you're running a million-dollar business out of that dump."

I didn't appreciate being called a liar, but was too disheartened and exhausted to argue. Instead of searching for other apartments, I began to travel more. Sometimes for business, sometimes for pleasure, sometimes just in search of some peace and quiet.

At the beginning of 1994 I was in England, and made what I semi-facetiously called a pilgrimage to Manchester. I wanted to see the bleak cityscape that had given birth to Joy Division and the Smiths.

Although I'd been a Joy Division fan since the late 70s, it hadn't been until the 90s that I started listening to the Smiths. Once I did, though, I became as obsessed as any gaunt, morbid 16-year-old goth. I also found myself suffering from increasingly severe bouts of depression.

I didn't know whether my newfound fascination with Morrissey's mournful crooning was the cause or effect of my darkening mood. My alcohol consumption, noticeably on the rise, posed a similar chicken-or-egg question.

Booze and I went back a long way, but our relationship had never been a stable one. There were times when I'd been all but straight edge, others when I was a stumble or two away from skid row. During the early Lookout years, I'd kept my drinking to a minimum, partly because I was too busy, partly because it wouldn't do the label's image any favors if the boss were regularly seen falling on his face.

I still limited myself to a beer or two when I was out in public, but showed no such moderation when drinking alone at home. I kind of knew this was a bad sign, even before taking one of those "Are you an alcoholic?" quizzes. Answering "yes" to three or four questions was supposed to indicate you had a problem. I got 15 out of 20, but laughed it off on the grounds I'd only scored 75%, barely a passing grade at most schools.

Things got worse instead of better when I finally got a place of my own, a tiny cubbyhole of a room in the house next door to Lookout. It was a tremendous relief, after four years of living in an office, to have an oasis of calm I could retreat to. The downside was that, free from the prying eyes of my co-workers, I could drink as much as I wanted. Once I got settled in, I proceeded to do just that.

It sounds grim, and it was. But it was also baffling. Why, now that so many of my dreams were coming true, did I want to hide in a darkened room and blot out my life?

It might have been like that old Peggy Lee song: "Is That All There Is?" I'd put so much of myself into Lookout without stopping to consider what success might look or feel like. Now it was here, and all I could think was, "So what?"

Was Lookout really that important? What had we actually accomplished except to make some silly punk rock records that kids would outgrow by the time they were ready for college? Thoughts like that slogged in a dismal cavalcade through my booze-clouded mind. When, like a groggy, grumpy bear, I wandered out of my cave and into the sunlight of public scrutiny, it felt ten times worse.

I was away when Green Day's album, *Dookie*, came out, and by the time I got home a few days later, it had already outsold both their Lookout releases combined. I went to see them play a Gilman-sized club in San Francisco, one of the last times they'd be able to do that without causing a mob scene.

Hanging out in the bookmobile Tre's dad had converted into a tour van, it felt like nothing had changed, but the minute we stepped outside, it was obvious everything had. Camera lights flashed to life, the media came fawning, the buzz in the air was palpable.

I didn't have cable, so I hadn't seen their video for "Longview," but it was in constant rotation on MTV. Apparently the band had been right to ignore my advice when I'd urged them to make "Welcome To Paradise" their first single.

"You could shoot the video in West Oakland," I told Tre. "Outside your old warehouse. Throw in some social commentary about the death of the American dream."

"Yeah, that'd be cool," he said.

He paused, as if seriously considering the idea. "Nah," he finally said. "I'd rather drive a car into a swimming pool."

The budget hadn't stretched that far, so they'd destroyed a sofa instead. Whether it was the music, the imagery, or both, "Longview" struck the perfect note with bored and frustrated teenagers everywhere.

Then Green Day were off to conquer the world, and I'd see them only now and again for the rest of the year. For a couple legs of their nearly nonstop tour, they took Pansy Division along as their opening act.

It was a gutsy move; the mainstream crowds flocking to Green Day shows had never encountered anything like Pansy Division's in-your-face gayness. But Green Day hadn't gotten where they were by being timid. When, at the last minute, promoters tried to kick Pansy Division off a Madison Square Garden Christmas bash to make room for Bon Jovi, Green Day didn't hesitate to say, "Either Pansy Division plays or we don't."

By the beginning of summer it was obvious Green Day were going to be bigger than anyone had dared imagine. In June, I watched from the back row as they played a sold-out London Astoria. Unable to navigate my way past security to see the guys in their dressing room, I set off down Oxford Street on foot.

As I was passing Marble Arch, a white van pulled alongside, its horn honking wildly. "Get in, you idiot!" yelled Mike. "What the hell are you doing out here?"

I tagged along with them for a session at the BBC studios in Maida Vale. While we waited for the engineers to get things set up, we messed around with some grand pianos in a giant concert hall, where, I was told, the Beatles had once recorded.

Elliot Cahn, Green Day's manager, showed up and took us to dinner. Just arrived from the States, he was carrying a copy of *Billboard*, which he opened with a flourish to reveal an ad that read: "Congratulations, Green Day. *Dookie* is gold."

Half a million records in less than five months. And that was barely the beginning. In moments like this, it was easy to imagine that I was part of their triumphant march to stardom, but in the morning, they'd be off to their next amphitheater, and I'd be headed back to California.

On the plane, they were showing a movie called *The Chase*, featuring songs by Rancid, Bad Religion, NOFX, and the Offspring. Was everybody I knew getting famous? I walked into the Lookout office, eager to tell Chris and Pat about it. "The Offspring aren't just in a movie," Chris said. "Their record is almost as big as Green Day's."

I thought he was joking. Only months earlier, I'd watched the Offspring play to a cold and nearly empty Gilman Street. Ten years as a band, I thought, and this was all they had to show for it? I felt so sorry for them that when Kamala asked me to drive Noodles, their guitarist, to the late-night liquor store, I instantly agreed. If anybody needed to drown their sorrows, these guys did. The last I heard, they'd gone on to sell something like 40 million records.

Generals are often accused of preparing to fight the previous war instead of the one to come. Something similar is true of major labels. They're supposed to have their eyes out for the next big thing, but usually wind up signing whatever sounds most like the last big thing.

They'd been all but ignoring punk rock since the end of the 70s, but suddenly punk bands were what was "happening," and every label rep felt compelled to sign a couple. They combed the Bay Area, apparently under the impression that we had half a dozen more Green Days hidden away somewhere.

Neither Samiam nor Jawbreaker sounded anything like Green Day, but they came from the same scene and had some decent indie releases under their belts. Both would sign to major labels, Atlantic and DGC respectively, before the year was out.

I wasn't asked for my opinion, but if I had been, I would have advised against that move. True, I'd said the same thing to Green Day, but in the case of Samiam and Jawbreaker, I'm pretty sure I was right.

Both bands had solid followings, and could have gone on making successful indie records for as long as they wanted. But they were never going to break through on a big enough scale to satisfy the majors.

Jawbreaker, with intricately crafted songs that walked a fine line between West Coast pop-punk and East Coast emo, had an especially intense and passionate fan base. Some of that passion turned to anger when they signed to DGC. Green Day had a similar experience when they signed to Reprise, but they'd gained hundreds of new fans for every disappointed punk that deserted them. It hadn't worked that way for Jawbreaker.

It took the major labels a year or two to figure out that the Green Day magic couldn't be replicated simply by signing any reasonably good East Bay band. In the meantime, we were at ground zero of a record industry gold rush.

"What's going down at the Gilman?" A&R guys would ask, after phoning, "just to say hi." The attention was flattering, but it didn't take long to realize that my new "friends" knew nothing—and cared less—about my label, the East Bay, or, for that matter, me.

Dealing with real-life friends could be a touchier business. Some weren't happy about the media circus, and didn't hesitate to let me know. Al Sobrante, for example, went ballistic when he discovered I'd given an interview to *Rolling Stone*.

"If you hadn't quit the band," I told him, "they might be doing things differently. But Billie, Mike, and Tre *want* to be in *Rolling Stone*."

That didn't help. Years would pass before I'd have another conversation with Al, who despite, or maybe because of his eccentricities, had been one of my favorite East Bay scenesters.

The attention being heaped on Green Day inevitably spilled over onto Lookout, and so did the fury of the punks. At least some of them thought it was all my fault. It didn't matter how many times I explained that Green Day were making their own decisions, and that anyone with a complaint should take it up with the band, not me.

At the same time, for every punk making "sellout" accusations, there were several others hoping I'd help them jump on board the major label gravy train. Everybody, it seemed, had a band that sounded "just like Green Day." If I pointed out that we were interested in original bands, not imitation ones, they'd come back with, "Like Green Day with a twist! Maybe better!"

Even a few bands already on Lookout gave me grief about not "promoting" them enough. If it weren't for my stinginess and mismanagement, it was implied, they'd be where Green Day was. "Try working as hard as Green Day and writing songs as good as Green Day" was not the answer they were looking for, but it's what I told them.

One Lookout band who had no complaints—and not just because they'd been broken up for five years—was Operation Ivy. They'd been our best-selling band from 1989 until 1994, and even when Green Day finally passed them, it wasn't by as much as you'd think.

Rancid try out a new guitarist. From left: Tim Armstrong, Matt Freeman, Billie Joe Armstrong. (Photo by Murray Bowles)

Nearly every Green Day show featured their irreverent cover of Op Ivy's "Knowledge," and the song had also appeared on the *Slappy* EP and the *1,039 Smoothed Out Slappy Hours* CD. All of Lookout's bands benefited from the "Green Day effect," but none so much as Operation Ivy.

Not that Op Ivy needed to ride anyone's coattails. They'd become a legendary band in their own right, and Tim and Matt were finding a whole new audience with Rancid, who'd just released their second album. In September, they and Green Day played a benefit at the Seattle Center, along with Hole, Weezer, and a few other bands I'd never heard of. I went along to check it out.

As arenas went, the one in Seattle was quite small, with a capacity of only about 5,000. Two days earlier, in Boston, 65,000 people had come to see Green Day play a free show that, when it was abruptly canceled, turned into the biggest rock and roll riot in that city's history. The previous month, when Green Day played Woodstock '94, an even larger crowd had staged history's biggest rock and roll mudfight.

But I hadn't been there for either of those events, nor had I ever seen Green Day or Rancid in an arena of any kind, so I was suitably wowed by the size of the Seattle audience. My all-access pass let me wander wherever I wanted, but with no idea where I was going or what I was looking for, it wasn't doing me a lot of good.

Stopping to get my bearings, I noticed a strange girl goofing around at the side of the stage. I don't know why, but the minute I looked at her, I heard myself say, "That girl is trouble."

Trouble or not, I couldn't keep my eyes off her. It wasn't because she was attractive, although she was. It was more the way her features moved like quicksilver, transforming not just her face, but her whole character, in the blink of an eye.

One second she'd look like a mischievous teenager, too young even to be here on her own, the next she'd resemble a suburban matron or a hard-edged hippie homesteader. It was as if she were trying on personalities the way other people try on clothes.

It was fascinating, but also disconcerting. I kept staring at her, trying to figure out what her deal was, then decided she must be some sort of groupie out to ensnare Billie Joe.

Billie was 22 years old, recently married with a kid on the way, and en route to becoming one of the biggest rock stars in the world. He had a whole entourage to look after his needs, yet somehow I thought I had to "protect" him, as if he were still the wide-eyed 16-year-old I'd met back in 1988. I gave the girl a stern glance, as if to say, "I know what you're up to." She wiggled her nose at me like Elizabeth Montgomery from *Bewitched*.

Just then Tim Armstrong came around the corner, and a few minutes later, Billie Joe showed up. We were catching up on East Bay gossip when a bodyguard shoved the three of us into a wall with a single burly forearm.

"Miss Love doesn't appreciate close personal contact with her fans," he barked.

"We're not fans!" I shouted back, but the words hadn't made it out of my mouth before "Miss Love" and her band swept past en route to the stage.

I shouldn't have spoken for Billie or Tim, but I really wasn't a fan, and Hole's show did little to change my mind. The most memorable thing about it was Courtney's infant daughter, wearing protective earmuffs that dwarfed her tiny head, set down in front of the amps like some sort of human stage prop.

Afterward, I spotted Hole's guitarist, Eric Erlandson, making out with the odd girl I'd been watching earlier. "I *knew* she was a groupie," I said triumphantly.

Wait a minute, I thought. Hadn't I read that Erlandson was dating the actress Drew Barrymore? What could he be thinking? There were cameras everywhere; she was bound to find out about this. That was when it sunk in the "groupie" was actually Barrymore herself.

I hung around with Green Day while the arena emptied out, then walked with them to their tour bus. Outside, where fans had been waiting for hours, it was like miniature Beatlemania.

I discovered that being with the band made me a superstar of sorts, too. If I smiled or waved to the crowd, kids would start shrieking and screaming, even though it was obvious they didn't have a clue who I was.

But once Green Day's bus had driven off, the fans melted away and I was left to wander alone across a deserted parking lot. Two girls stopped to ask how I knew the band, and if I could deliver a message to Tre. Apart from that, I'd been transformed back into a nobody.

It was my first glimpse at life inside the cocoon of celebrity. I could see the appeal: everything was provided for, all your needs catered to. But I also began to understand the gap that had opened up between the way I lived and life as experienced by Green Day.

Part of me envied them, of course, but I was also relieved to know that I could simply walk away anytime I got bored with the backstage hullabaloo. They no longer had that option.

What's more, the pressure they were under must have felt unrelenting. It doesn't matter how many hits you've had, how many arenas or stadiums you've filled, there's always the unspoken question of, "So what are you going to do for an encore?"

As I boarded a bus for the airport, I heard the Eagles croon from a passing car, something about every form of refuge having its price. I'd had a pleasant excursion into rock and roll fantasyland, but it was time to get back to the East Bay.

17.
The Year That Broke Punk

One of the great things about running a label was the ability to walk up to some band who'd just put on an incredible show and say, "Hey, would you guys like to do a record?" It was even better when they had no idea who you were, or that someone from a record label had been in the audience.

But now, at least around the East Bay, everyone knew who I was, and I didn't have to open my mouth to stir up drama. If I were seen simply watching a band—God forbid I should start tapping my foot or humming along—the word would go out: "Dude, the Green Day guy was at our show. I think he wants to sign us."

I hadn't "discovered" Green Day any more than Columbus had discovered America, but people like short, snappy descriptions. "The Green Day guy" had become mine.

Longtime friends joked about my newly acquired status in "the industry," but it wasn't always easy to tell where the joking left off and the unspoken "Why haven't you signed *my* band?" began.

That could be doubly so with friends whose bands were already on Lookout. The seemingly good-natured suggestions that I was favoring one band over another, that I had somehow made so-and-so's band more popular than someone else's, gradually grew less light-hearted.

"If I had that kind of power," I'd protest, "why wouldn't I use it to make all our bands famous? Starting with my own?"

Not every band was desperate to get—or stay—on Lookout. Some, like Spitboy, Fuel, and Cringer, chose to move to smaller labels. I was never sure whether it was because they weren't comfortable with the direction Lookout was headed, if I'd said or done something to offend them, or if they simply felt they'd fit in better somewhere else.

I was disappointed, but wished them well, and we parted on good terms. If only things had gone that smoothly with Sam McPheeters.

He'd suggested doing a CD version of the Born Against discography on Lookout. I'd enthusiastically agreed. I assumed it was a done deal, but as months went by without any further progress, I wondered if Sam was having second thoughts.

One night I decided things had dragged on long enough. I got Sam on the phone and started badgering him about when I could expect the masters and artwork. He hemmed and hawed, saying he wanted to think about it some more before committing to a release date.

Convinced this meant he'd decided to bail on the project altogether, I spent the next hour telling him, first nicely and then not so nicely, that he couldn't do this to me.

Sam was an easy-going guy, but not the sort of person who appreciated being told what he could or couldn't do. It didn't help that I hadn't bothered checking the clock before calling him. On the East Coast, where he lived, it was past midnight.

My biggest mistake, though, had been cracking open a fifth of Jameson's just before I dialed his number. While Sam couldn't see me punctuating every other sentence with a swig of whiskey, the longer I talked, the more I turned into that annoying drunk who corners you at a party and won't shut up.

"No, listen," I'd say, over and over, speaking more slowly each time in hopes he wouldn't hear me slurring, "Born Against *have* to be on Lookout."

Actually, as it turned out, they didn't, and it would be years before I saw or spoke to Sam again. When I sobered up the next morning I was deeply ashamed, but the damage had been done. There was no denying that I'd let drinking interfere with both my work and what had been a good relationship.

I denied it anyway. Alcohol wasn't the problem, I insisted. It was just a case of bad timing. In the future, I resolved, I'd stay off the phone once the cork was out of the bottle.

Technology, however, had already provided a new way of getting myself into trouble. I'd first heard of the internet back in the 1980s, when Shred Of Dignity's Tom Jennings told me how scientists were hooking computers together and teaching them to talk to each other.

I'd made some dumb crack about what a boring conversation that would be, but by 1994 Lookout was developing its own network and website. It hadn't yet become obvious how dramatically the internet would transform the music business, but I was already learning how effective it could be for sparking and prolonging controversy.

Until then, people who had a gripe with me had to write a letter of complaint to *MRR* or *Lookout* magazine. A month or two later, it would appear in print, along with my response. If they still weren't satisfied, they'd write a response to my response, and another month or two would go by before it was published. Few people had the energy to sustain a grudge much longer than that.

With the internet, all such time lags disappeared. Within minutes, sometimes seconds, of logging onto one of the many message boards or chat rooms, I'd have someone accusing me of selling out the scene and ruining punk.

Nowadays kids learn by the time they're in middle school that nobody ever "wins" an online argument. But in 1994 the rules were still being invented. I'd set out—often drunkenly—to defend myself with reason, logic, and eloquence, and get hit with a torrent of responses that ran the gamut from "FUCK YOU" to "YOU SUCK."

Maximum Rocknroll stayed off the internet, treating it with the same disdain they'd shown for CDs. Ben Weasel shared that view, memorably declaring in his *MRR* column: "I don't trust any motherfucker with an email address."

But while *MRR* couldn't conduct its inquisitions and witch hunts at the warp speed made possible by an internet connection, Tim Yohannan could still do plenty of damage in analog form. That spring, he launched a campaign against Jello Biafra that was both dishonest and a little scary.

Biafra, Tim charged, was a rock star who lived in a mansion. Never mind that the Dead Kennedys, Jello's closest claim to stardom, had been broken up for almost eight years, or that his "mansion" was a middle-class house in the pre-gentrification Mission District.

Nobody was sure why Tim was going after his longtime friend with such vehemence, but the sniping felt like the usual tempest in a punk rock teapot until a gang of crusties jumped Biafra at Gilman, leaving him with, among other injuries, a broken leg.

It was no random assault. As they punched and kicked him, his attackers shouted about the "rock star" and his "mansion." Biafra and I talked about it a few days later, and agreed that while Tim hadn't personally advocated this kind of violence, the tone of his remarks had helped create a climate where others might think it was acceptable.

Tim denied all responsibility, then made matters worse by trying to turn it into a joke. He printed a photo of the assault, and, almost visibly smirking between the lines, claimed it was impossible to tell whether the crusties were knocking Biafra down or helping him up.

What was left of my respect for Tim all but vanished. I spoke out about it, though maybe not as loudly as I should have (I wasn't eager to follow Biafra onto the *MRR* enemies list). I would have quit the magazine, too, if I hadn't already done so a few months earlier.

That was when Tim unilaterally fired *MRR* co-founder and longtime columnist

Jeff Bale. In almost the same breath, he announced that certain types of music would no longer be covered in the magazine because, in his opinion, they weren't "punk."

I'd known Jeff twice as long as I'd known anyone else at *MRR*. Though we often disagreed about music and politics, I'd always liked him. His columns added a much-needed diversity to the magazine's mostly monochromatic worldview. But as Tim saw it, Jeff might as well be taking his moderately agnostic cues directly "from the Republican Central Committee."

The anger and ill will stirred up by Tim's actions produced the biggest, loudest, and most divisive *MRR* meeting in the magazine's history. "A lot of people have been talking a lot of shit," Tim said, "I'm hoping we can get most of it cleared up before we leave here today."

That sounded promising, but Tim's idea of clearing it up turned out to be a cross between *Animal Farm* and the Chinese Cultural Revolution.

One reason so many of us volunteered at *MRR* was its image as a community-run institution. No one doubted that Tim was the hardest-working staffer, and the glue that kept the whole operation together, but that shouldn't, I argued, give him total authority over who wrote for the magazine and what they were allowed to write about.

"Either the magazine belongs to all of us," I said, "or it's Tim's magazine and we're just unpaid stooges. Which is it going to be?"

Egged on by Lefty Hooligan, a charmless *apparatchik* who played Madame Defarge to Tim's Robespierre, the crowd all but broke into a "Four legs good"-style chorus of "Tim's magazine!"

A vote followed, in which a clear majority ratified Tim's status as first among unequals. Many dissenters left as a result; several went on to start or join new magazines covering the music and ideas no longer allowed in *MRR*.

I agonized about it myself for a week or two. *MRR* had played a vital part in my life. Without the visibility it had given my band, my magazine, and especially my label, I might never have made it off Spy Rock. But *MRR* was changing into something I couldn't in good conscience be a part of.

Tim was good enough to let me explain my reasons for leaving in my final column, and I began writing for two new magazines, *Punk Planet* and Jeff Bale's *Hit List*. I continued to criticize *MRR*, maybe more harshly than was necessary, but Tim took it in stride, and refrained from denouncing me as an Enemy Of The People. For the time being, anyway.

"The Great Schism," as I called it, was not the only thing I wrote about in my last *MRR* column. The rest was devoted to Aldo Giorgini, who'd been diagnosed with a brain tumor, and was not expected to recover.

I went to visit him in Lafayette, where we whiled away the afternoon in a pizzeria decked out with cheery, red-checkered tablecloths that shimmered in stark counterpoint to the apocalyptic thunderstorm raging outside. Day turned into near-night, and flood waters filled the parking lot until it felt like we were in a ship adrift at sea.

Aldo, barely 60, was a fragile shell of the vigorous man I'd known, though he did his best to joke, talk, and laugh with his usual upbeat exuberance. By the time he died six months later, he was confined to bed and able to communicate only with an outstretched hand, a raised eyebrow, or a husky whisper. Even then his indomitable spirit shone through.

I had a less inspirational encounter with Ben Weasel in Chicago, where he was producing the new Queers album, *Beat Off*. The mood was distinctly different from the genial, drunken chaos that had accompanied the making of *Love Songs For The Retarded*.

During the *Love Songs* sessions, Ben had been efficient, good-natured, and accommodating. In Chicago I found him curt, brusque, and, at times, just plain rude.

Above all I was baffled by his refusal to let the Queers record the guitar and

Visiting with Aldo Giorgini, shortly before his death. (Photo by Mass Giorgini)

vocal overdubs that were fundamental to their Beach Boys-meet-the-Ramones style. He kept insisting that we needed to go for a more basic punk sound.

I'd been talking with Joe about this record for months. A more basic punk sound was not at all what he'd had in mind. But Ben was a hard guy to say no to, especially in light of all he'd done to help the Queers.

"It's your record, not his," I said to Joe. "I can talk to him for you."

Joe sighed, and told me there was no point in bringing it up, that it would just end in a big argument.

Erratic and inexplicable behavior was becoming the norm with Ben. To give him his due, it couldn't have been easy dealing with me, either. For example, when he confided that he didn't want to tour anymore because of his agoraphobia, I urged him to suck it up and get back to work.

This was as insensitive—and unrealistic—as telling a depressed person to "cheer up." Having never been in a band as popular as Screeching Weasel, I somehow imagined the excitement and adrenaline rush of playing huge shows would be more than enough to help someone get over a case of stage jitters.

I didn't understand—didn't even try to understand—that what Ben was going through wasn't just "jitters." He was having full-blown panic attacks, and all the cheering crowds in the world couldn't help that.

An unhappy side effect of Ben's withdrawal from touring was that it gave him more time to obsess over other things, like money. Especially money. Our long, rambling conversations seldom touched on music anymore. "I need to make enough to buy a house before this whole punk craze dies out," became his most frequent refrain.

Cool your jets, I told him. Punk crazes might come and go, but good songs are always in style. And if there was one talent Ben Weasel was blessed with, it was the ability to snatch an irresistible melody and an insightful or hilarious lyric out of what to anyone else would have looked like thin air.

If only he could have focused on pursuing that talent. Instead, he became his own worst enemy, unable to relax and enjoy his success, and often finding ways to undermine what he'd already achieved.

I spent a year begging him not to kick Dan Panic out of the band. Panic wasn't just one of the best drummers in punk rock; he was also a vital component of what most fans agreed was the definitive or "classic" Screeching Weasel lineup.

Ben sneered at my pleadings, telling me that drummers were a dime a dozen, and that Dan was just a hired monkey who got on his nerves.

Ben finally eased up on the idea of firing Panic, but before I could breathe a sigh of relief, he'd turned his ill will on Vapid, and forced him out of the band. The official story was that Vapid had voluntarily left, but when I saw Dan a couple days later, he could barely hold back his tears.

It was a shoddy move all around, weakening the band and dealing an especially harsh blow to Vapid, who could ill afford to lose the money he would have earned playing on the next record. Unlike many Lookout bands, Screeching Weasel didn't divide their royalties equally: Dan scraped by on a fraction of what Ben and Jughead earned.

Although Ben claimed Vapid's personal problems made it necessary for him to leave Screeching Weasel, within months he'd formed a new band with him, the Riverdales. Both Dans, Panic and Vapid, were also moonlighting with the Queers, and despite Ben's claims that they were "impossible" to work with, he seemed to have no problems recording *Beat Off* with them.

There could have been other things going on behind the scenes that I was unaware of, but kicking Vapid out of Screeching Weasel looked to me like a pointless power play. Even though no one ever questioned or challenged Ben's status as alpha Weasel, he still went out of his way to remind people of it.

It also meant Screeching Weasel would need a new bassist for the album they were getting set to record, *How To Make Enemies and Irritate People*. Ben asked

Danny Vapid reads about himself in Lookout *magazine.*
(Photo by Larry Livermore)

Green Day's Mike Dirnt to fill in.

It might have been a smart move in terms of publicity. This was, after all, the year of *Dookie*, and anything involving Green Day was sure to attract attention. But there was a major drawback, too: Mike was so busy touring with his own band that he was hard pressed to squeeze in more than the occasional practice or recording session with Screeching Weasel.

He got the job done, of course, and, being both a brilliant bassist and a longtime Weasel fan, did it well. But Mike's efforts alone couldn't salvage *How To Make Enemies*. It was an adequate record, but still Screeching Weasel's weakest release for Lookout up to that point.

Ben put more work into it than *Beat Off*, but it suffered from some of the same rushed, lackluster production that had marred the Queers record. His songwriting, too, sounded like it might be losing some of its sparkle.

Even mediocre Weasel stood head and shoulders above most punk rock. But I knew Ben could do better if he'd put as much energy into the record as he had into feuding with his bandmates and obsessing over money.

A bunch of us were in a bar in Chicago when the news broke about Kurt Cobain's suicide. Ben was the only one of us who'd met the guy, and Nirvana, even before they'd become superstars, had never really been part of our scene. But the news still cast a pall over the evening.

What was the point of struggling to get your music heard if, once you'd turned yourself into a household name, all you got in the end was that most clichéd of outcomes, drug addiction and death? Drugs had been killing rock stars—and musical unknowns—since I was a kid, yet generation after generation, the same tiresome pageant re-enacted itself.

Our scene was different, I'd wanted to believe, but drugs had been elbowing their way into the East Bay of late. They'd probably been there all along, but I'd been too busy or too oblivious to notice.

I started losing friends and acquaintances to overdoses and drug-related violence in the 1960s. Over the years I'd counted at least 35 or 40 such fatalities. It became clear that if I didn't distance myself—physically as well as emotionally— from people headed down that path, I'd go crazy.

So it came as a real kick in the gut when I discovered that heroin had played a huge part in the Queers' story. It was most likely what had kept them stuck out on the margins of the punk scene for so long.

Heroin was also why Hugh O'Neill, the band's second longest-serving member, wasn't there for the *Beat Off* sessions. A few months earlier, Joe had enlisted me, along with half a dozen friends and family members, to stage an intervention for Hugh, who even by Queers standards had been digging himself too deeply into the pit of addiction.

Hugh hadn't seen it coming; he was almost literally knocked backward when he walked in and found us sitting there. It was especially tough to see his dad, heartsick and bewildered, struggling to come to terms with what his son was going through.

We took turns explaining why Hugh, who sat on the edge of the sofa fighting back tears, needed to take a leave of absence from the band while he kicked his drug habit. The intervention felt doubly awkward because Joe, who'd organized and led it, hadn't been off heroin that long himself.

But when Joe did decide to clean up, there would be no half measures. The guy who'd helped litter the cover of *Love Songs For The Retarded* with empty Budweiser bottles laid down the law: no booze allowed in the studio or backstage anytime he was playing, recording, or practicing.

Joe talked a good game about alcohol, but his real problem, like Hugh's, was drugs. I would never see him take another drink, but there would be times when it was painfully obvious he was messed up on junk.

When he stayed clean—which, to his credit, was most of the time—he was a joy to work with. But as soon as heroin re-entered the picture, his songwriting would dry up, he'd grow irritable and contentious, and there'd be little point in even trying to talk to him.

Luckily, it would be a while before that happened again, and before leaving Chicago, Joe and I made plans—when Ben was out of earshot—to go into Sonic Iguana with Mass later that summer and work on some songs with bigger, lusher arrangements.

Then I headed to the airport for the trip home. For most of my life, no matter what else might have been going on, I'd never set out for California without an overwhelming, exhilarating sense of joy and relief.

But as we took off, I realized this was no longer true. California didn't feel special anymore. It didn't even feel that much like home. It was just a place I had to go back to.

Instead of looking forward to whatever challenges and adventures might await me there, I peered around corners, wondering who or what would turn into my next problem. The East Bay remained at the center of my punk rock universe, but part of me—perhaps the most important part—was drifting away.

18.
Moving On Up

One advantage of running your own label is that your band never has to worry about getting a record deal.

That's not always a good thing.

Like the dope dealer who's warned against getting high on his own supply, a label head needs to be careful when it comes to releasing music by his own band. It's easy to let perspective and common sense go flying out the window.

The Potatomen had made our name as "those guys who play acoustic guitars and a cardboard box outside of Gilman." People seemed to like us that way, but when we picked up electric instruments and effects pedals even some of our fans gave us the stink eye.

If we'd stuck with the original aesthetic, we could have recorded onto a cassette with a handheld microphone. We might even have wound up as some sort of lo-fi cult sensation.

But Lookout's success meant that we could now afford the full range of modern recording technology, and I was determined to use it. Though I'd always sneered at bands who said, "We'll fix it in the mix," who thought gimmickry and gimcrackery could overcome any deficiencies in their skill or imagination, once turned loose in the studio, I found myself in danger of slipping down that same electronic rabbit hole.

What started as a fun little project turned into a drama-fraught endurance test. Never again, I vowed, would I complain about how long it had taken Screeching Weasel to record *Wiggle*.

After months of agonizing insecurity and self-doubt interspersed with episodes of unbearable grandiosity (I still cringe when I read some of the interviews I gave about the "importance" of the Potatomen), we had finished enough songs to fill half an LP.

We took three of them and released a 7" EP, *On The Avenue*, that I was actually quite happy with. For a few days, at least, I thought all the time and effort had been worth it.

Quite a few people disagreed, especially those who'd expected us to be a little more punk. Instead of a new version of the Lookouts, they got our take on Buddy Holly, Hank Williams, and the Smiths. Kain Kong said I sounded like country-pop singer Mac Davis. He didn't mean it as a compliment.

Then we took a trip up the West Coast, from Berkeley to Vancouver, opening for the Queers. It was only five shows, but by the time it was over I'd gained a new appreciation for Ben Weasel's anti-tour stance. It wasn't that I'd had a bad time—much of the trip, in fact, was awesome—but the highs and lows were too intense, and too close on each other's heels, for my liking.

There were no flying beer cans or gobs of spit to dodge—we'd encounter those on future trips to Southern California—and there were a couple of nights when people clearly loved us. The worst reaction we got from an audience was mild apathy.

But I took everything way too much to heart.

Any band, no matter how long they've been at it, has nights they'd prefer to forget. A broken guitar string or kick pedal, a lost or misplaced voice, a crowd that fails to materialize or remains surly and hostile when it does: any of these things can send a show spinning off in the wrong direction.

Musicians seasoned in the ways of the road take these sorts of misadventures in stride. They know you can go from laughingstock to king of the world in the time it takes to drive from one town to the next.

I hadn't learned that lesson yet. I'd be up all night after every show, either searching for someone to blame for whatever I thought had gone wrong or—less often—exulting about how brilliant we'd been.

The first show of our tour went well, but on the second night, in Olympia, Chris and Pat disappeared the minute we hit town. I didn't see them again until we were due to go on. They were spectacularly drunk.

Though a little sloppy, they played fine. I, on the other hand, was so mad at them—and so preoccupied with watching for the mistakes I expected them to make—that I screwed up my own parts. You'd have thought I was the one who'd spent the afternoon warming up a barstool.

We had to sneak into Canada—free trade agreements work for oil tankers, but not so much for bands. That afternoon's show at a neighborhood rec center in Vancouver marked my first encounter with Nardwuar the Human Serviette, a zany polymath who, in between lecturing us about the United Empire Loyalists and the American plot to invade Canada, sang some songs with his band, the Evaporators.

Next up were the Smugglers. Two of them, Dave Carswell and John Collins, were also in the Evaporators, and for their day job ran JC/DC Studios, where the

A sharp-dressed Grant Lawrence, the Clark Kent of rock and roll. (Photo by Larry Livermore)

Potatomen would wind up doing much of our future recording.

Grant Lawrence, the Smugglers' frontman, bore an uncanny resemblance to Clark Kent's wimpier cousin. Until, that is, the music kicked in, when he abruptly morphed into a frantic, bespectacled dervish, chief driving force of one of the best live bands I'd ever seen.

Grant worked for the Smugglers' label, Mint Records, which was also home to Cub, three women who played in a wonderfully disarming style that some critics had dubbed "cuddle-core." Founded and run by Randy Iwata and Bill Baker, Mint played a role in the Canadian punk and indie scene that looked—to me, anyway—a lot like Lookout's in California.

They were struggling, however, to get consistent, reliable distribution in the USA. Since we'd been having similar problems north of the border, I thought some sort of Mint-Lookout alliance, or even merger, might help both of us.

It seemed like an excellent plan, but just as with Lookout UK, I was assuming that because something *should* work, it would. Mint and Lookout sunk a great deal of time, effort, and money into the partnership, but it never got more than partially off the ground.

Our being so much larger than Mint may have been part of the problem. It was, someone indelicately observed, like a hippopotamus trying to mate with a hummingbird. Fortunately, the hummingbird survived, and today, thanks to artists like Neko Case (a onetime Cub member) and the New Pornographers (featuring Neko and John Collins), Mint has grown into one of Canada's best-loved and most successful independent labels.

Even before our tour, I sensed that Chris's heart was no longer in the Potatomen, and he left the band soon after we got home. It was understandable. He was a good drummer and backup singer, but his looks and personality practically demanded he take a place at the front of the stage.

He'd been singing periodically with a reconstituted version of Bumblescrump, the Humboldt County band he'd formed while still in high school. They'd done one semi-legendary tour that, if I'm remembering the story right, led a couple of starstruck teenaged fans to steal a car and follow them around the Western United States.

Bumblescrump then did a second tour, this time partnering with Rice, a San Diego hardcore band who sang exclusively about . . . rice. It was around that time that Chris met Molly Neuman, co-editor of *Girl Germs* zine, drummer for Bratmobile and the Frumpies, and a founding mother of the riot grrrl movement. Romance ensued, and so did a band.

The PeeChees featured Chris, Molly, and two refugees from Rice (the tour with Bumblescrump had been that band's last hurrah). They were sharp-looking—you could mistake some of their record covers and posters for fashion shoots—and featured an edgy, almost jagged sound.

Bumblescrump with pasta. From left: Patrick Hynes, Chris Appelgren, Thadicus. (Photo by Murray Bowles)

All of them were good musicians—Molly being especially solid on the drums—but Chris was the star. He'd flamboyantly suck his thumb while writhing suggestively against the mic stand—actually, it wasn't suggestive at all; it was totally blatant—in a manner that unsettlingly melded the infantile and the lewd.

The PeeChees built up a strong following, but they never seemed like Lookout material to me, and we only put out one 7" for them. Kill Rock Stars, one of the quintessential Olympia labels, would be a better fit, and that's where they released the bulk of their material.

Molly knew KRS label head Slim Moon from her years in Olympia, and Chris had become friends with him as well. I knew and liked Slim myself, but if you looked at our respective musical tastes, you might think the two of us were from different planets.

Chris didn't see it that way. To him the two labels complemented each other nicely, and he began pushing for us to release a compilation with Kill Rock Stars, each label supplying half the songs.

The compilation would be Lookout's 100th record, and Chris thought of it as an ideal way to celebrate that milestone. I wasn't so sure. While open to doing a joint release, I thought Lookout 100 should embody more of the classic Lookout sound. *A Slice Of Lemon*, the compilation Chris and Slim came up with, did not exactly fit that bill.

It had enough middling-to-great songs to fill one solid album, but it was, unfortunately, a double LP. There were some real gems tucked amid the clunkers, like the Delightful Little Nothings or the track by Shaken 69, a short-lived Matt Freeman-Tim Armstrong project few people had heard of, let alone heard.

But just when I'd be happily grooving along to one of the more melodic numbers, thinking, "This comp's not that bad," a track would pop up that I found so infuriatingly unlistenable I'd want to toss both record and record player into the nearest garbage can.

Quality control issues weren't the fault of one label or the other. Kill Rock Stars and Lookout contributed good, bad, and mediocre songs in more or less equal measure. But for Lookout—at least Lookout as I'd always thought of it—*A Slice Of Lemon* marked a shift, both musically and aesthetically, not just into left field, but into a whole new ballpark.

Many longtime fans of the label agreed. I received more letters of complaint about *A Slice Of Lemon* than anything we'd done up to that point. I told Chris about this, but he didn't think it was a problem. It was our job, he argued, to challenge the listeners rather than continually spoonfeed them the same predictable pap.

If Chris considered *A Slice Of Lemon* a signpost pointing to Lookout's future, *Punk USA*, the compilation Ben Weasel had put together a few months earlier, kept its vision fixed firmly in the rear view mirror. It mostly showcased traditional-sounding bands, the kind I had taken to calling "meat and potatoes" punk.

It sold better than *A Slice Of Lemon* and received more positive reviews, but I didn't find it that much easier to listen to. There were none of the jarring changes in tempo or style that had marred the former record, but it all blurred together into a samey-samey stew.

Janelle Blarg at the OG Lookout office. Not sure if this was a workday. (Photo by Larry Livermore)

It's an age-old debate, whether you're a band or a label: do you keep cranking out the tried-and-true product, or push yourself and your audience to explore new sounds? Ideally the answer lies somewhere in between, but with Chris tilting in the direction of the North Oakland hipsters and Ben urging me toward an ever more fervent brand of punk fundamentalism, it wasn't always easy to find that balance.

Despite our diverging musical tastes, I still respected Chris's judgment, so when he asked if we could find a job for Molly Neuman, who'd recently moved to the East Bay, I said I didn't see why not.

We'd tried adding a fourth employee once before, but it hadn't worked out. Shortly after graduating from high school, Janelle Blarg had asked for a job. I'd given her a tryout, which she passed with flying colors, but the next morning she was nowhere to be found. When I tracked her down on the phone, she heaved a flabbergasted sigh. "What, you want me to come there *every* day?"

I hadn't bothered looking for anyone to replace her. I wasn't convinced we needed additional employees and had only taken Janelle on because she'd asked. Though business had tripled or quadrupled since then, I kind of felt the same way about Molly.

Chris, Pat, and I had been doing this so long it sometimes felt like we were a single organism. We seldom worried about formalities like "Excuse me" when we had to reach past or, for that matter, practically climb over someone to get at a ringing phone or jammed fax machine.

Similarly, we rarely felt the need to have long, involved discussions about label policy. Whether deciding which bands to sign or which drawer to keep the stapler in, we almost intuitively found ourselves on the same page most of the time— Chris's recent infatuation with *Slice of Lemon*-style bands notwithstanding.

So I was wary about introducing a relative stranger into the mix. Chris knew her of course—they were living together by now—but Pat and I were barely familiar with Molly at all, except by reputation.

That reputation was a formidable one, and it definitely influenced my decision to hire her. Between her bands, zines, and pioneering role in riot grrrl, she'd played a vital part in punk rock history. What I had failed to notice was that she wasn't really a punk.

Not an East Bay punk, anyway. From her first day on the job, it was clear that she wasn't impressed by Lookout's ramshackle and chaotic ways, nor by the constant clowning around that was woven into our daily routine. Even though I was twice her age, it felt like Chris, Pat, and I were poorly behaved kids, and Molly was the new nanny.

Our lackadaisical approach to business seemed to embarrass as well as annoy her. It was time, she informed us, that Lookout became a more "professional" operation.

I could see her point. I, too, was tired of filing cabinets where nothing was filed, desktops littered with the wreckage of a dozen half-completed projects, phone messages and letters that piled up unread and unanswered.

At the same time, childish or unrealistic as it might sound, my vision for Lookout had always involved keeping the label as resolutely unprofessional as possible. That had been fine in the past, Molly maintained, when we were pressing a few thousand 7"s for our friends' bands, but now it was time to grow up and begin acting like a "real" record company.

A vital step in this direction, in her view, would be to move the label out of my former bedroom and into a "real" office. She found an unlikely ally in this quest, someone she'd normally have little in common with: Ben Weasel.

Ben had been haranguing us all year about the need to establish ourselves in more businesslike quarters, but I hadn't been paying much attention. "Ben," I often reminded him, "if I spent as much time telling you how to write pop-punk songs as you do telling me how to run a record label, we'd both be out of business."

True, I couldn't blame him for losing patience with some of our more brazenly inept blunders. Album covers and lyric sheets were often riddled with typos; we'd had to throw out 2,000 7" covers because Pansy Division's name was spelled (in large, prominent letters) "PANSY DIVISON." A Green Day song called "One For The Razorback," dedicated to a girl from Arkansas, became "One For The Razorbacks," making it sound, said an exasperated Billie Joe, as if it were about "a goddam football team."

But how, I asked, would a bigger, more expensive office lead to better spellchecking and proofreading? Besides, operating out of our tiny rent-controlled room hadn't stopped us from growing into a multi-million dollar company. How could it possibly make sense to give up such a sweet deal?

The money we were saving wasn't my only motivation for wanting to stay on Berkeley Way. It also felt like we were putting one over on corporate America. Despite ignoring nearly every rule about how businesses were supposed to operate, we'd achieved the kind of success most conventional companies could only dream of.

But while Berkeley Way had been perfect for the three of us, introducing a fourth person upset the balance. We found ourselves playing musical chairs, desks, and phones. The ultimate tipping point was the toilet. With only a folding wicker curtain separating the bathroom from the rest of the room, there wasn't a lot of privacy. It hadn't been a big deal when it was just us guys, but it felt different with a woman on the premises.

Reluctantly, I began accompanying Molly on a search through downtown Berkeley for office space that was both cool and affordable. Nothing much was available in either category. Berkeley was full of vacant storefronts and half-empty commercial buildings, but landlords preferred to leave them that way rather than accept lower rents.

I halfheartedly toyed with the idea of moving into the Wells Fargo Building, a 1920s brick-clad structure, that, at 12 stories, was the closest thing Berkeley had to a skyscraper. It was a wildly improbable setting for a record label like ours, but that was what appealed to me: the prospect of punks and weirdos rubbing shoulders with bewildered bankers and insurance agents.

The space turned out to be too small and the price too exorbitant, and that was before I learned that the Wells Fargo tower had been declared an earthquake hazard. Then Molly talked me into looking at a third floor, six-room suite in what had once been Berkeley's first apartment house.

Ninety years old, and constructed entirely of wood, it was actually rather nice-looking, especially compared with the squat stucco and concrete monstrosities that make up most of California's commercial architecture. I couldn't complain about the commute, either: about a two-minute walk from my front door.

The rent was $2,000 a month; utilities and insurance would bump the total bill closer to $2,500, more than 15 times what were paying on Berkeley Way. But with record sales on track to top $10 million that year, it seemed silly to worry about pinching pennies. We signed a lease and moved into our new digs in April of 1995.

LOOKOUT RECORDS
H.Q.

19.
The Office

As reluctant as I'd been to leave our happy little hovel on Berkeley Way, I had to admit there were things to be said for our new headquarters.

It had been years, maybe decades, since anyone had lived there, but the place still felt more like an apartment than an office. I could almost see myself living there, though after years of making do with a single room, I had no idea what I'd do with six.

I didn't know how Lookout would use all that space, either, but Molly had plenty of plans. The rooms quickly filled up with furniture, office equipment, and new employees.

Molly deserved a lot of credit for furnishing and organizing our new home. If I'd been left in charge of it, we'd probably have spent years lounging around on the floor or on castoff chairs rescued from dumpsters.

I was ready to carry my door-and-filing cabinet "desk" over from the old office when Molly informed me that as president and CEO (the first time I'd heard either of those titles applied to me), I'd need something more "appropriate." She whipped out a catalog, and the next thing I knew, I was perched on an ergodynamic chair presiding over an imposing wooden desk nearly as big as some rooms I'd lived in.

On an impulse I'd also ordered a bleached-blue-denim sofa—I'd never seen one like it—thinking it would come in handy when I hosted meetings with bands or employees. It did, but saw more use as a place for me to stretch out and nap.

Mine was the only completely private office; few of the other rooms even had doors. This proved to be a mixed blessing.

Having quiet time to myself felt like an unbelievable luxury compared with the claustrophobic hubbub of Berkeley Way, but I missed a lot by not being within sight and earshot of my fellow workers. Phones, email, and instant messages could never replace the constant communication and camaraderie that came from being crammed together in that tiny room with Chris and Pat.

Only months had passed since I'd made the decision to hire Molly, but now we were taking on new employees almost faster than we could make up job descriptions for them.

First came a receptionist. People were so used to me picking up my own phone that they'd often start yammering without waiting for me to say hello. Now they'd be greeted with, "Let me see if he's available. Who may I say is calling?"

I felt a little self-conscious about that. Would my callers' feelings be hurt? Would they think I was acting like some kind of big shot? Still, it was hard to deny the advantages of having someone to say, "Sorry, he's in a meeting," when I wasn't in the mood for dealing with salespeople, marketers, or assorted crackpots.

Molly did most of the hiring. She'd usually clear it with me before putting someone on the payroll, but that often felt like an afterthought. I don't know why, after years of micro-managing every aspect of Lookout myself, I was willing to cede so much control to her. It made sense to let her manage the office—she was good at it, and it was an area I didn't have much interest or expertise in. It might not have been so smart to let her choose the people who worked there.

That was what happened, though, while I spent my time tucked away behind a closed door wrestling with the paperwork needed to turn Lookout into an LLC (limited liability company, the poor man's version of a corporation). As time went on, I realized I was also hiding out.

I'd accepted—reluctantly—that Lookout had to make certain changes. But I wasn't sure I liked the shape or direction those changes were taking.

So why didn't I do something about it instead of sulking in my office? I don't know if I'll ever be able to answer that. At times I felt depressed, at others, overwhelmed. The world outside my door had begun to feel like an alien environment, one where I didn't belong.

Our new employees were bright, energetic, and fun to be around, but I wondered if it wasn't possible to be a little *too* clean, perky, and upbeat. I'd never been a fan of the Spike Anarkie school of hygiene, nor the nihilistic attitudes that went with it. But sometimes I felt like the Eureka punks who complained about the time Tilt stayed at their house: "Man, they were hell of weird. They got up in the morning and took showers and put on cologne and deodorant, like they were going to the office or something!"

I'd laughed about it then, telling the kids that you didn't need to be dirty and smelly to play good music. But now it was my turn to feel like the odd man out in a room full of office punks.

There was another difference. When Pat and Chris came to work at Lookout, they were paid so little that it almost had to be a labor of love. Now we had people applying for jobs as if we were IBM or the Post Office. As talented and enthusiastic as the newcomers could be, it felt like at least some of them were thinking in terms of what Lookout could do for them rather than the other way around.

But then why wouldn't they see the label as a "normal" company instead of some bootstrap DIY operation? Where I'd once paid people out of petty cash or my own pocket, we now had a computerized payroll, complete with deductions for taxes, social security, and workers' compensation. We offered a range of employee benefits, including sick leave and fully paid health insurance.

Health insurance was one aspect of the new, more businesslike Lookout that I'd insisted on, and was proud of. Many companies had been cutting or abolishing employee health care programs, claiming they couldn't afford them. I was out to prove that the punks could do better, that we could run not just a successful business, but a socially responsible one.

Cathy Bauer would prove to be one of our most important new hires. I'd never met Cathy before Molly asked me to interview her, but I'd heard of her as far back as 1988, when, as a 16-year-old high school student in St. Louis, she'd booked shows for Operation Ivy and Crimpshrine.

I wasn't sure what exactly she was being hired to do, but she came across as smart, committed, and likable. Eventually she'd fill a vital role as operations manager, but at first she functioned more as an assistant to Molly.

Chris Imlay, who'd played guitar for Brent's TV, the Ne'er Do Wells, and, most recently, the Hi-Fives, was another new addition. He was a crack graphic designer, amiable, sociable, and energetic. He was also one of the worst spellers I'd ever met. Not that most of Lookout's college-educated staff were much better.

Maybe it was a generational thing. My Catholic elementary school had devoted as much attention to spelling and penmanship as to multiplication tables and saving our young souls. But whatever the reason, I saw red when documents riddled with misspellings went out to the public. No one else in the office seemed to notice or care.

Even Molly's otherwise well-written and important-sounding press releases were marred by this tendency. What really got to me, though—especially considering how bright she was—was her reaction when I pointed out mistakes, usually some version of an eye-rolling "Whatever."

It became more effective to intercept her documents and proofread them myself, which annoyed her and made more work for me. It was not a huge deal, but helped underline what was becoming obvious: Molly was not your typical sort of employee.

A stranger walking into our office might have mistaken her for the boss, partly because of her strong-willed, confident, and outspoken manner, but also because of her highly specific—and routinely articulated—vision about the kind of label she wanted Lookout to be.

I sometimes wonder if she was as sure of herself as she appeared, or if her unrelenting certitude was at least partly a means of coping with her own insecurities. In any event, she usually wound up getting her way, often by sheer force of personality.

Her determination to move into a new office had been only a starting point. Now it was time to get busy doing the things that—at least in her view—legitimate record labels did.

Most of these involved spending money, in some cases quite a lot of it. That was how major labels operated: throwing vast amounts of cash at producing, promoting, and publicizing every band they signed, on the theory that one or two of them would become the next U2 or REM. The rest—the overwhelming majority, actually—could be written off as bad investments.

It's a business model that can work, as long as you've got enormous financial reserves to tide you over until one of your acts hits it big. But I'm talking about tens or even hundreds of millions of dollars, not the piddling one or two million Lookout had accumulated.

My philosophy hadn't changed much since Lookout began: keep things smart, simple, and cheap. No matter how many Green Days or Operation Ivys we nurtured, we'd never have enough money to beat the big boys at their own game. Most indies who tried crashed and burned pretty quickly.

Whenever Molly brought up the need to hire publicists, make videos, run ads in mainstream magazines, I'd point out that we'd always done fine—more than fine—without taking on all those additional expenses. "The business is changing," she'd retort. "You can't keep acting like it's still the 1980s."

Personally, I didn't see why not. What we'd done in the 80s had worked well for us, and was working even better in the 90s. But Molly kept pressuring me to try some of her ideas, and a number of other Lookout staffers and bands came to share that view. I finally decided it couldn't hurt to loosen the purse strings a little.

It wasn't as if we couldn't afford it. In 1989, when the Operation Ivy album came out, we were thrilled to sell 2,000 copies of it in a year. By 1995 we were selling 2,000 Op Ivy albums every week. And they weren't even our biggest band anymore.

I wrote checks for $1.2 million to cover just three months' worth of Green Day royalties, and sent a similar amount to the IRS. My father, who'd always brushed off inquiries about my mostly nonexistent accomplishments, began one-upping his cronies with, "My son pays over a million bucks a year in taxes."

Cathy Bauer, shortly after joining Lookout.
She'd go on to become operations manager.
(Photo by Larry Livermore)

Dad had graduated high school in 1931, during the depths of the Great Depression. That same year my mother's family lost their home because her father, an unemployed autoworker, couldn't keep up with the payments. Having grown up steeped in such lore, and having done time as a penniless squatter myself, my first inclination when I came into money was to stuff it under a mattress.

But there was no longer a mattress big enough to encase Lookout's riches, so when I was asked for the umpteenth time about making a video, I said, "Sure, why not? Let's try it and see what happens."

Love Is Dead, by the Mr. T Experience, was the first release we treated and budgeted for as if it were certain to be a hit. MTX had been bubbling beneath the surface ever since coming to Lookout. Their records sold well but not spectacularly; while they were closely identified with the label, they'd never broken through to the level of popularity enjoyed by Screeching Weasel or the Queers, let alone Green Day or Op Ivy.

But with East Bay pop punk the flavor of the day, we were sure Mr. T's moment had finally arrived. I was as caught up in the excitement as anyone. When we got the test pressing, I slipped my headphones on, dropped the needle on the first track, and was blown away.

The extra time and money spent on production had paid off. The record sounded thoroughly—for once I didn't mind using Molly's word—professional, measuring up to almost anything out there, major or indie.

We made a video for the anthemic "Ba Ba Ba Ba Ba" and submitted it to MTV, expecting it to get tons of airplay. The sly nod to Green Day wouldn't hurt either, I thought. In that band's "When I Come Around" video, Billie Joe casually knocks a pay phone off the hook while striding through a BART station; in "Ba Ba Ba Ba Ba," Dr. Frank thoughtfully stops to hang it back up.

The tune was catchy, the concept cute, but "Ba Ba Ba Ba Ba" was played once or twice on *120 Minutes*, MTV's "alternative" show, and that was about it. *Love Is Dead* sold twice as well as the Mr. T Experience's previous records, but nearly everything we released that year enjoyed a similar uptick.

Artistically, the album was a triumph, and many MTX fans cite it as their favorite, but from a strictly financial standpoint, the deal had been a wash: the extra money we'd put into it was only slightly more than balanced out by the increased sales.

I'd been a Mr. T Experience fan for as long as they'd been a band, but I began to realize they'd probably never make it too far out of the underground. They were just that little bit too arch, quirky, and offbeat, what the British sometimes call "too clever by half."

Unless Frank—the only remaining member from the original lineup—was willing to make some fundamental changes, both musically and lyrically, I suspected the Mr. T Experience had gotten about as big as they were going to get. But record executives (which was what I was now, at least according to the media and my most recent tax return) aren't supposed to think like that.

They're expected to be uninterruptedly upbeat, promising the moon and the stars, and at least once in a while delivering. There's little room for negativity, or what people in other businesses might call realism. Utter a slightly discouraging word about a band's prospects and people looked at you as if you'd farted in church.

The reality was that most of our bands were never going to earn much more than a decent middle-class income. Given the hardscrabble life of the average musician, that in itself is a major accomplishment. But in the middle of the 1990s, hardly anybody wanted to think that small.

You couldn't blame bands for dreaming. They'd seen lightning strike for others; they wouldn't have been human if they didn't wonder, "Why not us?"

In their song "Dumb Little Band" the Mr. T Experience noted that they were still taping flyers to telephone poles, while their friends had gone on to become punk rock millionaires "taping their live album at the Hollywood Bowl."

Ben Weasel put it more bluntly, complaining in "My Friends are Getting Famous," that he ought to be, too. He might have been joking, but as with many of the best jokes, it was funny because it was true. He *did* think he should be as successful as his former contemporaries, but couldn't bring himself to believe it would ever happen.

Other bands, too, made a regular schtick out of asking when I was going to launch the full press marketing campaign that would turn them into the next Green Day, or at least the next Screeching Weasel. They might play it off as if they were just fooling around, but their light-hearted gripes came with what felt like an undercurrent of seriousness.

I don't want to make those years sound as if they were nothing but a case of "more money, more problems." So many great records came out, so many outstanding bands were able to get their music heard, and Lookout's success had a knock-on effect, creating opportunities not just for musicians, but also for artists, designers, engineers, printers, and other creative types. People accustomed to thinking of themselves as useless punks had become linchpins in a burgeoning sub-economy.

It all happened so fast, or at least seemed to. One of my biggest regrets about the mid-90s is that I seldom stopped to take stock, let alone savor and appreciate what was going on around me. It was one of the most rewarding, depressing, exhilarating, and terrifying times of my life, but at any given moment, I'd have been hard pressed to tell you exactly how I was feeling about it. My personal problems hadn't gone away, and may have been getting worse, but I was too busy to notice more than a vague, gnawing discontent that occasionally bubbled over into a disgruntled "Oh, what's the use of it all, anyway?"

Spring was in the air, and I sat staring out my window, the phone pressed halfheartedly to my ear as some Hollywood executive droned on about using some songs by Lookout bands in an upcoming film.

We'd had this conversation three or four times already, and I had no idea why we were having it again. The bands were willing, I was willing, the price and terms had been agreed, and still he showed no sign of hanging up. It was as if I were the first human being he'd encountered after years of being lost in the wilderness.

"You never know with soundtrack albums," he said. "Sometimes they'll go platinum, like *Reality Bites*."

That would be nice, I agreed.

"I have a good feeling about this one," he continued. "I think it might be another *Reality Bites*."

I'd never seen *Reality Bites*, had only vaguely heard of it, but if some Lookout bands were to make it onto a million-selling soundtrack, you wouldn't catch me complaining. What was the point, though, of sitting around speculating about something that might happen, probably wouldn't, and over which we had little or no control?

The sun flashed with a crystalline sparkle off the metal facing of an industrial building several blocks to the south. A flock of birds landed on the roof next door, preened and ruffled their feathers, then languidly took off again, tacking effortlessly into the edge of a stiffening sea breeze.

"It's like when you're surfing," the movie exec was saying. For a minute I thought he was referring to the birds, then remembered he was in Los Angeles and had been describing the feeling of having your film or record become an unexpectedly massive hit.

"You catch a wave, a bigger wave than you ever imagined. There's no time to think about where it came from or where it's going or how long it's going to last. You just hang on and ride that sucker for all it's worth. And you make sure you enjoy the ride, because the one sure thing is that it will end. Probably a lot sooner than you expect or want it to."

I didn't know much about surfing, but it sounded like good advice, so I tried my best to do as he'd recommended. Never in my wildest dreams had I pictured my shambolic little enterprise turning into such an enormous deal; never in my worst nightmares could I have foreseen feeling so empty and unfulfilled despite it all. Lookout might still bask voluptuously in pools of golden light, but for me at least, the light was beginning to dim.

20.
Iceland

A few days before *Dookie* was released, I started keeping a diary. Originally inspired by some dark thoughts that crept into my brain during a long late-night walk home, it evolved into what I half-jokingly called "the longest suicide note in history."

I wasn't kidding about the suicide bit; I fully intended to kill myself. But a simple overdose or bullet to the head wouldn't do, let alone a generic leap off the Golden Gate Bridge. I wanted to give the world a suicide to remember, and that would require a suitably elaborate manifesto.

Despite all my efforts, it never developed into more than a long-winded rant to the effect of, "You'll be sorry when I'm gone." Like many people absorbed in depression and self-pity, I had a severely distorted view of my own importance. I thought everyone would want to know—would need to know—every last exquisite detail of how and why I'd been forced to end my life.

Even the phenomenal sums of money flowing in and out of the Lookout bank account weren't enough to distract me. When our accountant called to say, "Congratulations! You're a millionaire!" I didn't bother explaining that because of Lookout's profit-sharing arrangement, not all that money was mine. I just said, "Um, okay, thanks," and went back to work on my suicide note.

Two years later, I'd written 450 pages and the end was nowhere in sight. With Lookout at the peak of its success, I despaired of ever finding time to knock out the last couple hundred pages. I also worried that I'd written too much, that people might not read it because it was so long. If there's anything more dispiriting than writing a suicide note, it's having to edit it for length and content.

My plan was to fly to London, catch a train to the end of the line in Scotland, and board a tramp freighter to Iceland. Once there, I'd make my way to the remote northwestern fjords, where I'd find a suitably desolate outcropping jutting out into the Arctic Ocean.

There I'd sit, with my whiskey, my codeine, and my Walkman soundtrack—an endless loop of the Smiths' "Asleep" and Joy Division's "The Eternal"—until I expired from a combination of cold, chemicals, and sadness.

The whole concept felt so beautifully tragic that I could hardly wait to get started. But first I'd have to make sure everything at Lookout was organized well enough so that Pat and Chris could easily step in and take over. That proved harder and more time-consuming than putting the final touches on my goodbye note.

I never officially gave up on my suicide plan, but finally had to accept that it was semi-permanently on hold, and settled for turning it into a Potatomen song. The realization that I wasn't going to be dying soon did little to cheer me up. What kind of a loser, I asked, couldn't even get it together to kill himself?

My isolation deepened. I spent whole days alone in my office, not seeing or interacting with anyone. One night, near closing time, I wandered out to use the xerox machine and ran into a young woman who I supposed must be our new receptionist.

"Excuse me," she said, "but who are you?"

I did manage to put in an appearance at the party we threw to mark the opening of the Lookout Recordshop. Although the new store, on the ground floor of our building, had been primarily my idea, I felt hopelessly out of place. Everyone seemed better dressed and more at ease than me.

I wandered around the periphery, waiting for a chance to slip away unnoticed. A sidewalk reunion of the original Potatomen lineup did little to lift my mood, and neither did a surprise appearance by Green Day.

Long before the festivities ended, I was back at my desk going over some recording budgets. When asked why I hadn't stuck around, I said the affair had reminded me too much of a high school reunion.

It was an odd thing to say, considering I'd never been to a high school reunion. I wasn't even sure what I meant, until I realized it reminded me of a similar experience I'd had as a young hippie.

I'd been on the road for six or eight months, a long time, apparently, in hippie years, because I came home to find my "family"—the couple dozen of us who'd infested an off-campus house like so many pot-smoking cockroaches—transformed into adults who sipped cocktails, wore makeup, and chatted about jazz.

Most of the people at the Lookout Recordshop party were in their 20s while I was not far off from 50, but I felt much as I had in 1968: like the last kid standing in a room full of grownups.

A shrink could have a field day with that kind of thinking, and in fact I'd recently started going to one. I got the feeling he didn't really like me.

"Your life is going great," he snapped at me one day. "And all you ever do is complain about it."

I stopped going after that. I didn't see the point of paying someone to tell me what I'd already been telling myself for years.

Social situations had always been a problem for me, but work, once a reliable escape route, now began to feel similarly unmanageable.

On paper I might still be Lookout's president and principal owner, and people still asked my approval—most of the time—before launching major projects, but there were days when I wondered if there was any point to my being there.

I wasn't the only one feeling alienated. Several bands asked me what was happening to the label they'd signed up with. Joe Queer even wrote a song complaining that Molly Neuman "don't wanna talk to me, won't return my calls."

I don't think Molly was deliberately freezing him out, but I don't think she was that comfortable around him either. It could easily have been a case of her riot grrrl ideals clashing with his not particularly feminist-friendly lyrics and manner, but I think there was more to it than that.

Molly was the product of a relatively privileged middle class, maybe even upper middle class background. She was never snooty or snobbish about it, but her life experiences had been different from Joe's, or, for that matter, mine. I'm pretty sure she didn't grow up around people who worked at places like Zug Island.

There was probably a generational aspect to it, too. Joe was closer to my age than Molly's. He and I had emerged from a punk scene far more ragged and rough than this shiny mid-90s version. She never said so overtly, but I got the impression Molly—and several other staffers—thought classic East Bay punk rock, the kind Lookout was built on, was kind of, well, out of date.

Andy Ernst phoned to tell me about Screw 32 and AFI, a couple of young bands he'd been recording. "They're right up your alley," he said. "Plus they're nice kids who deserve a break. I bet you could sell a lot of records for them."

He sent over cassettes for me to check out. Andy was right: both bands would do well on Lookout. Unfortunately, I couldn't find the time or energy just then to shepherd them through the production process.

I went around the office trying to find someone else to take on the project, but everyone was "too busy" or "not really into it." The subtext seemed to be, "That's not the kind of music we do anymore."

Our catalog, packed with the likes of Screeching Weasel, the Queers, the Mr. T Experience, the Vindictives, and many more, would have indicated otherwise, but it was obvious that unless I did all the work myself, Screw 32 and AFI weren't going to be on Lookout.

I still wish I'd tried harder. Turning down those bands felt like turning our back on the kind of label Lookout had originally been. Which made it all the more baffling when Molly and Chris set up a record deal with a band called Furious George, whose simplistic three-chord ditties made Screw 32 and AFI sound like Mozart and Beethoven.

I couldn't picture Molly or Chris listening to Furious George's music, let alone liking it. As much of a three-chord, pop-punk guy as I could be, I'd unhesitatingly given the thumbs down when George Tabb, Furious George's frontman, had asked me about being on Lookout.

George, a popular *MRR* columnist, had been a hero of 1987's "Great Skinhead Battle" outside Gilman, and could be charming, personable, and a world-class schmoozer. I'd put out records by Raooul, Filth, Blatz, and Isocracy, none of whose lyrics were going to be confused with Ph.D. dissertations, but songs like Furious George's "Betty Crocker, Punk Rocker," consisting of little more than those four words repeated *ad infinitum*, represented, as far as I was concerned, the one-step-beyonding of dumb.

But George had done an end-around while I was out of town, pressuring Chris and Molly with the help of a strongly worded recommendation from Tim Yohannan. By the time I got wind of it, the "Betty Crocker" single was in the works, with a full-length LP to follow. It was too late to stop the single, but I canceled the LP.

"What are we supposed to tell George?" Molly protested.

"Tell him whatever you want," I said. "That record's not coming out on Lookout."

George was, pardon the expression, furious, but his reaction was mild compared with Tim Yohannan's. The following month's *MRR* was a theme issue, the theme being "Lookout sucks."

The cover featured the Furious George mascot being nailed to a cross by a hammer-wielding arm labeled "Lookout." When Chris called to ask why our usual ad was missing from that issue, a chortling Tim told him, "You'll have to speak to our new account manager, Furious George."

It wasn't as vicious as Tim's anti-Biafra campaign, but it was just as dishonest and sleazy. Because I'd refused to do a special "favor" for his friend, Tim was trying to dump a metaphorical horsehead in my bed.

It was the final breaking point in our decade-long friendship. Tim and I didn't officially stop speaking to each other, but . . . we never spoke to each other again. When, a couple years later, I heard he was seriously ill, I thought it might be time to end the feud and go see him, but, sadly, I was still thinking about it when he died.

Chris Gambin was someone else I never got to say goodbye to. A preternaturally bright and happy-go-lucky kid who tagged along with the downtown Eureka punks, he developed health problems that forced him onto crutches during his mid-teens. His mood seemed to darken, to the point where it wasn't always easy to be around him.

His behavior grew more erratic after he moved to the East Bay, where, it's believed, he became the inspiration for the character "Little G" in Aaron Cometbus's novel *Double Duce*. Still only 19, he was found in a car parked near the San Francisco waterfront, a bullet through his head, presumably the victim of a drug deal gone bad.

Rich "Lucky Dog" Gargano was yet another casualty. Ten years before, as a wisecracking high school student, he would send letters to *Lookout* magazine talking about his band, No Dogs. Later, he and a gifted guitarist named Jean Repetto formed East Bay Mud (the name was borrowed from the East Bay Municipal Utility District, aka the water company). For several years he tried halfheartedly but persistently to talk me into putting out their record.

They had a song on the *Floyd* compilation, and their debut 7" was supposed to be Lookout 33, part of 1990's 10-EP series. But the tape they handed me was just a little too sloppy and didn't make the cut. It was only when Lucky joined Jeff Ott's band, Fifteen, that he finally became a full-fledged Lookout artist.

Billie Joe Armstong with Lucky Dog at Gilman.
(Photo by Murray Bowles)

By that time little evidence remained of the carefree kid he'd been. Gaunt, haggard, and unwashed, he put in regular appearances at the Lookout office, always wanting to know if he had any money coming.

We paid bands every three months, though they could usually get an advance in case of emergency. But with Lucky, it was always an emergency. Some Lookout staffers told me they found him a little frightening.

There was nothing to be afraid of; Lucky was only dangerous to himself. I told him to come directly to me when it was time to get paid, but even though it was none of my business what he did with the money he'd earned, it pained me to hand him his check. It would be only a matter of time, I guessed, before the substances he was spending it on would kill him. Before that could happen, however, he took his own life with a shotgun.

I was still drinking heavily myself, but hadn't used drugs in years. The longer I stayed away from them, ironically, the more I got dragged into other people's drug problems.

This was especially true when it came to the Queers. The intervention we'd staged for Hugh had worked for a while, but now he was back in the band—and back on drugs. So, unfortunately, was Joe, which I didn't realize until I flew out to Indiana to produce their fourth album, *Move Back Home*.

Joe and I had spent hours on the phone talking about the amazing new songs he was writing, but when we started recording, I discovered that only a couple of those songs actually existed. The rest were just snippets of melody or a catchy hook. In some cases, he hadn't gotten farther than a title.

The previous summer, Joe, Hugh, B-Face, and I, taking full advantage of the overdubs and effects spurned by Ben Weasel on *Beat Off*, had spent a couple of truly enjoyable days in the studio producing one of my favorite Queers records, the *Surf Goddess* EP. I'd been looking forward to a repeat of that experience, but the *Move Back Home* sessions proved to be anything but.

The new record was essentially written in the studio, with Mass Giorgini waiting patiently at his mixing board while we struggled to come up with ideas, riffs, and choruses. Even when something interesting did develop, Joe was seldom in the mood to pursue it.

"It's fine like it is," he'd snarl when I suggested another take or some additional harmonies. It felt like his primary purpose was to get this thing done as quickly as possible, collect the advance I'd promised him, and skedaddle back to the dope man in New Hampshire.

Move Back Home wasn't a terrible record. Considering the state Joe and Hugh were in, it's impressive that it got made at all. Still, I was unhappy enough about it that I refused to let myself be credited as producer.

When Joe was clean, you couldn't ask for a funnier, more enjoyable character to work with. But for several years, I was never sure which Joe I'd be getting. Fortunately he was in far better shape the next time I saw him at his home in Portsmouth.

Joe was putting together a compilation for Lookout called *More Bounce To The Ounce*, and Cletus, a Charleston, South Carolina band, were in town to record two songs for it. I'd always liked and gotten along with Cletus's singer, a garrulous, congenial fellow who went by the name of Johnny Puke.

But Johnny had a little problem, though he didn't see it as one. In fact he practically bragged about his heroin use. It had been in his apartment that feces-hurling shock-rocker G.G. Allin had overdosed and died, something Johnny usually made sure you knew within minutes of meeting him.

Cletus were recording a cover of one of my favorite Queers' songs, "Granola-Head." I thought that was a great idea until I heard the vocal track. Johnny had replaced a lyric about getting drunk with one about "shootin' junk."

"You're not putting that song out on Lookout," I told him. "Not like that."

My objection wasn't to the drug reference per se—you could find those on a number of Lookout releases—but the way it was framed, making it sound as though injecting heroin was a typical, even defining characteristic of being punk.

"That's censorship!" Johnny protested.

No, I told him, censorship is when the government stops you from saying something. I wasn't the government, and I wasn't stopping him from saying anything. He just wasn't going to say it on Lookout.

"I'll fucking kick your ass right here, Livermore!" he yelled, loud enough to be heard up and down the block.

I invited him to try, but no ass-kicking ensued. The next day Johnny sang "Granola-Head" with the original lyrics, though he was none too happy about it. A few months later, I was in the studio with the Queers as they recorded their *Don't Back Down* album. In between takes, Joe was clowning around doing Johnny Puke imitations.

Mass Giorgini hit the record button as Joe delivered his umpteenth rendition of "I'll fucking kick your ass right here, Livermore!" It wound up as a bonus track on the *Don't Back Down* CD.

Johnny Puke's bluster had been more comical than menacing, but Neko Case was a tougher customer. Hanging out at the Whiskey—or was it the Trocadero?—

during the Muffs/Queers/Cub tour, I was trying to convince B-Face and Vapid to take their beers somewhere else before Joe, who'd reinstated his backstage drinking ban, wandered in and saw them.

Neko overheard me and butted in.

"They're big boys," she said, "They can drink where they want."

"Yeah, but Joe doesn't . . . "

I didn't finish the sentence, because Neko wasn't interested in Joe's opinion. Or mine. She was ready to strike a blow for freedom, and I had a queasy feeling that that blow might be more than just a figure of speech. She was squaring up in one of those "Oh yeah? Sez who?" postures when I decided to vacate the premises and let Joe police his own backstage.

In late October I sat down at my desk to get started on the year-end accounts. It also happened to be my birthday, but the only party I was planning involved a mile-high stack of Lookout spreadsheets.

An intern from UC Berkeley walked past, looking for some floor space where he could fold and pack some catalogs. My office had plenty of room, so I invited him to set up there, and we got to talking.

This kid had only been working there a few days, but he'd obviously been paying attention. When I asked how he thought the label was doing, he offered a detailed critique, comparing Lookout to Detroit automakers and the Soviet Union: driven more by momentum than purpose, with no regard for efficiency, and cranking out products without any sense for whether they were wanted or needed.

I offered him a job on the spot. It had been years since I'd made a snap decision to hire someone I barely knew, but that was how I'd run the label in the early days, and it had produced some good results.

I knew his blunt assessments would put him at odds with the amped-up cheeriness and forced enthusiasm percolating around the office, but that was exactly what Lookout needed: someone willing to cut through the bullshit and deliver some hard truths.

He surprised me by turning the offer down, saying he'd rather finish college first. We talked some more about careers and education, and the subject of it being my birthday came up. "Why aren't you spending it with your family?" he demanded. He seemed genuinely disturbed to hear I'd never married or had children.

He hung around a couple hours past quitting time, until he'd folded all his catalogs and I'd put a large dent in my spreadsheet pile. As he was leaving, he wished me happy birthday and returned to the subject of my nonexistent wife and kids.

"I hope you don't mind me telling you this," he said, "but if I were your age and in your position, I'd consider myself a failure."

His words hung in the room long after he'd gone. Yellowish-white light from the just-past-full moon cascaded through the cantilevered blinds and spilled across the carpet.

Was I a failure? Or was the kid—much as I'd been at 19—too quick to offer opinions about things he didn't yet understand?

I turned back to my spreadsheets. The moon followed my progress, creeping past each of the three windows in turn, illuminating the room as if from within.

It had begun its descent toward San Francisco and the sea by the time I finished and filed my paperwork. My desktop, gleaming in the last bit of moonlight, was completely and utterly clear. First time that had happened in years.

21.
As The Weasel Turns

Even before that marathon bit of birthday accounting, I could see that Lookout's electrifying expansion was slowing down, maybe even coming to a halt.

1995 would prove to have been our high water mark. Sales dropped from $10 million that year to $6 million in 1996.

That was no reason to panic. The pop punk craze was cooling down a little, and 1995, when three out of every four records we sold were by Green Day, had been something of an aberration.

Still, it was the first time in our history that annual sales had gone down rather than up. It was hard not to be a little concerned.

Digital file sharing hadn't really begun to cut into record sales yet, but already some of my fellow label heads were muttering darkly about the "gold rush" being over. To hear them tell it, the music business itself—the punk rock part of it, especially—was headed for extinction.

People had been saying the same thing back in the 1980s. If I'd listened to them then, there never would have been a Lookout Records. Forget "industry trends," I said; if nobody was buying your records, it was probably because they weren't any good.

I'd glibly repeated that mantra while our sales multiplied, but now that they were headed in the opposite direction, some soul-searching seemed in order. Was Lookout making crappy records? Were we losing touch with our audience? Or was that audience growing up and moving on without us?

I wasn't ready to believe any of those things. Most of our bands were still doing fine; the only one that had suffered a significant falloff was Green Day, and that might be because their second major label release, the darker, less accessible *Insomniac*, hadn't been as well received as the mega-platinum *Dookie*.

What did worry me was the way Lookout seemed to be hemorrhaging cash. Even $6 million was hardly chump change, and should have given us a hefty profit, but at the end of the year, we weren't noticeably better off than we'd been at the beginning.

That was something else that had never happened before, even in the earliest days when were selling records by the thousands rather than the millions. Obviously we were spending way too much money.

But on what? There was no single expenditure I could point to, but a host of costly and inefficient practices had become baked into the system.

Massive promo campaigns, for example, sometimes saw us mailing out more free copies of a release than we'd end up selling. The ridiculously high-priced ads we placed in mainstream magazines looked like a blatant form of payola, aimed at guaranteeing good reviews and coverage. It made for pleasant reading but accomplished little else.

Then there were the industry conferences like CMJ in New York, South by Southwest in Texas, or Midem in France. I'd always thought of them as pointless circle jerks, but Chris and Molly loved them. Not content with attending themselves, they began flying bands out to play Lookout showcases.

When I griped about the cost, they argued that it was only a few thousand bucks here and there. It wasn't like we were talking about serious money, was it?

A similar attitude set in when bands asked for bigger recording budgets, or advances to buy equipment or tour vans. I had a well-deserved reputation for being tight-fisted about such requests, but Molly and Chris were more accommodating, and as often as not I went along with their decisions.

The Lookout Recordshop was a bigger financial drain than I'd expected, and for that I had no one but myself to blame. It was never a disaster, but the shop didn't come close to turning a profit. As with my misjudgments on the Lookout UK and Mint deals, I'd fallen prey to wishful thinking.

Having our own retail outlet would have made sense a few years earlier, when not many stores were interested in carrying our releases. But now that you could buy our records almost anywhere, the shop functioned more as a social space and Lookout museum.

Jane Taatjes, our smart, no-nonsense manager, kept it running smoothly and made it an enjoyable place to hang out. Spend enough time there and you'd meet people not just from the local scene, but from all over the world. It was mainly visitors, though, who actually bought things.

The Recordshop also became the new home for our mail order department, which had been languishing in a windowless storeroom upstairs, and suffering serious hiccups in quality. That would change dramatically when Erika, Patrick's then-fiancée, took over.

Mail order might not be the most glamorous occupation, but Erika loved it, treating it like a work of art. She always found time to answer people's questions, and routinely enclosed little notes and bonus items in the packages she sent out. She was especially good at dealing with parents who called to find out about this "Lookout Records" their kids were sending so much money to.

One thing that tested Erika's patience, though, was fielding inquiries and complaints from customers who wanted to know when they'd be getting that Downfall album they'd ordered and paid in advance for. "When's Downfall coming out?" became the longest-running punchline to any and all Lookout jokes.

At various times the record was supposed to be released as a 10" on David Hayes's Very Small label, an LP on Jesse Luscious's Zafio label, or a CD/LP on Lookout. The more Operation Ivy's reputation grew, the greater the buzz became around Downfall, which featured three of Op Ivy's four members.

Orders flooded in the instant Matt and Tim gave us the go-ahead for Lookout to release the ten-song *Get Ready For Action* LP. But then there was a complication. The first of many.

While most of Matt and Tim's post-Op Ivy projects had, like Downfall, been short-lived, Rancid had stuck around, and in the wake of their second album,

Downfall at the Berkeley Square. From left: Dave Mello (also formerly of Opeartion Ivy), Jason Hammon, Tim Armstrong, Matt Freeman. (Photo by Murray Bowles)

Let's Go, were becoming extremely popular. It grew difficult, then impossible, to pin anyone down long enough to decide on release dates, artwork, or track listings.

When they finally got in touch again, it was to let us know they wanted Brett Gurewitz to remix the record before it came out. Brett's work didn't come cheap, but the new master he handed back was well worth the extra expense. It sounded nothing short of astounding; I hadn't been this excited about a new release in years.

Then we were told to put the album on hold again, this time because Matt and Tim were too busy recording the new Rancid LP. "Once that's out and everything has quieted down," said Tim, "we can concentrate on Downfall."

But things never quieted down. *And Out Come The Wolves* would be Rancid's biggest record by far, setting off a major label feeding frenzy that saw the likes of Madonna turning up at their shows and trying (unsuccessfully) to sign them.

Calls and questions again went unanswered, and I finally gave up asking. People still occasionally corner me at shows brandishing a Lookout credit slip and half-seriously wondering if that Downfall album will ever materialize. "You never know," I tell them.

1996 also marked an end to my ever more stressful relationship with Ben Weasel. Not *the* end, as it turned out, but a dramatic tapering off. Or so I hoped, anyway.

Although Screeching Weasel had again "broken up" after their 1994 album, *How To Make Enemies And Irritate People*, I no longer took these breakups and reunions seriously. The band existed or ceased to exist when Ben wanted it to.

Why he'd pulled the plug on the Weasel machine just as the demand for snotty three-chord punk was at its apex was anybody's guess. For someone who never tried to deny that he was in this business at least partially for the money, Ben had a funny way of going about it.

With Green Day having blown open the doors for virtually any punk band that cared to stroll through them, a new Screeching Weasel album would have done phenomenally well in 1995. Instead, we got *Kill The Musicians*, an interesting but far from sensational collection of old demos, singles, and live performances.

Ben, meanwhile, busied himself with a new band that looked suspiciously like the old band—it contained three out of the four Weasels—but sounded noticeably different. Some people accused the Riverdales of being a straight-up Ramones tribute, but I saw them more as trying to play original songs while channeling the Ramones.

The Riverdales' first single, the Ben-penned "Fun Tonight," was arguably their worst. "'Ben Weasel' and 'fun'?" Joe Queer cracked. "Those are words you don't usually hear in the same sentence." But their second, Dan Vapid's sublime "Back To You," literally fooled me into thinking it was a lost Ramones track the first time I heard it.

Their LP, alternating between Vapid and Ben songs, was a solid effort. "In Your Dreams," in which an uncharacteristically vulnerable Ben lets his voice crack with emotion, was one of several high points. But though it sold well, the Riverdales were never going to rival Screeching Weasel, commercially or artistically.

Ben was not pleased. He'd grown more obsessed than ever with making enough money to buy a house, but could see his new band wasn't likely to generate that kind of revenue. Although we'd spent more promoting the Riverdales LP than on all the Screeching Weasel records combined, Ben bitterly accused Lookout of "dropping the ball."

"You want money?" I told him. "Make a Weasel record." It was sound advice, but he wasn't in the mood to hear it.

I sometimes wondered if Ben was out to prove it was his own genius, not the Screeching Weasel brand, that sold records. That would explain not only the Riverdales, but also the Gore Gore Girls, and even the Shotdowns, an odd little prank that saw Ben, Jughead, and *Chicago Sun-Times* columnist Jim DeRogatis record and release a Lookout single that pretended to be the work of an obscure hardcore band from backwoods Maine.

Everything Ben did musically ranged between good and great, but just as Screeching Weasel were a cut—several cuts, really—above their many imitators, so too did Screeching Weasel as a unit surpass anything Ben ever managed on his own. Ben, however, seemed to have trouble grasping this.

But grasp it he finally did, and it came as no surprise when he called to tell me Screeching Weasel were back in business and ready to make a new album. We talked about studios, release dates, cover art, and songwriting, but most of all we talked about money. Money and house prices.

I sensed from the start this was not likely to end well. Until now Screeching Weasel had never asked for nor been given a cash advance by Lookout. But this time Ben was demanding one big enough to cover the cost of a house for himself—or at least a hefty down payment.

A quick calculation revealed that if we gave him what he was asking for, we'd need to sell 75,000 copies—more than we'd sold of any previous Weasel release— just to break even. It was almost as if Ben wanted to make it difficult or impossible for Lookout to profit from the deal at all.

I told Ben the advance he was asking for was out of the question, and he responded with a series of ever more convoluted counter-offers, including one where we'd give him (him personally, not the band) an interest-free loan that would enable him to buy a house.

Not a hint remained of the cooperation and partnership that had produced releases like *My Brain Hurts*. Ben made it painfully clear he didn't care what happened to Lookout as long as he got what he was after.

Sick of the constant bickering, and seeing no sign that things were likely to get better, I encouraged him to look around for another label. I suggested Epitaph, but Ben was afraid he'd be in their bad graces because of rude things he'd previously said and written about them. Fat, however, looked like a possibility.

It's a nutty way to run a business, you might think, deliberately trying to get rid of one of your best-selling artists. On a strict dollars-and-cents basis, you'd be right, but signing great bands had been only part of the Lookout formula. Just as vital was the relationship we had with those bands. While I still got along well with the other members of Screeching Weasel, I was beginning to feel I could no longer trust or believe anything Ben said.

Maybe Fat Mike would have better luck with him. I was pretty sure he'd treat Ben fairly, but I could also see him laughing out loud at some of Ben's more outlandish demands, or dismissing them with a definitive, "No way, man."

"Fat Mike" Burkett of Fat Wreck Chords.
(Photo by Larry Livermore)

Chris Appelgren, ever the idealist, still thought he could salvage a Screeching Weasel deal, so against my better judgment, I stepped aside and let him try. He flew to Chicago and came back with an agreement barely different from the one I'd been rejecting all along. He meant well, but was no match for Ben's bluster.

I vetoed it, Ben furiously accused me of ruining everything, and with that, took himself off to Fat.

Their Fat debut, *Bark Like A Dog*, wasn't Screeching Weasel's best record; it probably wasn't even their second or third best. But it was well produced, packaged, and promoted—and its front cover prominently featured the Weasel head. It quickly became their best-selling record ever.

And that, I thought, was that. Sitting in my suddenly tranquil office, I reflected that, at least for now, all was right with the world. Ben was making enough money to buy his house, weeks had passed without having to deal with his litanies of complaints, and sales of our Weasel back catalog were picking up nicely.

Then came the letter. On multiple handwritten sheets of yellow, legal-sized paper, Ben accused Lookout of systematically shorting him on royalties for the entire time we'd worked together. He demanded that we either pay him the money he claimed we owed, or hand over rights to all the records we'd released for Screeching Weasel and the Riverdales.

I knew—I'd been writing the checks, after all—that we'd paid both of Ben's bands every penny they were due, on time, and often, when Ben was short of cash, in advance. They got 60% of the profits on each record, tape, or CD we sold, and the label kept 40%. Every Lookout band had the exact same deal, whether they sold a million records or a couple hundred.

I'd explained this profit share system to Ben in great detail, both before and after he'd signed a contract that spelled out how it worked. He'd agreed that it was both fair and generous, and had said so many times, both privately and publicly. Yet now he was claiming he'd never understood it, and that we'd used his ignorance to defraud him.

Ben was smart, well-read, and articulate, but the reasoning he was using to "prove" we'd been ripping him off was so incoherent—not to mention math-defying—that it was impossible to take seriously.

His main piece of "evidence" was that Fat was paying him a higher per-record royalty rate than Lookout. But Fat, like most labels, paid their artists based on a percentage of a record's list price. And Fat's list price was two dollars higher than Lookout's.

Our system was actually more generous. If we raised the price of Screeching

Weasel releases by just one dollar, we'd be able to pay them more per record than Fat was. I offered to do just that, but Ben furiously ordered me not to. He wanted me to leave the price unchanged and pay him more money out of Lookout's share of the profits.

I told him—as nicely as possible—to go to hell, and raised the price anyway. It meant thousands of dollars in extra income for Weasels, Inc., but you'd think I'd stabbed him in the eyeball with a rusty spoon. Even though, as I pointed out, our Weasel records were still selling for a dollar less than *Bark Like A Dog.*

Ben was talking a lot about his lawyers, and throwing around legal terms like "breach of contract." It sounded—I think he meant it to—as if he were threatening to sue us. I reluctantly concluded it was time to talk to a lawyer of our own to see where we stood.

A prominent point in every Lookout contract was the clause stating that if we ever fell more than six months behind on royalties, the contract became void, and the band could take back ownership of their recordings. It was an extremely unusual provision to find in any record deal. The lawyer advising us had all but begged me to leave it out.

"You can always release a band from their contract if you feel it's the right thing to do," he'd said. "There's no need to give them a built-in escape clause."

I insisted that the language stay. As long as we paid bands everything we owed them, it was irrelevant. If we stopped paying them, then what right did we have to keep them on our label?

What it meant was that if we'd really been underpaying the Weasels, as Ben was charging, they wouldn't even need to sue us to be released from their contract.

But that wasn't the case.

"I've got financial records and canceled checks to show we paid them everything we owed them, on time or ahead of time," I told our lawyer. "Do they have any kind of legitimate claim against us?"

"Not really," he said.

I breathed a sigh of relief, but he wasn't through talking.

"Even though you're in the right," he continued, "this Weasel character could still run you through the wringer."

"How?" I asked.

"Most contracts specify where disputes should be adjudicated, but yours doesn't. That means he could sue you in his home state, and make you spend a fortune flying yourself and your lawyer back and forth, or, alternatively, hiring a local attorney and setting up camp out there in Chicago. The case could drag on for years. His lawyers would know how much it was costing you, so they'd stretch it out as long as possible."

"Seriously?"

"I'm very serious. I've seen it happen. Also, Mr. Weasel would have home field advantage. His lawyers could paint him as the poor but honest local boy being victimized by the big bad California record company."

"So what are you saying? That I should sue him here in California before he can sue me in Illinois?"

"You don't have to sue him. There's a much simpler remedy. You can petition a judge for declaratory relief."

I looked at him blankly.

"You ask a judge to examine the contract and rule on whether or not you're in breach. Show him your paperwork, your payment records, any other evidence you might have. Mr. Weasel will be allowed to do the same. The whole thing could be done in a day or two."

"So if the judge says the contract is valid...?"

"Your troubles are over, unless Weasel is insane enough to blow tens of thousands of dollars on a pointless appeal. Things would return to the status quo. You'd continue to sell his records and pay him the amount stipulated in the contract, just as you've been doing."

"What if the judge rules in his favor?"

"He'd be released from his contract and be free to do whatever he wanted with the records. But based on what you've shown me, that's highly unlikely."

I left his office feeling somewhat relieved. At last, it seemed, there might be a way out of this endless wrangling.

But I was also deeply troubled. I'd started putting out records because I loved music and DIY culture, not because I wanted to hang around courtrooms arguing about contracts. Yet this declaratory relief thing sounded like the cheapest, fastest, and fairest way of ending the dispute.

I spent a long, sleepless night trying to decide whether to go ahead with the lawyer's suggestion, still puzzling over why Ben had started this fight. He couldn't really believe I'd cheated him, could he? I tried putting myself in his place, tried to figure out what might be going through his head.

In the end I realized it didn't matter what Ben's motives were. Whether he was acting out of ignorance, greed, or full-fledged malice, if he got what he was after, Lookout would lose a quarter of its revenue, I'd have to lay off most of our staff, and our label would be permanently—and falsely—branded as dishonest.

Just ahead of a cold, bleary dawn, I decided that while I didn't like any of my options, fighting for what I knew was right was the only real choice. I tried unsuccessfully to get a little sleep, then walked over to the office, sat down at my desk, and dialed the lawyer's number.

"Okay," I said, "I guess we'd better do this."

22.
Journey To The End

I wasn't naive enough to think our legal battle would go unnoticed, but the firestorm of argument and accusation that erupted still came as a shock.

MRR wasted no time declaring me the villain. I'd expected that, but was surprised—and disappointed—at how many people automatically took Ben's side without bothering to learn what the dispute was about.

I shouldn't have been. Whenever there's a conflict between an artist and a record company, the public tends to assume it's the artist who's being wronged. More often than not, that's a safe assumption.

Besides, let's face it: musicians come across as more lovable—or at least more interesting—than the guys behind the scenes who collect and count the money.

"Lovable" might be stretching a point when it came to Ben Weasel, especially since getting people mad at him had always been one of his chief marketing strategies. But even if they only loved to hate him, Ben evoked passionate reactions in his fans, as much for his persona as his music.

That left people willing—as I too had once been—to cut him a lot of slack. Nobody quizzed him too hard about the glaring inconsistencies in his story. No one knew that Ben had been threatening me with lawyers and legal action for months; what they heard now was him bellowing like a wounded animal about the injustice of "punks suing punks."

It didn't matter how many times I explained that no one was suing anyone, that we were simply having a judge rule on the validity of the Lookout-Weasel contract, much as a referee might review a decision via instant replay. "Punks suing punks" had a snappier ring to it than "Lookout asks for declaratory relief."

As bad as it felt to have people believe Lookout would defraud one of its artists, it was far worse to stand accused of lying and cheating by a longtime friend who had to know that what he was saying wasn't true. If nothing else, it made no sense. Why embezzle money from one of my favorite bands when I could make far more—legally and honestly—by simply charging the higher prices that labels like Fat and Epitaph did?

I felt completely isolated and alone. Regardless of how they might feel personally, people didn't want to be seen taking sides, especially if they were in other Lookout bands.

Some let me know they had complete confidence in Lookout, but couldn't risk alienating Ben by publicly contradicting his story. Most tried to avoid the subject altogether.

One exception was Joey Vindictive, Ben's neighbor and, depending what day it was, best friend or worst enemy.

Ben had brought Joey's band, the Vindictives, to Lookout, much as he'd done with the Queers. It had worked out well, with one slight exception: I'd never been able to get Joey's signature on a contract.

In the early days, we'd put out dozens of records without worrying about such formalities. But by 1997 the nature of the business had changed (as evidenced by the Weasel drama), and we usually insisted on having a signed contract in hand before laying out significant sums of money on a new artist.

It wasn't that Joey *refused* to sign a contract. He'd be happy to, he assured me. But there was always some reason he couldn't do it at that particular moment.

Typically, he'd tell me he was under too much stress to deal with it just then. How much stress, I wondered, could be involved in signing your name to a piece of paper? I knew about his struggle with mental health issues—Joey often spoke publicly about it—which made the excuse sound semi-plausible. Apart from that, though, he was a charismatic guy, and a lot of fun to hang around with. It was easy to overlook any suspicions that he might be giving me the runaround.

Joey and his wife, Jen, lived upstairs from Ben and his then-wife, Portia, in a three-apartment building owned by Joey's parents, who lived on the ground floor. It was the perfect setting for a punk rock sitcom—or soap opera.

Though I was a frequent visitor to Vindictive-Weasel Towers, I never knew what scenario might await me there. On happier days, everyone might be clustered around Mr. and Mrs. Weasel's living room, with one of Ben's nonstop harangues competing for attention with the constantly blaring TV.

Joey was one of the few people able to get a word in when Ben was in full flow, and kept us in hysterics with his well-timed wisecracks. He also had a running gag about the ever-deepening dent Ben's rear end had left in the sofa. Joey only had to pat his own seat cushion and smirk knowingly to render us helpless with laughter. Ben hated not being in on the joke, especially when suspecting he might be the butt of it. I don't know if he ever figured it out.

But those were the good days. I might just as easily find Ben and Joey at war with each other, often over something as trivial as an argument about a band or

TV show. Ben would greet me at the door with a terse grimace that let me know I'd better not even mention Joey's name, let alone go upstairs to visit him.

"I'm only here to see you, Ben," I'd have to assure him. Later I'd come back and sneak up the stairs to take care of business with Joey, who had his own grudges to vent. He was convinced, among other things, that Ben was downstairs trying to listen in on him with a drinking glass pressed up against the ceiling.

Most of these feuds blew over eventually, but when the two fell out over some mixing work Ben had done for the Vindictives, it looked like their friendship might truly be at an end.

Joey refused to pay for the work, calling it substandard. He added insult to injury by erasing some rhythm guitar tracks Ben had laid down and having them re-recorded by another guitarist.

Ben demanded that I kick the Vindictives off the label, much as he'd done with the Queers a year earlier when he was mad about something. He'd gotten over that pretty quickly, so much so that Joe Queer might never had known he'd been in the Weaselmeister's doghouse. But Ben and Joey Vindictive remained at each other's throats up until the day our legal action was filed.

Joey immediately announced that because of the way we'd treated his "friend" Ben Weasel, he would never sign a contract with Lookout. It felt a little self-serving—and naive, considering the things Ben had been saying about him—but it was a minor annoyance in light of everything else on my mind.

I still felt confident that the ill feelings between Ben and me would blow over once the dispute was settled. We might never be close friends again, but it was in both of our interests to have a mutually respectful business relationship.

However the legal matter played out, things had to change at Lookout. I couldn't see myself sticking around much longer if they didn't. The Weasel crisis had stirred me into taking action and reasserting some measure of leadership, but how long would that last? Was my heart still sufficiently in it? Would it ever be again?

I'd been thinking about leaving Lookout as far back as 1994. I liked building and creating things. I didn't like sitting at a desk, I didn't like being "the boss," and I hated not having enough time for my own music and writing.

Yet since I was going to be stuck there at least until the Ben Weasel problem was resolved, I thought I might as well draw up some plans for getting the label back on track once the court business was over.

Molly would have to go. She wasn't a bad person or a bad employee, but she wasn't a good fit for Lookout. I'd kind of known that from the start, but her relationship with Chris, combined with the major role she'd come to play in the label, had made me hesitant to do anything about it.

Chris could stay—would have to stay. Like Patrick, he was a full partner now, both of them having served the five years laid out in our 1991 agreement. But his role needed to be redefined. As an artist and graphic designer, he was invaluable, and his infectious, bubbly personality made him an excellent schmoozer-in-chief.

But he wasn't management material. He had too strong a need to be liked, and was too eager for everyone to be happy. When bands wanted bigger recording budgets or animated videos or miniature action figures of themselves (I exaggerate, but not by much), they knew Chris was the one to see.

Even if they asked for something impractical, unaffordable, or simply ridiculous, he found it hard to deliver a flat "No." He'd respond with something vague, like, "Let's see what we can do!" or "Maybe we could make that happen."

Although Molly officially worked for him rather than the other way around, you wouldn't have always guessed it from the way they interacted. As his wife— they'd been married since 1996—she wielded an authority that transcended job classifications, and her personality was as forceful as his was flexible.

That meant it might be difficult or impossible to convince Chris it was time for Lookout and Molly to go their separate ways. Maybe I could find different duties for her, ones that gave her less influence over major policy decisions.

Other employees would have to be replaced or reassigned, too, but the more I thought about it, the more I came to believe the label's problems might not be as intractable as they'd seemed. After several days of going over the various projects and boondoggles I intended to scale back or eliminate, I was feeling more upbeat and enthusiastic about Lookout than I had in years.

Spring was settling in over the East Bay, and I strolled into the office in an almost sunny mood. Chris came in to see me, looking unusually grim, not at all like himself.

"I think we should cancel the court case and make a deal with Ben," he said.

"Are you crazy? After all the work and money we've put into it? In another week or two, it'll be settled, and we can go back to being a regular record company again."

"I've been talking to Ben," Chris told me. "He's upset because he thinks we don't trust him. I think it'd help if we made some kind of good faith gesture to show we're willing to work things out."

"Of course we don't trust him! Why would we? All that garbage he's been spouting about us cheating him out of royalties? You of all people should know that's not true."

"Yeah, but I think he just feels backed into a corner, and that's why he's overreacting. Would it be so bad if we gave him a new contract like he's asking for, and maybe paid him a little more?"

I looked at Chris as if he'd taken leave of his senses, which, at that moment, I probably believed he had.

"What Ben wants," I said, "is a deal that would give him a higher royalty rate than all the other bands. How could we do that and not give everyone else the same raise? Where would the extra money come from?"

"We could figure something out," Chris said brightly. He didn't offer specifics.

"And remember," I added, "the contract Ben's asking for would give him the right to take his records away from us anytime he's unhappy or doesn't get what he wants. Which, as you may have noticed, happens every other week."

"Yeah, maybe," Chris acknowledged, "but don't you think if we were willing to compromise, he'd be happier, and wouldn't feel like he had to fight with us all the time?"

"If a grizzly bear corners you on a mountain he might just eat one of your arms or legs now, but don't you think he'll be back for more when he gets hungry again?"

"Larry, you're making Ben sound like some kind of super-villain. Think about how long you guys have been friends."

"I am. After this many years, I've got a pretty good idea how he operates."

"Well, I can't go along with you," Chris said, with a determination I'd rarely seen. "Unless you cancel the court thing, I'm going to have to quit."

It was the most devastating of sucker punches. The wind in my sails went rushing away, and I stood there lacking the faintest idea of what to do next.

Part of me thought, fine, if Chris left, Molly would, too, and just like that, we'd be on our way to a slimmed-down, more efficient and functional Lookout.

But it wasn't that simple.

Chris was fundamental to Lookout. I could barely imagine the label without him. Patrick and I might be able to take over his responsibilities, but it would represent a massive upheaval.

"I don't know, Larry," said Pat, when I told him about Chris's ultimatum. "To be honest, I'm not sure how much longer I want to keep doing this."

His feelings mirrored my own. We looked at each other and simultaneously let slip a weary sigh of resignation.

Pat had always been supremely loyal. I knew without having to ask that he'd stick around to help if I went through with my plans to rebuild the label. What I didn't know was how fully his heart would be in it. I was wondering the same thing about myself.

We sleepwalked through our duties and routines for the rest of the day. On the surface everything seemed normal. Apart from Chris, Pat, myself, and probably Molly, no one in the office knew anything was amiss.

I had to decide what I was going to do—and fast. The court hearing was coming up in a matter of days. Whatever course I took, Lookout would never be the same again.

Looking uncharacteristically happy and at ease behind my great big desk. (Photographer unknown)

I stayed in my office all night, mulling over possible solutions. I'd pace the floor for a while, then flop back in my chair with my hands wrapped around my head. Suddenly the phone rang, seeming to almost jump off my desk.

Normally I would have ignored it, but curious about who might be calling in the middle of the night—and eager for some distraction—I picked it up and said hello. It was Ben.

It was the first time in weeks that I'd heard his voice, and it was obvious he hadn't been expecting to hear mine. Hesitating briefly, he cleared his throat and launched into what sounded like a prepared speech he'd been planning to leave on my voicemail.

It was a 30-second torrent of verbal abuse—a concise rehash of everything he'd been accusing me of for the past couple months—that only stopped when he ran out of breath. When the line finally went silent, I opened my mouth to reply, only to realize he'd already hung up. I caught a glimpse of my reflection in the window, still holding the receiver in my hand and looking at it as if it were a coiled snake.

Why, I asked myself, hadn't I thought more seriously about just selling the label and getting out of this business altogether? It had been a fantasy that regularly crossed my mind, but I'd always wound up dismissing it because it would have most likely meant selling to a major label.

Judging from the deal that had seen Warner take over half of Sub Pop—a label roughly the same size as ours but with a less valuable back catalog—I could probably count on getting 20 or 30 million bucks for Lookout, maybe even a good bit more. Given the Green Day connection, Warner was almost sure to be interested.

But that payday would come at a price. It would mean committing to a year or two's worth of restructuring, reorganizing, drawing up and negotiating contracts, hanging out more or less constantly with accountants and lawyers—all the stuff, in other words, that I liked least about running a record company.

That wasn't the worst of it. Chris, Pat, and I would become multi-millionaires, but most members of the Lookout family wouldn't be so lucky.

A major label buyer would want Lookout's indie cred, but would keep only a handful of our bands: the proven moneymakers like Operation Ivy, Green Day, and Screeching Weasel, and probably a few others like Avail, the Queers, or the Mr. T Experience. Dozens of other bands—the vast majority, really—would be unceremoniously dumped.

Most of our employees would lose their jobs, and business would dry up or disappear for the artists, printers, and manufacturers who did production work for us. Hardest hit of all might be Mordam, who relied on us for about half their sales, and who'd just invested in a new warehouse made necessary by our vast inventory.

Letting Lookout become a major label subsidiary would mark a bitter and ignominious end to pretty much every dream I'd started out with, yet as I sat there stewing in the aftermath of Ben's diatribe, I couldn't help wondering if it would be that much worse than the fix I found myself in now.

In the end, though, I knew I'd never do it. *Maximum Rocknroll* might have excommunicated me from the scene, but the independent ideal remained deeply embedded in my punk rock DNA. Whatever others might say, I still had to live with myself.

At around 3 or 4 in the morning I hit upon the idea of handing the label over to Chris. Unlike Patrick and me, he was fully committed to staying with Lookout, and though he and I didn't see eye to eye on everything, I felt confident we shared the same essential values.

True, once I'd signed the company over to him, there'd be nothing to stop him from giving in to Ben's demands or instituting other changes I disagreed with, but I was so tired, so frazzled, that I was even ready to surrender my belief that mine had to be the "right" way to handle things. Maybe it was time to let someone try a different approach.

The more I turned it over in my head, the more it seemed like the only choice that made sense. Everything that had once felt so bright and shiny about Lookout was turning to ashes for me anyway. Why not leave now, before it got any worse?

It was already getting light outside when I started typing my letter of resignation. Addressed to all the employees, it assured them that their jobs and benefits remained secure, that Lookout would carry on as always, only with Chris running the label instead of me.

It wasn't long, a page and a half at most. I tried, but couldn't picture how people might react when they found it waiting in their email that morning. I reread the letter one last time. It sounded as if it had been written by a stranger.

My finger hovered over the "send" button. It wasn't too late to change my mind. Should I maybe think about it a little longer before giving up the company I'd spent ten years of my life building? Could there possibly be some other way out?

Heartsick yet resolute, feeling more certain in my course than I had in years, I let my finger fall, and the deed was done. I sat quietly for a quarter of an hour, then began cleaning out my desk.

23.
After The Gold Rush

Fulfilling a long-deferred dream, I moved to London. Putting some distance between myself and Lookout felt like a good idea, though it was never my plan to sever all connections.

I'd made it clear that I'd be available to answer questions or offer advice, but while some employees kept in touch, Chris and Molly's attitude seemed to be, "We can do it ourselves, thanks."

I found that a little surprising, but didn't give it as much thought as I might have. For a while, in fact, I wasn't giving much thought to anything. The separation hit me harder than I'd expected. I stumbled through my first year away from Lookout in something resembling a state of shock.

For much of that time I could barely stand to listen to music at all, even—or especially—my favorite records. I'd put on *My Brain Hurts* or *Energy* or Nuisance's *Confusion Hill*, and before the verse had dissolved into the chorus, the emotions and memories would become too painful, and I'd have to shut it off.

I'd planned to live permanently in London, but had to return to California for a while when my father's health began to decline. I stopped by the Lookout office and was greeted like a conquering hero.

Everyone crowded around to ask what I'd been up to and to fill me in on their current projects and the latest gossip. I loved it: all the camaraderie and laughter of the old days, with none of the stress and pressure.

But during subsequent visits, I got a more muted reception. People had work to do; they couldn't stop to chat every time I happened to drop in. Before long I only went there if I had specific business, which wasn't often.

While they showed little interest in my opinions about how to run the label, both Chris and Molly wanted me to attend the weekend of shows and parties they'd planned in honor of Lookout's 10th anniversary. Reluctant to deal with the bright lights and crowds, I only made it to the last couple hours of the weekend's final event. When the 15th anniversary rolled around, they didn't bother inviting me at all.

I don't want to make it sound like I was completely alienated from the label. I

I arrive in London after stepping down from Lookout, and take solace in a nice cup of tea. (Photographer unknown)

still loved most things about Lookout. But when asked what was going on there, as I often was by both friends and strangers, I had to answer, "I'm not really sure."

I socialized with Lookout people when I was in California, and went to see Lookout bands when they played in London, so I was exposed to a steady stream of news, rumors, and speculation. But even then it wasn't easy to put together a coherent picture of the changes that were happening.

Chris sometimes gave or sent me packages of the latest releases. Some were by familiar bands like the Mr. T Experience, the Hi-Fives, Avail, or Pansy Division, and others featured newer signings that blended in well with the Lookout tradition, like the Groovie Ghoulies or the Crumbs.

But mixed among them were records I didn't quite get. I'd loved Exene Cervenka's vocals in X, for example—they more or less made that band. But her new project, Auntie Christ, was something of a directionless muddle. I wondered if Molly had been a little starstruck when she agreed to release it on Lookout.

Chris seemed to have fallen in love with the Phantom Surfers, a surf-punk instrumental combo who'd played at his and Molly's wedding, and the Go-Nuts, who sang exclusively about (and assaulted their audiences with) snack foods.

Both bands could be fun—depending on your sense of humor—and Chris was entitled to experiment with quirky, less commercial projects, just as I'd done in my day. But judging from the way he handled and promoted the releases, you'd think he was expecting them to be the next Op Ivy or Green Day.

Emo-hipsterish acts like Black Cat Music, Pretty Girls Make Graves, and Chris's own band, the Pattern, were actually pretty decent, but maybe not best suited to the Lookout demographic. Devo wannabes Servotron had talent, but seemed to be operating, if not in the wrong decade, at least on the wrong label.

It felt like Lookout was throwing a little of everything against the wall, and not nearly enough of it was sticking. "I used to automatically buy everything that came out on Lookout," people told me. "Now I don't know what to expect anymore. It's like a whole different label."

Equally worrying was the way Lookout no longer seemed able to distinguish between bands with potential to sell a ton of records, and those who, like Brent's TV (or Raooul, or, for that matter, the Potatomen), would probably only attract a niche audience.

It's true that apart from the occasional conversation with Chris, I had no way of knowing for sure what Lookout was spending on their releases, but I'd been in the business long enough to make an educated guess. I'd also developed a pretty good instinct for estimating how many copies a record would sell.

From where I sat, the two figures seemed wildly out of sync. It was as if Lookout thought they could spend and promote every band, no matter how quirky or obscure, into superstardom.

The question of whether this was wise or even possible had been one of the philosophical differences that regularly flared up during my last years at the label. Now that I was no longer there to veto some of the more exorbitant outlays, I sensed that spending might be spiraling dangerously out of control.

When I mentioned this to Chris, he pooh-poohed my concerns, assuring me that the label was on as sound a footing as ever. And since I was only guessing, whereas he had access to all the facts and figures, I had no choice but to take his word for it.

One other thing bothered me about the new Lookout: the way their image seemed to be changing into something more slick and corporate. Ad copy and catalog commentary, once one of the label's strong points, rang forced and hollow.

The lighthearted irreverence that had been our hallmark was replaced by strangely joyless exhortations to get "pumped" or "stoked" about whatever new release was about to "drop."

That sort of jargon was endemic in the more commercial sectors of the industry, but only someone with severe tin-ear-itis would expect it to resonate with a Lookout audience. Coupled with the increasingly erratic quality of its releases, I feared the label might be driving away old fans faster than it could attract new ones.

Patrick Hynes had resigned from our partnership at the same time I had, leaving Chris, Molly, and Cathy (who'd moved into a management role) in full charge. He'd stayed on, however, as a contract employee, maintaining the label's database and computer network. He probably knew as much about Lookout's finances as any of the three people ostensibly in charge.

He didn't like to talk about it—"complicated" was his favorite one-word description for the figures he had to juggle—but I could tell he was finding the work stressful. I urged him to be more assertive about letting Chris, Molly, and Cathy know what the label could and could not afford, but as he put it during one such discussion, "They're not going to listen to me anyway."

"What are you going to do if they wind up going broke?" I countered.

"Find a new job, I guess."

Not since the very early days, when David Hayes and I were running the label and Mordam hadn't yet taken over our distribution, had Lookout had to worry about running out of cash. Nobody working there now knew what that was like; for them, money had always been so abundant that it was all but taken for granted.

But to continue its free-spending ways, Lookout would have to come up with some new breakout acts. Chris and Molly seemed to think they'd found one in the Donnas, four young women who played metal-tinged rock in a style echoing that of the Runaways.

I didn't think it was likely to happen. The Donnas had undeniable appeal to a certain core audience, but their sound, their look, their whole schtick, really, was too much of a throwback to 1970s and 80s hair-rock and butt-metal. It had little in common with punk except a certain amateurishness and naiveté that disappeared once the band got more adept with their instruments and more ambitious about their careers.

I don't know if the Donnas chose to market themselves as sex objects—or what role Lookout played in that decision—but it's essentially what happened. Some of their lyrics were merely playful and suggestive, but others ("Come on and stick it in") were straight out of a porn flick.

That might explain why their audiences differed noticeably from those usually drawn to Lookout bands. The teenaged boys who pushed their way to the front did more gaping than dancing, and mixed among them were a number of older men who looked like candidates for the dirty raincoat brigade.

In their defense, the Donnas were young, and maybe not fully aware of how they were being perceived. The one time I hung out with them—in, of all places, the Vancouver branch of Hooters—they came across as bright, polite, and well-spoken, not at all like the raunchy image they presented on stage.

Even before the label started heavily promoting them, the mainstream rock media showed more interest in the Donnas than they had in any Lookout band, including pre-*Dookie* Green Day. It was the novelty factor, I warned, and wouldn't have staying power, but nobody was interested in my naysaying. Chris also didn't think it was funny when I snarkily suggested that sending every kid in America a $15 check to spend on a Donnas CD might be cheaper than the marketing campaign he was running.

The Donnas did rack up some respectable sales figures, and landed a major label deal with Atlantic. Unlike my ambivalent attitude when Green Day had announced their departure, Chris and Molly seemed bent on greasing the skids for the Donnas' move. Molly actually became the band's co-manager, putting herself in the questionable position of representing both band and label.

Although they got a lot of attention, briefly cracked the *Billboard* charts, and licensed several songs for movies and video games, the Donnas didn't live up to expectations and were dropped ("mutually parted ways," as the band preferred to put it) shortly after their second Atlantic LP. If Chris and Molly had been counting on another Green Day-style windfall, they would have been severely disappointed.

Chris swore that Lookout had come out ahead on the deal, though his math seemed a little fuzzy. He could be similarly vague when I asked about certain rumors I'd heard.

One story, sounding almost like a *Saturday Night Live* skit, had Molly bringing in a *feng shui* expert to rearrange the office furniture. A disgruntled staffer claimed Molly's real motive, rather than optimizing "energy flow," was to reinforce her claim to the private office I'd once occupied.

Molly loved "consultants" and "experts," often urging me to hire them to show us better ways of running the label. "Given what we've accomplished on our own," I'd retorted, "they should be paying us."

Despite its excesses, Lookout should have had sufficient resources to carry on far into the future, perhaps indefinitely. It might have, too, if it weren't for several crucial mistakes. The first, not surprisingly, was Ben Weasel-related.

I'd all but begged Chris not to follow through on his plan to release Ben from his contract. "It's like giving him a gun to hold to your head every time he wants something," I'd warned.

Chris was undeterred. "It's important to start fresh," he'd insisted. "Besides, why would Ben try to take advantage of us when we're giving him everything he asked for?"

Late 90s Potatomen graphic. (Drawing by Patrick Hynes)

Chris's optimism seemed to pay off at first. After releasing two records on Fat, a new version of Screeching Weasel—Vapid and Panic having been replaced by Zac Damon, Dan Lumley, and Mass Giorgini—returned to Lookout.

It was a mixed blessing. Anything named "Screeching Weasel" was bound to sell records, but the band would never again enjoy anything like the commercial success of its first Fat release. Nor would this rebooted version, gifted as its individual members might be, reach the artistic heights attained by the "classic" lineup.

Ben's new relationship with Lookout came with some baggage. He'd started his own label, Panic Button, concentrating on good but mostly by-the-numbers punk and pop-punk bands in the Screeching Weasel/Queers/Vindictives vein. He demanded and got a co-release arrangement with Lookout that meant Mordam had to distribute anything Panic Button put out.

Ben had a good ear for that style of music, and with Mordam's and Lookout's clout behind it, his label should have been far more successful than it was. Unfortunately, nobody at Lookout had much time, energy, or interest to devote to Panic Button bands.

Band members complained about phone calls and emails going unanswered, about having no idea whether their records were still in print. "I finally got through to somebody at Lookout," one disgruntled guitarist told me, "and they'd literally never heard of us."

Screeching Weasel's first release on returning to Lookout was titled *Major Label Debut*, perhaps an ironic reference to the band's downsizing from Fat. I thought the record was surprisingly poor, but my judgment might have been skewed by the fact that one stunningly hateful and dishonest song seemed clearly directed at me.

It resembled that invective-filled phone call I'd received from Ben on my last night at Lookout, set to the sort of furious thrash beat that Screeching Weasel had mostly abandoned back in the 1980s. There was little melody or "singing"; a near-apoplectic Ben could barely stuff the epithets and accusations into his mouth fast enough to spit them back onto the tape.

Nothing Ben said or did surprised me anymore. But I was baffled—and hurt—that others had gone along with it, especially Mass Giorgini, who'd I'd become quite close with over the years. And by releasing the record, my former partners and co-workers at Lookout appeared to at least tacitly endorse Ben's accusations.

I could sort of see the musicians' point of view: playing in even a watered-down version of Screeching Weasel represented a prestigious feather in their caps, and it's not like the boss was going to be interested in their opinions about his lyrics anyway. And thanks to the new contract Chris had given him, Ben had become the tail that wagged the Lookout dog. Saying no to anything he "asked" for could, especially in financial terms, prove disastrous.

I didn't bother taking it up with Chris—or anyone, really. Though I tried to shrug off the whole ugly business, the label that had represented one of my life's proudest accomplishments began to feel like a creepy albatross hung round my past and fated to follow me forever into the future.

Instead, I tried to distance myself from Lookout, which may be why rumors about bands not getting paid took so long to reach me. Even when they did, I dismissed them as just another bit of Lookout gossip that might or might not be true.

But I couldn't keep ignoring them. One of the last things I'd done before leaving the label was to broker a compromise between a still-not-speaking-to-each-other Jeff Ott and Aaron Cometbus, making it possible to release Crimpshrine on CD. I told them, as I'd told Avail, the Queers, and a dozen other bands, that if they ever had any questions or problems with Lookout, they could always call on me.

Now they were calling.

"Hey, do you know what's going on?" I'd hear from one band after another. "We haven't seen a statement or a check all year."

All year? That didn't even make sense. A computer glitch or some missing data could explain a delay of a week or two, but even that had rarely happened during my time at Lookout. And whatever I might think of Chris's and Molly's spending habits, it seemed impossible that they could have burned through so much cash that they couldn't meet the label's most fundamental responsibility.

My father was terminally ill at that point, so I was spending most of my time in California. I tried contacting Chris to ask him what was going on, but it wasn't always easy to get hold of him. It was harder still to get answers that made sense.

There'd been "mistakes" and "misunderstandings," he admitted, but promised everything would soon be straightened out.

Instead matters went from bad to worse. Lookout employees had their hours and benefits cut, including the health insurance I'd been so proud of. I began asking band members, whenever I ran into them, if they'd been paid lately. Almost none had.

But where had all the money gone? At the time I left, Lookout had at least a million dollars in assets, and must have taken in several million more in record sales since then. It's possible—though it would have taken some doing—that the label had squandered all its own resources on a combination of high living, ill-conceived marketing campaigns, and new releases that didn't pan out. But that didn't explain what had happened to the bands' share of the profits.

If you were running a legit label, you didn't touch that money, because it wasn't yours. You didn't dip into or "borrow" part of it to tide you over until some new income came along.

I'd heard rumors—never verified—that soon after I left, Chris and Molly had taken out a bank loan, presumably to expand Lookout's operations. It made no sense—apart from the couple of times Ruth at Mordam had given us an advance on an upcoming check, we'd never needed to borrow money in the label's history.

But whether it was to repay the bank, or to fund new releases, or just to accommodate a more luxurious lifestyle, obviously at some point a decision had been made to put off paying bands in favor of covering expenses that were deemed more important.

The need—or at least the perceived need—to raise more cash must have figured heavily in another costly mistake: Lookout ended its longstanding relationship with Mordam and signed an exclusive distribution deal with RED.

I'd been begging Ruth to sell directly to RED before I left, but the deal Chris and Molly agreed to was something entirely different. It gave RED the right to cherry-pick the releases it wanted, leaving much of Lookout's catalog available only by mail order. Thousands of records and CDs wound up in the landfill, creating an unexpected bonanza for Berkeley's sharp-eyed scavenger punks.

It was more or less what would have happened if we'd sold Lookout to a major label—minus the multi-million dollar payday. In fact, the costs of making the transition, which included repackaging its inventory to fit the RED format, meant Lookout paid a stiff price for the privilege of being taken over.

The timing could hardly have been worse. The deal also forced Lookout to sharply raise its prices just as record sales began to lag industry-wide, thanks to the double whammy of economic recession and illegal downloading.

I tried not to care, to focus instead on family matters and personal concerns. Besides, I kept reminding myself, it wasn't my label anymore, and had little in common with the label that once had been mine.

It was like watching a shipwreck in slow motion, with Lookout as a modern-day Titanic drifting helplessly to its doom. Up above the band still played and the party carried on, glitzy and glamorous as ever. But down below, where no one ever seemed to venture, the engines had failed, the hull was torn open, and water was pouring in at what would prove to be a fatal pace.

24.
There Is A Light That
Never Goes Out

It was 2004, maybe early 2005, when I got a call from a desperate-sounding Joe Queer.

"Geez, Larry," he said, "do you have any idea what's going on at Lookout? I can't even remember the last time we got paid. At least I can still make some money playing shows, but what am I supposed to tell Hugh's family?"

Hugh had died a few years earlier following a long, painful illness. I preferred to remember him from that oddly warm November afternoon in Portsmouth before he got sick, when the two of us stepped out to get some fresh air and wound up walking all the way out to the mouth of the Piscataqua River. He pointed out some of his favorite 17th century houses, and we talked about history, architecture, science, and religion in a way we never had before or would again.

After he passed away, Lookout sent Hugh's royalty checks to his dad, but then, like Joe's and B-Face's, they stopped coming. I heard similar complaints from Jeff Ott. Part of Crimpshrine's royalties were supposed to be donated to the Berkeley Free Clinic and Food Not Bombs, but neither institution had seen any money in quite a while.

I'd all but given up on asking Chris about stories like this, because I never got much in the way of answers or action. But when I called him this time, he invited me—with unusual enthusiasm, it seemed—to come see him.

Lookout had closed the Recordshop and relocated to a sprawling low-rise brick building on an as yet ungentrified stretch of Adeline Street in South Berkeley. Just down the block sat the storefront that had once been home to Own's Pizza, scene of the 1986 show that had inadvertently launched us on the road to Gilman Street.

Inside, the new headquarters were pleasant enough, but from the street, they made for an unlovely sight, with grimy windows permanently barred by rusty iron gates. Chris greeted me warmly, but it wasn't hard to tell he had serious troubles on his mind.

He didn't bother hemming or hawing or beating around the bush, and freely acknowledged that he was having problems keeping up with royalty payments. While remaining vague about why this was happening, he said he hoped things would be sorted out soon. "Hoped" was not nearly as strong as "expected," the word he'd used the last time we'd talked.

His breezy assurances sounded sincere, but Chris always tended to err on the side of optimism. When I asked exactly how he planned to get things back on track, he jumped up and offered to take me on a tour of the new warehouse and office space.

It was getting dark outside, and everyone else had left for the night. We tramped up and down the aisles of the warehouse, our footsteps echoing morosely through the gloom that seemed to spill in from the street. Periodically Chris would pluck a record or CD from the shelves and suggest I take it home with me.

At times we had to detour around boxes of unsold records, many by bands I'd barely heard of. Moments later we'd hit a stretch of empty shelves that should have been stocked with perennial best-sellers from the label's heyday.

"There's not as much demand for that old stuff as there used to be," Chris told me. But I'd heard a different story from Lookout employees: many of the records that had been the label's bread and butter were out of print because manufacturers, who in the 90s had happily offered us a million-dollar credit line, were demanding cash in advance before they'd fill new orders.

Molly and Chris had split up, and she had moved to New York. She was still on the Lookout payroll, and still part-owner of the company, but most of her time seemed to be taken up with managing the Donnas. I tried to ask Chris how the label could afford an East Coast rep when they couldn't cover their West Coast bills and royalties, but he shunted that question aside.

He was willing, though, to talk about a much bigger financial headache: the deal he'd made with Ben Weasel to buy Panic Button Records for what sounded like a wildly inflated price. The money involved would have been enough to pay the lion's share of Lookout's past-due royalties.

It made no sense, Chris readily admitted now. Panic Button had languished even when Ben was managing it; there simply wasn't anyone at Lookout with enough passion for snotty three-chord punk to make the partnership work. It wasn't hard to imagine what would happen once Ben, whose world revolved around that style of music, had cashed in his chips and gone.

Regardless of whether anybody could have made a go of Panic Button, the brutal fact remained: Lookout was spending money it didn't have—that actually belonged to others—to buy something it didn't want and definitely didn't need. The only question was why.

Chris was reluctant to spell it out in detail, but I could picture how the deal

Robynn Iwata, Lisa Marr, and Grant Lawrence make a punk rock pilgrimage to the place it all began. The Spy Rock sign is no longer there; it's been stolen so many times that the county stopped replacing it. (Photo by Chris Imlay)

might have gone down. Ben would have started whining about how running Panic Button was stressing him out, how he needed more time for his writing and music, and how it would make sense for Lookout to take the label off his hands. For a "reasonable" price, of course.

Any demurral on Chris's part would have been met with dark mutterings from Ben about "trust" and "respect," and if that wasn't sufficient, pointed references to finding some other label where he'd be more appreciated.

He'd be bluffing. Nobody else was likely to lay out that kind of cash for Panic Button. But, thanks to Chris's generous rewriting of Ben's contract back in 1997, the threat to yank the Weasel and Riverdales back catalog would have been real.

It was a terrible position for Chris to be in. He couldn't afford to lose those records, but he also couldn't afford to take over Panic Button, especially at the price Ben was demanding. When he gave in and accepted Ben's "offer," I suspect he saw it as a double-or-nothing sort of gamble, buying time in hopes something might turn up that would enable him to balance the books again.

The gamble didn't pay off. Not long afterward, Ben took back his records anyway, and began threatening to sue for the unpaid balance from the Panic Button deal. If any chance remained of pulling Lookout back from the brink, that probably ended it.

You wouldn't have guessed it, though, from the spate of new records that came out that year, featuring the likes of the Oranges Band, Troubled Hubble, Hockey Night, The Reputation, Engine Down, and Mary Timony. None of them was likely to rescue the label's fortunes; some probably drove it deeper into debt.

Ted Leo was one of the few remaining bright spots in Lookout's rapidly dimming constellation, but though beloved by critics and steadily growing in popularity, he hadn't yet become the kind of star who could sustain a label. That role, even all these years later, was still filled by Operation Ivy and Green Day.

I assumed Lookout was still paying those two bands, because neither had complained to me, and because it would have been insane not to. I was wrong.

The relationship between Lookout and Green Day had always been relaxed and easy-going. As far as I could remember, there'd never been a serious question or misunderstanding about money. Following their major label success, managers and accountants had taken charge of their financial affairs, and since then we'd rarely needed to talk about business at all.

Maybe things had gotten a little too comfortable. I can't conceive of any other reason Chris would have thought he could put off paying them while dealing instead with his more aggressive creditors. The past-due royalties kept mounting; Chris later told me he'd owed them about $400,000. Green Day thought it might be considerably more.

Exercising the clause I'd put in their contract to protect them against such an eventuality, Green Day took back their records and ended their 17-year relationship with Lookout. Operation Ivy, also owed hundreds of thousands of dollars, stuck around a little longer, but eventually followed suit. Chris talked bravely of a relaunch, but all scheduled releases were canceled and all the employees except Cathy were let go.

Lookout had felt like a dead label walking for some time already, but this sudden, ignominious end hit me hard nonetheless. I vented my anger in a post on the Pop Punk Message Board, a relatively tiny website frequented by a few friends and fans of old-school Lookout-type bands:

> I don't know too many details, but I know the problem has been going on for a long time, and that Green Day have been more than patient. If anyone should be griping, it should be me: I basically gave those Green Day records to the current Lookout owners, and they basically threw them away. Lookout has been failing to pay Green Day (and other bands) for years now, and apparently using the money to put out a series of terrible records that very few people wanted to buy. Gambling on new bands is part of what a record label does, but you don't do it with other people's money. Green Day could have taken their records away several years ago when Lookout first breached their contract, but they were generous enough to allow Lookout to keep licensing them in hopes that the label would get back on its feet. No matter how rich a band is, they shouldn't be expected to subsidize a failing label forever, especially when that label isn't doing anything particularly worthwhile. Sorry if that sounds harsh, but it kind of makes me sick to see what's happened to a label that I put so much of my heart and soul into.

I never expected those unguarded and intemperate comments to go rocketing around the internet, be picked up by the wire services, and wind up in the pages of my former hometown newspaper, the *San Francisco Chronicle*.

My mother phoned to tell me about it.

"You sounded so . . . vindicative," she said.

"Um, Mom, I think you mean 'vindictive.'"

"I *know* what I mean," she snapped. "And you were very vindicative."

My mother is probably the smartest member of our family, especially when it comes to words. It was so unusual to hear her make that kind of mistake that I realized she must be genuinely rattled. And if it bothered her that much, I hated to think how people actually involved with Lookout might have taken it.

I soon found out. Reporters called to ask if I'd been misquoted, or if I'd meant to be that scathing. When Chris got in touch to say how badly my words had hurt him, I knew I'd overstepped the mark.

The next time I was in California, I met him at Cafe Hell and apologized. He relaxed, and for the first time in years loosened up enough to talk freely about what he'd been going through.

"I was barely 24 years old when you left me in charge," he said, a number he repeated several times.

Put that way, it did sound crazy. When I was 24, I could barely organize a beer run to the corner store, never mind step in as chief executive of a multi-million dollar company.

The Panic Button deal had been a bad idea, Chris acknowledged, but rather than pile all the blame on Ben, he took responsibility for going along with it. He also tried to explain how Lookout had racked up so much in unpaid royalties.

"We thought we'd be able pay it all back when money came in from the new releases, but there was never enough. There'd always be some new bill or expense we weren't expecting. It seemed like the more we tried to catch up, the farther we got behind."

He seemed dazed and shaken about the way things had turned out, but as he spoke I became aware that I was in no position to judge him. I was the one, after all, who had impulsively bailed out on Lookout and handed it over to that inexperienced 24-year-old.

We sat commiserating and reminiscing for hours. What remained in the end was a shared sadness, and a renewed appreciation for each other that in recent years seemed to have all but vanished.

Despite the air of finality that hung over that 2005 conversation, it wouldn't be until January of 2012 that Chris, via a post on the label's website, officially put Lookout out of its misery.

A few weeks later, the two of us appeared on KQED, San Francisco's NPR station, to discuss, mourn, and celebrate the label's history. It was a surprisingly sweet affair, free from rancor or bitterness, focusing mostly on happy memories.

KQED is primarily a news and talk station, with an older, not especially punk rock audience. Our segment opened with Operation Ivy's "The Crowd," and I pictured listeners being jolted out of their easy chairs, reaching to turn off this unfamiliar racket but instead becoming entranced by that little catch in Jesse's voice as he hurtled into the line that always got me: "Drink, drink in the badlands, liquid bread for the poor."

Strange, I thought, how after all these years that song had lost none of its power, how it could still ring out so jarringly, stirringly raw and true. Over the past quarter century, millions of people must have heard it, yet like all the best rebel music, it had reached the mainstream without becoming part of it.

That was the essence of everything I'd tried to accomplish with Lookout. At heart, at my core, I'd never stopped being that Detroit kid with a chip on his shoulder, out to show the world that ordinary people from ordinary places could, given half a chance, do extraordinary things.

Had I succeeded? More than I'd dared to hope, less than I'd dared to dream.

In the years after leaving Lookout, especially when the label began running into trouble, I'd devoted an unhealthy amount of energy to speculating about what I'd do differently if I were still in charge. It wasn't until Chris helped me to see things from his point of view that I was able to fully accept where I'd been at fault, how my cowardice and weakness had led me to abandon one of the best and most amazing things I'd ever done.

Quitting when I did had felt like an act of self-preservation. I honestly believed my sanity was at stake, and perhaps even my life. Whether that was really true, or if I was being over-dramatic and self-indulgent, I'll probably never know. But when people ask, as they often do, how such a shining success story could have gone so horribly wrong, I'm pretty forthright about admitting: "I gave up, walked away, and let it."

Of course it would be as arrogant of me to claim full responsibility for Lookout's failure as it would be to take full credit for its success. I may have played a crucial role, but I was only one of hundreds of people who participated in the label's rise and fall. Maybe more to the point, Lookout was probably never going to be one of those institutions that takes permanent root and prospers down through the ages.

Epitaph's Brett Gurewitz, interviewed by Myspace for an oral history of

*Dead Lookout graphic created by Tom Meehan for his radio tribute
to Lookout Records. (Graphic by Tom Meehan)*

Lookout, had a nice way of putting it: "Record labels never really go away. Stax Records is still there for us to enjoy. Sun Records might not exist, but on some level it will always exist. Lookout Records is a moment in time that was wonderful."

Ultimately, Lookout will be remembered not for how long it lasted or how big it got, but for the quality of what we accomplished. Everyone knows about the Lookout alumni who went on to sell millions of records, win Grammy awards, and reshape popular culture, but as proud as I am of them, I'm just as proud of the professors and urban planners, the social workers and shopkeepers, the scientists, artists, writers, and engineers who crawled out of our tempestuous little tide pool.

And the mothers and fathers, citizens, idealists, and activists, all of whom carry some mark, some life-changing memory from the work we did and the fun we had together. It might have been the time they saw an amazing band at Gilman and thought, "Hey, maybe I could do that!" Or the moment they slipped the needle into the groove of a mail-ordered 7", or opened the pages of a hand-xeroxed zine and understood that they were no longer alone in the universe.

Some still proclaim themselves "Punk Till I Die," while others chuckle indulgently at the crazy stuff they did before they "grew up." And there are those— myself, for example—who walk both sides of that street.

A year or two might slip away between visits to Gilman—but I still come back. I complain about nihilistic drunk punks who think in slogans and speak in gobbledygook, but haven't forgotten I was once one of them. Every time I find myself on the brink of writing off the whole subculture as an exercise in low self-esteem, I meet a new band or hear a new story that inspires me all over again.

Not because it's "punk" or "alternative" or "underground" or whatever nickname you want to hang on it, but because it gets to the heart of what it is to be human: the never-ending need to re-imagine, re-invent, and, above all, transcend ourselves.

If there's one thing I hate about memoirs or documentaries, it's that they all seem to wind up with some version of, "We did this amazing thing, it was awesome, and then it ended. Too bad you weren't there, because you'll never see anything like it again."

That's not the story of Lookout, or of Gilman, or the East Bay. The music, the culture, and friendships we found there grew out of soil tilled by artists, philosophers, rebels, and misfits dating back to the dawn of time.

If you lived in a different part of the world, if you were too young or too old to be there, if perhaps you weren't even born yet, never let anyone tell you that you missed out or that you couldn't possibly understand what it was like.

Staple a flyer to a telephone pole for a basement show in Poughkeepsie, Kokomo, or Las Cruces, and you're treading in the footsteps of Operation Ivy, Crimpshrine, and generations of bands, poets, and troubadours who came before and since. Sing a song, write a book, upload a video that tells the story of what it means to be you, and only the calendar will divide your efforts from ours.

You may never have been at Gilman, but your songs, dreams, and visions will carry you to places we can barely imagine. To other planets, perhaps, or to a deeper, more constructive understanding of this one. We all get our moments, and where they begin or how they end is less important than how we experience them, what we do with them, and how they transform us.

The story of Lookout Records was not simply one of bands, or punk rock, or even music itself. Its true essence was the indomitability of the human spirit: a handful of sub-cultural schmucks, with no money and less sense, relying on bargain basement guitars, homemade cassettes, and scammed xerox copies, created something whose legacy still reverberates, and will outlive us all.

Outro:
The Neon Boneyard

O n the outskirts of Las Vegas, where the bright lights and tatty architecture dissolve into the desert, sits a park and museum known as the Neon Boneyard.

It's a showcase for antique, obsolete, and historic neon signs. As I was wrapping up the first draft of this book, a group of us gathered there to celebrate Billie Joe and Adrienne Armstrong's 20th wedding anniversary.

Flanked by their teenaged sons Joey and Jakob, Billie and Adrienne renewed their vows in a ceremony led by Jason White, part-time minister and full-time Green Day guitarist. As darkness fell, the neon signs around us flickered to life.

The colors they gave off combined with those of the sunset, scattering a soft orange glow across the sand. It bore an eerie resemblance to the steel mill skies of my youth, while the warm breeze that sprang up could have come straight from the maw of that long-ago blast furnace.

A DJ fired up some 1960s tunes, and Joey and Jakob scampered onto the dance floor, followed by three generations of family and friends. As the boys danced together with an easy grace, my mind drifted back to the day Billie visited me at Lookout to give me a framed photo of his then one-year-old son.

"I want you to have this picture to remind you of what this is really all about," he said. "And if I ever forget, so you can remind me."

Now Joey was a fully-grown young man, finishing his first year of college and headed out on tour with a band of his own. The world had moved on in so many ways, but while it would have been easy to focus on everything that had changed, what fascinated me more was how much had stayed the same.

A year later, with this book all but done, I watched as Green Day were inducted into the Rock and Roll Hall of Fame. There'd been rock stars and celebrities sprinkled among the crowd at the Las Vegas event, but in Cleveland you could hardly take a step without tripping over one or two.

Despite the glitz and glamour, Gilman and the East Bay never felt far away. Especially when, at a preshow two days earlier, Al Sobrante rejoined the band for the first time in 25 years to play a set almost identical—complete with between-songs banter—to what we would have heard in 1989.

Or when, midway through his acceptance speech, Billie said with unmistakable reverence: "We come from this place called Gilman Street." It's rare for performers who've risen so far to remain so closely connected to their roots, but Gilman inspired—and continues to inspire—that kind of devotion.

As I listened, I couldn't help reflecting on all the turning points, tiny and enormous, that conspired to bring me to the East Bay, and to launch me on an adventure that would transform my life in ways I couldn't possibly have foreseen. Many of them began as no more than a word, a song, an image, or a gesture delivered by someone I met in passing—or maybe never met at all.

I haven't always used my time wisely or productively. Many people who knew me as a young man would be astonished to learn that I ever accomplished anything at all, though none of them could be more surprised than me. As a teenager, I saw no point in living past the age of 20; my 21st birthday came not just as a shock and disappointment, but carried with it a genuine sense of failure.

Today, I'm more than three times that age, and regularly wake up astounded and delighted by all that I've seen and what I still have to look forward to. There've been close calls, times when a single misstep or bad judgment could have—perhaps should have—ended it all, but somehow I've survived and even, after a fashion, flourished.

Without the assistance, inspiration, and companionship of those I met along the way, my journey out of Zug Island desperation would never have been possible, or even worthwhile. One day, when we've trundled off to the ultimate neon boneyard, I'd like to picture the light of our collected efforts continuing to spread itself across the sky, testimony to all of us who, told we had no future to live up to, insisted on having one anyway.

Larry Livermore was born in Detroit and arrived in California in 1968. He was co-founder of Lookout Records, editor and publisher of *Lookout* magazine, and a longtime columnist for *Maximum Rocknroll* and *Punk Planet*. His first memoir, *Spy Rock Memories*, was published in 2013 by Don Giovanni Records. A contributor to numerous other magazines, books, and anthologies, he has also sung and played guitar for the Lookouts and the Potatomen. He lives in Brooklyn.

Read more of Larry's work at www.larrylivermore.com.